Library of
Davidson College

Political Culture
in Israel

Eva Etzioni-Halevy
with Rina Shapira

The Praeger Special Studies program—utilizing the most modern and efficient book production techniques and a selective worldwide distribution network—makes available to the academic, government, and business communities significant, timely research in U.S. and international economic, social, and political development.

Political Culture in Israel
Cleavage and Integration among Israeli Jews

PRAEGER SPECIAL STUDIES IN INTERNATIONAL POLITICS AND GOVERNMENT

Praeger Publishers New York London

Library of Congress Cataloging in Publication Data

Etzioni-Halevy, Eva.
   Political culture in Israel.

   (Praeger special studies in international politics
and government)
   Bibliography
   Includes indexes.
   1. Israel—Politics and government. 2. Political
socialization. I. Shapira, Rina, joint author.
II. Title.
JQ1825.P3E85   320.9'5694'05   76-24350
ISBN 0-275-23790-7

320.9569
E85p

PRAEGER PUBLISHERS

200 Park Avenue, New York, N.Y. 10017, U.S.A.

Published in the United States of America in 1977
by Praeger Publishers, Inc.

All rights reserved

© 1977 by Praeger Publishers, Inc.

Printed in the United States of America

To
Irene Esther Glücksohn

PREFACE

Israel has been called a paradise for social scientists because of the great variety of social settings in this small-scale society and the manifold social processes that have been compressed into relatively short time periods. Unique opportunities for social research, which should be of international interest, are provided by the kibbutz movement (sometimes referred to as a venture in utopia); the absorption of many groups with the most diverse cultural traditions into a common social framework; and the fact that Israel, throughout its short existence, unfortunately has had to face a series of external conflicts (alternating with periods of relative relaxation of tension). Professionally speaking, what more could a social scientist ask for?

And yet, Israel's social setting has also placed many difficulties in the way of the social scientist; the character of Israeli society and many of its social phenomena and processes elude classification. Is it torn by major tensions or is it basically an integrated society? Is it a society in rapid change or is it rather stable in its most basic features? Is it a Western-type democracy or a developing country? It is doubtful whether any clearcut answers are possible. The present study does not pretend to supply them. Rather, it attempts to bring out the convergence of opposites: political tensions as well as integrative mechanisms; trends of change as well as stabilizing forces; democratic procedures as well as undemocratic practices.

It is our intention to bring out particularly the points of stress in the Israeli political system, the integrative mechanisms that mitigate this stress, and the vulnerability of these integrative mechanisms themselves. We shall argue that several points of stress have recently been evident, expressed in far-reaching cleavages between the Israeli public and the political establishment and in decreasing rapport between the two; that despite this, the Israeli political scene has been basically quiescent and, in contrast to recent occurrences on the American scene, protest phenomena in Israel have been limited, mild, and moderate. This, we shall argue, is due to the fact that the various cleavages between the public and the establishment have been counteracted by two integrative mechanisms that are not part of the Center-Periphery relationship: opening channels of individual advancement and relatively strong collective commitments of Israelis. At the same time, the integrative effect of these mechanisms is precarious and may well decline in the foreseeable future.

This is not the first study of Israeli politics. It draws on (and greatly benefits from) some excellent previous studies. But these were based either on general observations and insights, or else on single research projects. This essay, however, presents a systematic secondary analysis, and, hopefully, a synthesis of the existing body of previous research (including a great amount of recent survey research by eminent social research institutes, many of whose findings have not yet been incorporated into sociopolitical analyses).

Israelis underwent traumatic experiences recently—especially those of the Yom Kippur War and its aftermath. It is widely believed that these have had far-reaching sociopolitical effects, but no systematic evidence has been presented to support this view. Scattered pieces of empirical data have been available, but they have not been integrated into a systematic analysis of recent developments. Our analysis attempts to fill this void.

We do not deal with any of the topics that have formed the major, unique Israeli contributions to sociology, such as the kibbutz and the absorption of immigrants. Ours is a more pedestrian topic that might just as well have been analyzed in any other country. But it is precisely because of this that both the similarities and the peculiarities of the Israeli social setting can best be brought into relief. Therefore, the analysis should interest not only those with a special affinity to Israel, but also those who seek a comparative perspective on other societies.

ACKNOWLEDGMENTS

This study was planned jointly by both authors. It was carried out in part by Eva Etzioni-Halevy alone and, for Chapter 1 and Part II, in collaboration with Rina Shapira. The study attempts to integrate the body of research on political culture in Israel; hence, it draws on many previous studies and analyses. We owe a special debt of gratitude to Professor Louis Guttman, director of the Israel Institute of Applied Social Research, for his kind permission to reprint data from the institute's surveys; and to Ms. Shlomit Levy for her kind assistance in making the data available to us. We are also deeply grateful to Professor Asher Arian and Dr. E. Turgovnik of the Department of Political Science, Tel Aviv University, for their generous permission to use the data from the 1973 General and Panel Study; and to Dr. Michael Lotan for his kind permission to review the data collected by the Society for Sociological Services, which he heads. Thanks are also due to Professor Simon N. Herman, Dr. Abraham Zloczower, Ms. Ruth Schrift, and Professor Asher Arian for their kind permission to reprint tables from their respective studies.

Among the analyses drawn on, special mention should be made of those by S. N. Eisenstadt, Y. Shapiro, S. Deshen, S. Smocha and Y. Peres, A. Arian and D. Horowitz, and M. Lissak. Our debt to these and a great many other analyses (mentioned in the text itself) is hereby gratefully acknowledged. However, we claim sole responsibility for whatever errors may have been made in the interpretation of these analyses—and for the conclusions we have drawn therefrom, with which the authors may not concur.

We are greatly indebted to our colleagues, Dr. Yochanan Peres, Professor Shlomo Deshen, Professor Ephraim Yaar, Dr. Moshe Schwartz, and Dr. Yitzchak Samuel, who commented on several chapters of the manuscript and contributed greatly to their improvement.

We would also like to express our gratitude to the Institute for Sociological Research of the Department of Sociology and Anthropology, Tel Aviv University, for supplying the financial aid without which this study could not have come into being.

Finally, we would like to express our deepest appreciation to Lew Golan for his outstanding work in editing the text, Mrs. Ruth Parnas and Mrs. Tina Asher for their most skillful and patient typing and retyping of the manuscript, and Mrs. Liora Lev-Ami and Moshe Livne for their unfailing assistance at various stages of the project.

CONTENTS

	Page
PREFACE	vii
ACKNOWLEDGMENTS	ix
LIST OF TABLES	xiii
LIST OF MATRIXES	xvi
LIST OF FIGURES	xvi
INTRODUCTION	xvii

PART I: POLITICAL CLEAVAGES

Chapter

1 THE SETTING: IDEOLOGICAL DEVELOPMENT AND THE ACCUMULATION OF POWER 3

    The Prestate (Yishuv) Era 3
    The Political Framework of Israel 12
    Conclusion 20
    The Political Significance of Extra Political Processes 21

2 THE LEFT-RIGHT CONTINUUM: THE SIGNIFICANCE OF POLITICAL ORIENTATIONS 25

    Analytical Framework: The Significance of Political Orientations 26
    The Significance of Political Orientations in Israel 30
    Conclusion 40

3 CHANGES IN POLITICAL ORIENTATIONS AND IDEOLOGICAL INCONGRUENCE 44

    Changes in Political Orientations: An Empirical Analysis 45
    Trends of Change—An Interpretation 60

4 THE BLOCKING OF POLITICAL INVOLVEMENT 67

    How Israelis Confront Politics 68

Chapter		Page
	Confrontation of Politics and Confidence in the Israeli Establishment	82
	Conclusion	86
5	THE DECLINE OF CONSENT?	88
	Consent and the Establishment	88
	Consent and the Israeli Establishment	92
6	THE POLITICS OF ISRAELI PROTEST	112
	Introduction	112
	Three Cases of Protest	114
	The Response to Protest	121
	The Limitations of Protest: An Interpretation	129
	Conclusion	133

PART II: INTEGRATIVE MECHANISMS

7	SOCIAL POSITION, SOCIAL MOBILITY, AND POLITICAL INTEGRATION	137
	The Relevance of Social Position	138
	The Relevance of Social Mobility	142
	Conclusion	154
8	NATIONAL IDENTIFICATION AND POLITICAL INTEGRATION	157
	National Identification and the Political Establishment	157
	National Identifications: The Integrative Commitments of Israelis	159
	National Identifications: The Collective Commitments of Israelis	163
	The Vulnerability of National Commitments: Some Indications for the Future	169
	Conclusion	176
9	SOLIDARITY, MORALE, AND POLITICAL INTEGRATION	179
	Solidarity, Morale, and the Political Establishment	179
	Solidarity and Morale: Facing External Conflict	180
	Morale and Solidarity: How Israelis Face External Conflict	183
	Morale, Solidarity, and the Israeli Establishment	199

Chapter			Page
10	CONCLUSION		205
		Political Cleavages	205
		Integrative Mechanisms	208
		The War Impact	211

Appendix

A	LIST OF QUESTIONS	214
B	MILESTONES IN THE ISRAELI-ARAB CONFLICT	221
C	GLOSSARY OF MAJOR PARTIES IN THE YISHUV AND IN ISRAEL	222
D	ELECTORAL BASIS OF ISRAEL'S GOVERNMENTS AND OF THE MAJOR OPPOSITION PARTIES	225

BIBLIOGRAPHY	229
NAME INDEX	244
SUBJECT INDEX	246
ABOUT THE AUTHORS	251

LIST OF TABLES

		Page
2.1	Political Involvement Percentage Difference Indexes (PDI) by Political Orientation, in 1973	31
2.2	Participation and Involvement According to Political Adherence in Haifa, 1964	32
2.3	Election Image Percentage Difference Indexes (PDI) by Political Orientation, in 1973	33
2.4	Political Orientations by Preferences on Stand vis-a-vis the Arab Countries and on Economic Patterns, in 1969	34
2.5	Percentage Difference Indexes (PDI) for Preferences on Territories and on Two Domestic Issues, by Political Orientations, in 1973	35
2.6	Differences among Left, Center, and Right-Wing Adherents, by Country of Origin, in 1973	38
2.7	Percentages of Leftists, Centrists, and Rightists Who Think Problems of Socioeconomic Gaps Will Influence Their Voting, by Education and by Country of Origin, in 1973	39
3.1	Distribution of Votes among Parties and Blocs in Knesset Elections, 1949–73	46
3.2	Net Effect (Standardized Regression Coefficients) on Voting Decision of Political Orientation and of Opinion on Concrete Policy Issues, in 1973	50
3.3	Political Orientations of Adults and Youngsters, as Revealed by Various Surveys, in 1973	53
3.4	Political Orientations by Country of Origin, in 1973	57
3.5	Political Orientations by Age and Country of Origin, in 1973	58
3.6	Political Orientations of Israelis at Various Time Periods	59

4.1	Political Involvement and Political Efficacy among the Israeli Public, 1960–73	70
4.2	Political Participation among the Israeli Public, 1960–73	73
4.3	Types of Citizens Who Do Not Express Confidence in the Government, in 1973	85
5.1	Net Effect (Standardized Regression Coefficients) of Opinions on Domestic and Foreign Affairs on Support for the Government, in 1971	105
6.1	Average Gross Annual Income of Urban Employees' Families by Continent of Birth, in 1970 and 1973	123
6.2	Index of Salaries and Prices in Israel, 1968–74	125
6.3	Relative Yearly Increases in Prices, 1960–72	126
7.1	Approval of the Government's General Policy, by Education, in 1971 and 1972	141
7.2	Percentage of Socialist Adherents among Five Categories of Respondents—According to Status Satisfaction and According to Intergenerational Mobility, in 1964	143
7.3	Net Effect (Standardized Regression Coefficients) of Political Orientations and of Concern over Advancement on Satisfaction with the Government	146
7.4	Numbers and Percentages of Workers in Various Economic Branches, Average Monthly Salary, and Rank Order of Salary, in 1961 and in 1974	147
7.5	Jewish Employed Persons by Occupation and Continent of Origin, in 1954 and in 1974	149
7.6	Rates of Interethnic Marriages in Israel and Interracial Marriages in the United States	153
8.1	Students with Strong Attachment to Israel (Disapproving of Emigration) by Jewish Identification, Israeli Identification, and Sense of Affinity with Jews in the Diaspora, in 1969	161

8.2	Centrality of Jewishness and Israeliness for High School Students, in 1964–65	164
8.3	Israeli Identification and Jewish Identification of Tel Aviv University Students	165
8.4	Israelis' Sense of Belonging to the Jewish People in the World, Commitment to Zionism and to the Land of Israel, 1970–1975	166
8.5	Israeli High School Students' Sense of Belonging to the Jewish People and Zionist Commitment, in 1973	170
8.6	Zionist Commitment and Desire to Live in Israel—Percentage Difference Indices (PDI) by Age, in 1973 and 1974	171
8.7	Centrality of Jewishness for Religious, Traditionalist, and Nonreligious High School Students and Their Parents, in 1964–65	172
8.8	High School Students' Sense of Belonging to the Jewish People and Zionist Commitment PDI by Religiousness and Type of School, in 1973	176
9.1	Net Effect (Standardized Regression Coefficients) of Morale, Solidarity, and Social Background Variables on Support for Government Policy, in 1971	200

LIST OF MATRIXES

		Page
5.1	Correlations (Monotonous Coefficients) among Support for Various Aspects of Government Policy, in 1974	106
7.1	Correlations (Monotonous Coefficients) between Past, Present, and Expected Economic Situation and Approval of Government Policy, in 1971	145
8.1	Correlations (Monotonous Coefficients) between National Commitments and Tolerance of the Regime, in 1974	163

LIST OF FIGURES

4.1	Typology of Citizens	84
5.1	Consent for Government Policy, 1967–75	98
5.2	Three Types of Consent, 1967–75	102
9.1	Morale, 1967–75	184
9.2	Sense of Intergroup Solidarity, 1967–75	190
9.3	Morale and Solidarity, 1967–75	195
9.4	Morale, Solidarity, and Consent for Government Policy, 1967–75	201

INTRODUCTION

FRAMEWORK OF THE ANALYSIS

The term "political culture" has been used by social scientists (such as Almond and Verba 1965; Pye 1965; DiPalma 1970; Devine 1972; Kavanagh 1972; Bluhm 1974; Rosenbaum 1975; and others(to designate a set of beliefs, orientations, and attitudes in the political realm. One distinctive feature of the political culture approach is that it seeks to derive the contours of a society's culture from the distribution of attitudes among its individual members, and thus to provide a bridge between the microlevel and the macrolevel. This approach has been adopted in the present analysis.

In addition, the analysis revolves around actual patterns of political action, because (on both the micro and macrolevels), these are so closely interwoven with attitudes that one can hardly be understood except in close conjunction with the other. Thus, if we say that the analysis is concerned with Israel's political culture, we are stretching the concept a bit beyond its original definition. We hope, however, that we gain in understanding what we lose in precision.

Since this essay is based mainly on reanalysis of existing data, the discussion must follow the footsteps of empirical research. Nevertheless, it is guided by two central analytical concerns. In the discussion itself, these themes are interwoven; analytically, they should be kept apart.

Our first concern is with the multifaceted relationship in Israel between what have been variously referred to as the "political center" and the "periphery," the "ruling class" and the "masses," the "power elite" and the "rank and file," or the "establishment" and the "public."* We view this relationship as an intricate balance of various components. One such component, for instance, concerns the relative distribution of power between the elite and the rank and file. While a political elite, by definition, wields more power than do members of the general public, there are variations in the difference in access to resources, and in the resulting power advantage that the elite has over the rank and file (and in the rewards it derives thereof). As Huntington put it: "The most important political distinction among countries concerns not their form

---

*The demarcation between the two must be regarded as a gray area rather than a sharp line. This, however, does not render the distinction any less valid. We deal only with the relationship between the establishment and the public, and not with the internal structure of the establishment itself. On the latter topic, see, for instance, Medding (1972); Aronoff (1972); and Brichta (1972).

of government but their *degree* of government" (Huntington 1968, p. 1, emphasis supplied). We shall argue that the Israeli establishment has had a specially great power advantage over the Israeli public and that an excessive power disparity has thus developed between the elite and the rank and file (Chapter 1).

Another element in the political balance is the ideological affinity between the establishment and the rank and file. Duverger (1964, p. 307) pointed out that each period tends to have a dominant doctrine, and the dominant party identifies itself with this major ideology. As time passes, the dominant doctrine may shift. If the dominant party does not keep in tune with the changing dominant mood, its position vis-à-vis the public may be weakened. Citing this conception, Arian (1975) points out that for many years Israel's dominant party (the epitome of the Israeli establishment) has had such special affinity with Israel's dominant doctrine. He then asks whether this is still so, or if the dominant party is losing step with the times. We trace the changes that have occurred in the political orientations of the Israeli public, and argue that an ideological incongruence has indeed developed between the public and the establishment (Chapter 3).

A further element in the center-periphery interaction concerns the involvement of the public in the political sphere and its sense of political efficacy. We show that a sizable proportion of Israelis have been blocked in their political involvement by a sense of political futility and that this has had negative implications on their confidence in the political leadership (Chapter 4).

Another cluster of components concerns the degree of support (or consent) the public extends to the political establishment (whether at election times or in between), and the opposition (whether institutionalized or uninstitutionalized) it presents—for instance, in the form of "direct action" or protest activities. We shall see that support for the political establishment has been declining in recent years, even though the establishment has been successful in absorbing and mitigating the resultant protest activities, and that the rapport between the public and the establishment has been decreasing (Chapters 5, 6).

These components of the interaction between the public and the establishment each have their inner dynamics; at the same time, they continuously affect each other. Their joint exploration in this study is intended to show that certain interrelated cleavages between the Israeli political elite and the public have been developed in recent years.

In addition, it is our contention that there are two sets of factors that, although outside the proper domain of the center-periphery interaction, impinge on it significantly: first, the individual aspirations and expectations of Israelis, and the manner in which they can be realized in Israeli society; and second, the collective national commitments of Israelis. In making this point we draw on two disparate theoretical approaches in an attempt to consolidate them into a common framework of analysis.

First there is the well-known thesis that neither the people's objective situation nor their aspirations determine their social satisfaction; but, rather, the juxtaposition of the two. Where an excessive gap develops between expectations and what is actually attainable, social frustration may be channeled into resentment of the political regime, and may eventually result in social unrest, protest, or rebellion.

Observers of revolutions and rebellions, for instance, have long pointed out that these are precipitated not when the objective situation is the worst. They occur when improvements lag behind rising expectations, or when an improving situation subsequently takes a turn for the worse—resulting in a pronounced gap between expectations and reality.* The protest of specific groups has also been interpreted in this light. Lipset and Altbach (1966) have suggested that student protest is most likely to erupt where the blocking of social mobility occurs; that is, where opportunities for social mobility do not match the students' aspirations and expectations. Conversely, it has been suggested, when mobility expectations are widely diffused, and when expectations and actual mobility are balanced, this tends to promote the acceptance of the sociopolitical order (Germani 1966, p. 376).

Lately, this widely accepted conception has been questioned, the claim being that the political establishment itself has an important share of such expectations. Edelman (1971, p. 7) claims that, "Political actions chiefly arouse or satisfy people not by granting or withholding their stable, substantive demands, but rather by changing the demands and the expectations." He adds: "To make this point is to deny or seriously qualify what may be the most widely held assumption about political interaction: that political arousal and quiescence depend on how much of what they want, people get." (Also see Edelman 1964, esp. pp. 24 and 153.)

It seems, however, that people's individual aspirations and expectations for their own life goals spring largely from prevalent values—those that Merton referred to as "cultural goals." In Western society, for instance, these are the achievement-oriented values commonly thought to have their source in the "Protestant ethic" and similar sets of values,† which set the standard for

---

*See De Tocqueville (1955); Brinton (1959); Davies (1962); and Huntington (1968).
†There is an extensive literature arguing this point. See Weber (1958); McClelland (1961); Sombardt (1951); Riesman (1973); Kluckhohn (1953). Also see Green (1959) and Etzioni-Halevy and Zvi Halevy (forthcoming).

individual achievements. Such aspirations are further influenced by people's previous attainments, and by reference groups whose attainments people set up as standards for their own.

These factors are largely beyond the control of the political establishment —so the leeway that it has in influencing aspirations and expectations is not as great as Edelman and like-minded thinkers would lead one to believe. In fact, if the political establishment had as much control over the public's expectations as emerges from this approach, the question would inevitably arise: Where do social dissent, rebellion, and revolutions spring from? It is only when individual aspirations are regarded in large part as independent of the establishment (as the previous tradition has held them to be, and as, in fact, seem to be the case) that we can view the relationship between aspirations and their realization as affecting the harmony between the establishment and the public.

The second approach is a remote descendant of the Durkheimian tradition with its emphasis on the general importance of collective values and cohesiveness in society. The additional contribution of this approach is that cohesiveness, which involves the commitment of men and groups to each other and to collective traditions, identities, or ideologies, is closely related to political integration. The level of community a society achieves is reflected in the relationship between the political authorities and the social groups that compose the public. Where political communities are fragmented against themselves, where attachments center chiefly upon groups or classes with their own sense of separateness, common political institutions have little authority and command little stable, dependable support. A basic prerequisite for the acceptance of the regime is that the population be pervaded by a sense of collectivity that transcends its various segments, that social divisions be bridged over by national loyalties and commitments, and that these loyalties and commitments be coextensive with the political system (Key 1961; Verba 1965; and Huntington 1968). To paraphrase Huntington's succinct statement, we may say: "In the total absence of social cleavages, political institutions are unnecessary; in the total absence of cohesiveness, they are impossible."

Assuming then, that individual aspirations and expectations, on one hand, and collective identifications and loyalties on the other, are to some extent independent on the political establishment, we suggest that the latter's relationship with the public is likely to be affected by both. Even where potential cleavages between the establishment and the public are indicated, the tension between them may well be attenuated where concern over the blocking of individual aspirations is weak, and where collective commitments are strong. We argue that this has in fact been the case in Israel; that there is no certainty, however, that this will continue to be so, that there are some indications in fact that the integrative effect of these processes may be declining in the future, and that political tensions may therefore become increasingly prominent (Chapters 7, 8, and 9).

Our second concern is with the role of value orientations and attitudes in Israel's sociopolitical reality. In recent years, the old debate about the relationship between values and social practice has tended to become polarized by extremist views. Some scholars emphasize the formative influence of values on social reality, and even view them as governing or determining such reality. Others regard them as mere legitimators of existing conglomerations of interests and power structures or their opposition, which implies the view of values as employed in the service of power (see Chapter 2).

It is our contention that neither of these have focused on one of the most important roles of value orientations, namely, that they lend significance to sociopolitical reality. They do so by sensitizing individuals selectively to different aspects of that reality; by influencing the manner in which individuals define the reality and their own situation in it; and by influencing what individuals want from it. While value orientations are a source of sociopolitical preferences, some value commitments may foster tolerance of a political system even when these preferences are not realized. We substantiate these theses by examining the implications of Israelis' political orientations and national commitments on the political scene and by tracing the political significance of recent changes in these orientations (Chapters 2, 3, 8, and 9).

Another controversy concerns the consistency and dependability of value orientations and attitudes. On one hand, there is the political culture school that takes attitudes rather seriously and treats them with a marked degree of deference. In Pye's (1965, p. 7) words: "The notion of political culture assumes that the attitudes, sentiments and cognitions that inform and govern political behavior in any society are not just random congeries, but represent coherent patterns which fit together. . . ." In contrast, it has been argued (Edelman 1971, p. 3) that political attitudes are "frequently sporadic in appearance, fluctuating in intensity, ambivalent in composition and, therefore, logically inconsistent. . . ."

We shall attempt to show that contrary to the latter conception, the political attitudes of Israelis do tend to crystallize into meaningful patterns. Although they sometimes undergo rapid shifts, these shifts usually make sense in the light of sociopolitical developments at that particular time.

The Predicaments of Secondary Analysis

This secondary analysis attempts to incorporate into a common framework data from various sources: official statistics, especially those of election turnout and results; empirical research by social scientists (including our own); content analysis of newspapers; and survey research data. Each of these sources is, in a certain sense, problematic. Official statistics are fine as far as they go; the trouble is, they do not go very far. They supply at best the merest skeleton, which must be filled out or supplemented with different types of data before their broader significance can even be approximated.

Empirical research in the social sciences in Israel is of the highest standard, in no way inferior to similar research in the United States, for instance. Unfortunately, however, not enough research has been done on relevant topics, and several loopholes remain. Still, while the relevant research data are not as abundant as could have been wished, neither are they as sparse as could have been feared. The results of two major types of empirical research by social scientists have been included: first, anthropological research based mainly on participant observation; and second, research based on questionnaires, administered to various samples or groups of the population. Each has its advantages and drawbacks.

Anthropological research is possibly the more penetrating, but it is confined to small segments of the population (usually a village here, a small town there), and its evidence is frequently based on the statements of small numbers of respondents. We have sought to overcome this problem by presenting the joint conclusions of various projects of this kind. Surprisingly, we found that, although carried out in different parts of the country, they usually corroborate each other (see especially Chapter 5).

Research based on questionnaires by different scholars has sometimes been carried out with different frames of reference and with differently worded questions submitted to different types of samples. Consequently there are some difficulties in comparing their results. Luckily these difficulties do not exist in all cases. Sometimes, when fate is especially kind, it happens that diverse scholars have resorted to identically worded questions. Frequently, however, it seems that communication among scholars has been somewhat deficient and whenever identical questions have been included this is more by haphazard improvisation than by deliberate design. As a result, some comparisons had to be made on the basis of single or small numbers of questions, which obviously reduces the confidence to be placed in the conclusions. At the same time, in view of the lack of joint planning of projects, it is fortunate that even these few identical questions could be located. To make up for this deficiency in the data, we resorted, whenever possible, to a combination of a variety of data that supplement each other's credibility (see especially Chapter 3).

In addition, survey research by Israel's Institutes for Social Research has been included.* Most of it has been carried out on cross sections of the Israeli Jewish urban population. A few surveys include the Jewish population in

---

*Some of the research projects by Israeli scholars have been based on survey data collected by an institute of social research, so that research by single scholars and research by institutes sometimes shade into each other.

towns of 5,000 inhabitants or over, or the Jewish population in general, but most have been carried out in Israel's four main urban centers: the Jerusalem, Tel Aviv, Haifa, and Beersheba areas. The reason is obvious: these surveys are designed to gauge public opinion at certain points in time; hence they must be carried out as quickly as possible, since any drawing out of the investigation would defeat its very purpose. Also, budget limitations require that the cost per respondent be kept as low as possible—which is more feasible in the cities.

This means, however, that Israel's rural population, including members of collective settlements (kibbutzim and moshavim), is automatically excluded. While this is certainly a shortcoming, it should not be considered detrimental. After all, the bulk of the Israeli population (90.6 percent) resides in urban areas. Despite the special significance that has always been accorded to Israel's collective settlements, the fact remains that, quantitatively, the mainstream of Isreali society is in and around urban centers. The survey research data, then, appertain to this mainstream.

An additional drawback is that the Arab population of Israel is not included. While this might seem undemocratic, it does have its methodological justifications. Most Israeli Arabs reside in villages. In addition, their position in Israeli society, the vantage point from which they view it, is very different from that of the Jewish population; therefore, presenting survey results of the Jewish and Arab populations as one entity would only confuse the issues.

A problem that besets survey research data in general (and, thus, in Israel as well) has to do with the nature of the questions asked and the precoded replies presented to the respondents. This method has been criticized because it resorts to crude categories (disregarding the fact that similar responses may actually hold diverse meanings) and hence misses out on significant nuances of the data. It "forces" some people to express opinions even when they have none; it coerces other people into condensing into simplistic statements opinions to which they have given a great deal of thought and that may be the result of much inner trepidation. For these and other reasons, it is claimed that survey research comes up with oversimplified results.*

It is not our intention to repel this kind of criticism, which undeniably has a point. However, when the opinions of large numbers of people are examined, it is doubtful whether any other method would be feasible. Comparison of the participant observation method with the survey research method illustrates the dilemma of knowing much about a few versus knowing a little about many. At any rate, as pointed out by Free and Cantril (1967), secondary analysts cannot be choosers. Hence we utilize, without undue misgivings, data

---

*This criticism has been voiced especially in regard to survey research on religious commitments and national identities. See, for instance, Deshen (1975).

from both types of sources. Certainly, we feel that when the alternatives are knowing little and knowing even less, the first is preferable.

While the above-mentioned problems, which beset all research, cannot be solved, they can be circumscribed when the surveys are carried out by well-qualified bodies. This condition has luckily prevailed in Israel. Research institutes of the highest standard, the Israeli Institute of Applied Social Research (IIASR), under the directorship of Professor Louis Guttman, in conjunction with the Communications Institute of the Hebrew University, headed by Professor Elihu Katz, have been carrying out periodic surveys ever since the Six-Day War. Also of the highest quality is the Society for Sociological Services, under the directorship of Dr. Michael Lotan, which has also carried out surveys on political attitudes and whose results we have been privileged to review.

All in all, in spite of some problems besetting survey research, the data collected in Israel constitute a veritable treasure. This information has not yet been fully utilized—and social scientists, the Israeli public, and anybody interested in Israel can ill afford to disregard it.

PART

I

**POLITICAL
CLEAVAGES**

CHAPTER 1

THE SETTING: IDEOLOGICAL DEVELOPMENT AND THE ACCUMULATION OF POWER

Israel's political system like those of other new nations, was not created *de novo* on the day of its declaration of independence but is partly the product of political developments in its preindependence period. In fact, it will be seen that one of the major features of Israel's political system is the excessive concentration of economic power in the hands of the political elite and the pronounced power discrepancy that has thus developed between the elite and the public, and that this feature is a direct outgrowth of the sociopolitical patterns developed in the prestate era.

THE PRESTATE (YISHUV) ERA*

The Aliyot

The reconstruction of the Jewish community in Palestine began at the end of the 19th century (when the country was under Turkish-Ottoman rule) and gained impetus after World War I (when the country became a British mandate). This development is the outgrowth of several waves of immigration (aliyot).† These aliyot differed from each other in their social character and in

---

*Yishuv: the term used to designate the Jewish community in Palestine (literally, "settlement"). This all too short analysis draws chiefly on the following studies: Shapiro (1975); Eisenstadt (1967); and Horowitz and Lissak (1971).

†Singular: aliya. Before the onset of the modern aliyot, there existed a small Jewish (mostly observant) community known as the old yishuv; it does not concern us for the present analysis.

the contribution they made to the budding political system. The second and third aliyot were clearly the most influential and their ascendancy was to be highly significant for the sociopolitical development of the yishuv.

The First Aliya, during 1882–1903, comprised 20,000 to 30,000 immigrants from Eastern Europe. These immigrants founded a number of agricultural colonies (moshavot) in which land was privately owned. They soon faced grave difficulties in the largely unsettled country. They were assisted by Baron Rothschild's philanthropic enterprise, but at the price of being subjected to the administration of his French-Jewish officials whose outlook was alien to theirs. As a consequence, the nationalist ideals that had brought them to the country were practically stifled. Agricultural work came to be carried out by an increasing number of hired Arab peasants. Demoralization and, finally, stagnation set in, relieved only by the advent of the next wave of immigration.

The Second Aliya, composed of 35,000 to 40,000 immigrants, reached the country in 1904–15. These newcomers were mostly young intellectuals from Russia who had been influenced by the socialist trends of the 1905 Revolution. They strongly rejected the colonial-capitalist leanings of the first settlers and their exploitation of Arab labor. Instead, they advocated socialist-Zionism, Jewish self-labor, and "pioneering"—which implied a willingness to harness themselves to the service of the yishuv, and to make personal sacrifices in order to further its development.

Thus, the fervor of the immigrants of the Second Aliya was in marked contrast to the patterns adopted by their predecessors. However, the confrontation between the two groups was not confined to the ideological level; seeking employment, the new immigrants expected to be hired by the veteran colonists, while the latter preferred the better qualified and cheaper Arab labor.

The Third Aliya arrived in 1919–23, composed of 35,000 young people most of whom had no independent financial means. They came from Eastern Europe and, like the Second Aliya, they adhered to socialist and pioneering ideologies.

The Fourth Aliya comprised 80,000 to 85,000 immigrants, mostly from Eastern Europe, during 1924–31.* The Fifth Aliya—the last until the establishment of the state, and also the largest one—reached the country in 1932–47; it comprised more than 300,000 immigrants. Many of the immigrants of the Fourth and Fifth Aliyot came from middle-class backgrounds and brought capital with them; they also brought a bourgeois orientation that differed greatly from the socialist Zionism and pioneering commitment of the Second and Third Aliyot. Most of them settled in urban centers and gave a strong

---

*A sizable proportion of the immigrants who came with the first waves of immigration later reemigrated, although the exact number is not known.

THE SETTING

impetus to the development of the professions and of private enterprise in crafts, industry, and commerce.

However, although the Fourth and Fifth Aliyot were the largest in numbers, and although they made a significant contribution to economic development, the impact they made on the yishuv's sociopolitical system clearly fell below that of the two previous ones. It was the fusion of Zionist socialism with the collectivist pioneering ideals of the Second and Third Aliyot and the sociopolitical structures they created that came to be dominant in the yishuv.

The confrontation of the immigrants of the Second Aliya with the colonists of the First Aliya over the question of Jewish labor prompted those of the Second Aliya to establish separate labor parties and trade unions; these later formed the basis of the Histadrut.* Thus, the Second Aliya (and later the Third Aliya) laid the foundation for the labor movement that was to dominate the social structure of the yishuv, and for its various political entities (many of which have been maintained to the present time).

The difficulties of the new immigrants in finding employment, together with their socialist ideals, led them to create new forms of collectives (cooperative social organizations) in agriculture and in urban centers; today they constitute some of the most distinctive characteristics of Israeli society. The collective agricultural settlements (kibbutzim and moshavim) started by immigrants of the Second Aliya and further developed by settlers of the Third Aliya assumed special importance; they provided subsistence for large numbers of people, they constituted a major force in the reclamation and resettlement of the land, and they played a prominent role in the defense of the yishuv.

The Second and Third Aliyot with their pioneering-socialist orientations may thus be seen as decisive stages in the formation of the sociopolitical patterns of the yishuv and of Israeli society. As Eisenstadt (1967, p. 15) put it: "The ideals and organizational patterns created by them were not only maintained and perpetuated in the social structure of the Yishuv, but were to guide and shape its further development." This is closely associated with the ascendancy of the left-of-center socialist oriented labor movement over the center-right.

The Political Sectors: The Ascendancy of the Labor Movement

Almost from the beginning, the political spectrum of the yishuv was differentiated along left/right and religiously observant/nonobservant continua. Accordingly, three political sectors developed: the left-of-center labor

---

*The General Federation of Labor.

movement, the center-right "citizens," and the religious groups. Each of these was subdivided into moderate and extremist sectors as follows:

- *The moderate left* included Hapoel Hatzair and Poalei Zion—and, later, Achdut Ha'avoda (Mapai) (see below) and Hashomer Hatzair.*
- *The extreme left* included the communists and Poalei Zion Smol (the latter in the 1920s and early 1930s).
- *The moderate center-right* included the General Zionists† and the progressives (Aliya Chadascha).
- *The extreme right wing* included the Revisionists.
- *The moderate religious sector* included Hamizrachi and Hapoel Hamizrachi.
- *The extreme religious sector* included Agudat Israel and Poalei Agudat Israel.

Of these three sectors, the leftist one (the labor movement)—most of whose members and leaders were immigrants of the Second and Third Aliyot —came to be the most powerful and the most influential. By the early 1930s it had gained hegemony in all the central political organizations of the yishuv. This ascendancy came about by various stages of organizational evolvement.

The labor movement was the first to organize on a relatively large scale.‡ In 1906 the first two labor parties were founded: Hapoel Hatzair, composed mainly of agricultural laborers; and Poalei Zion, a Marxist party that initially aimed at furthering the urban proletariat, eventually coming to stress agricultural labor as well. Most workers could not align themselves with the political orientations of these parties and did not become members. In addition, however, various trade associations and a worker's sick fund were established that attracted a larger membership. The farmers followed in the workers' footsteps, founding the farmers' association in 1913, but their organization was clearly on a smaller scale.

In 1919 the Achdut Ha'avoda organization was founded to help absorb the immigrants of the Third Aliya. The new organization established agricultural settlements, trade unions, and an office for public works to alleviate unemployment, as well as various welfare projects. But initially most laborers refused to join the new political body, which was organized as the local branch of the World Poalei Zion Party.

---

*For a translation of the parties' names, see Appendix C.

†Appeared as a united party only in the elections to the World Zionist Organization. In the yishuv elections there were various "Citizen's Groups" that did not present a united front until after the proclamation of the state.

‡Although, in 1902, a branch of the world organization of Mizrachi was opened in Palestine.

In order to overcome this obstacle and to organize all new immigrant and veteran laborers in a common framework, the leaders of Achdut Ha'avoda and other labor groups founded the Histadrut in 1920. This was a countrywide general federation of labor unions embracing all occupations, but it did not confine itself to trade union activities. It assumed many of the economic functions previously fulfilled by Achdut Ha'avoda; it also provided employment for its members by establishing its own economic enterprises.

Within a few years the Histadrut succeeded in organizing the majority of Jewish laborers,* and by the early 1920s, most laborers were employed in economic institutions connected directly or indirectly with the Histadrut (including collective settlements). Gradually growing in size and importance, the Histadrut developed into one of the most powerful organizations of the yishuv; its economic enterprises evolved into some of the yishuv's (and Israel's) major economic concerns.

From the outset, the Histadrut established itself not only as an economic body but as a political body as well; it included in its framework various labor parties.† In the 1920 Histadrut election (following a system of proportional representation) Achdut Ha'avoda won over 50 percent of the votes and thus gained control of the Histadrut's executive bodies. Within a few years, Achdut Ha'avoda succeeded in taking charge of the Histadrut's various functions and enterprises as well.

In 1930 Achdut Ha'avoda joined with Hapoel Hatzair to form Mapai (Mifleget Poalei Eretz Israel); thereafter Mapai received 75 percent of the votes in the Histadrut elections, thus enhancing its control over that organization's executive bodies. The economic power that the party now wielded enabled it to set itself up as the dominant force not only in the Histadrut, but also in the yishuv as a whole.

In the 1920s the influence of the labor movement on the national political center of the yishuv had been limited.‡ But the establishment of Mapai as a unified, powerful party marked the beginning of the political hegemony of the workers' groups in the yishuv.

The moderate center-right "citizens" groups, despite their major contribution to economic development, accepted the labor movement's dominance. In contrast, the Revisionist Party (which was more rightist than other groups on domestic affairs, and more activist on relations with the British and the Arabs) challenged the supremacy of labor in national leadership. Accordingly, it seceded from the institutional framework of the so-called "Organized Yi-

---

*By 1926, 70 percent of all laborers were members of the Histadrut.
†Gradually, nonlabor parties gained representation too, but remained a minority.
‡Described below.

shuv" in 1935; however, this did not undermine labor's dominant position—and perhaps even facilitated its control over key political positions.

Why was the labor movement so successful in establishing its ascendancy over the other political sectors? Several explanations have been offered. First of all, the timing and pattern of its organization were influential. Being the first to organize on a large scale, labor was better equipped to take charge of the absorption of immigrants. The labor parties supervised the vocational and ideological training of future immigrants while they were still abroad, organized their immigration and their economic, social, and cultural absorption, and continued their political socialization upon their arrival in the country. In doing so, they succeeded in incorporating large numbers of newcomers into their ranks. The center-right was a late comer to the scene and did not measure up to labor in this respect.

The labor movement was also the most effective in its organization. Its potential adherents usually reached the country without adequate private means, and hence were dependent on the labor organizations. On the other hand, immigrants with capital, the potential adherents of center-right parties, were not dependent on the assistance of organized bodies to the same extent; hence their ties with the parties were more tenuous, and the parties themselves were more loosely organized. At the beginning of the 1940s an attempt was made to organize the center-right "citizens" groups more tightly as a counterweight to the labor movement; but this was after the left had entrenched itself in its dominant position, and the right was not able to dislodge it.

Furthermore, it seems that the labor movement's manner of organizing immigration and settlement was the more appropriate under the circumstances. In the early 1920s the Zionist movement was beset by a controversy concerning the most desirable way to settle the country. Some favored nationally financed pioneering types of settlements, others stressed the advantages of privately financed colonization. Since most immigrants in the early years lacked adequate private means, the emphasis had to be on nationally financed settlements. This helped create the conditions for the hegemony of the labor movement, which was the sponsor and promoter of this pattern.

Arab opposition to Jewish settlement, in the form of intermittent attacks, made it necessary to provide for self-defense. The labor movement greatly strengthened its leadership position by its involvement in this activity. In 1920 the Histadrut established the Haganah—the yishuv's major clandestine defense organization—which continued to be under the predominant influence of the labor movement until the establishment of the state.*

---

*Since 1930 the Haganah was under the control of the national institutions (see below), but in reality the labor movement's influence remained predominant. The dissident armed groups—Irgun Zvai-Leumi and Lechi—were not attached to the labor movement, but these were marginal groups that carried less weight in the yishuv.

Another source of the labor movement's strength may be found in its ideology of pioneering socialist-Zionism. This ideology includes the utopian image of a classless society with but small differences in wealth (Eisenstadt 1967, p. 147). In addition to this relatively egalitarian element, the ideology asserts the primacy of the collective over the individual; it expects the individual to realize himself by serving the collective; and it favors publicly owned means of production and collective forms of social organization.

This ideology seemed to be the most appropriate for the harsh conditions that initially prevailed in the country. It was especially apt for motivating the early immigrants to fulfill the various tasks required for the development of the yishuv, and to adopt the austere way of life that the conditions necessitated. The center-right did not succeed in presenting a countermyth of comparable stature. Its ideology of individualism and private enterprise was not nearly as attractive to the majority of the community. The labor movement also was highly successful in disseminating its ideology through the educational system, while the center-right lagged behind in this area as well.* Thus, the principles of collectivist-socialist Zionism became the dominant ideology of the yishuv.

The primacy of the pioneering ideology found expression, inter alia, in the predominance of the pioneers (for example, members of collective settlements, usually from the Second and Third Aliyot) in the political elites of the yishuv. This, in turn, strengthened the primacy of this ideology, as well as the predominance of the labor movement (of which the pioneers were part) in all key positions of the yishuv.

It was a major tenet of the collectivist-socialist ideology that the collective (as represented by its political organizations) was to play a major role in organizing and supervising all facets of socioeconomic life. Accordingly, the collectivist-socialist orientation furnished the ideological basis for concentrating great economic power in the hands of the labor movement (including the Histadrut), thus aiding the movement in establishing itself as the major political power in the country. This pattern of concentration of economic power in the hands of political organizations, as devised by the labor movements, was later perpetuated in the State of Israel as well, and came to be a central characteristic of its sociopolitical system.

---

*Lacking a centralized school system, education was sponsored by political movements. Accordingly, there were three "trends" in education: the labor trend, the general trend, and the religious trend. The labor trend was more zealous than was the general trend in inculcating the pupils with its ideology. In this it was aided by highly influential, labor-affiliated, pioneering youth movements. Some center-right-affiliated youth movements existed as well, but most of these were less ideological in their orientation.

Self Government: The National Institutions

To prepare itself for eventual independence, the Jewish community under the British mandate set up a semiautonomous political authority that was formally recognized by the British government in 1927.* While the British were concerned mainly with maintaining law and order, the Jewish political authority known as the "state in the making" took charge of the internal organization of the yishuv.

This political authority was composed of two bodies known as the "national institutions." One was the Elected Assembly[†] and its executive body, the National Council; it was concerned primarily with culture, education, health, and welfare. More important and more powerful, however, was the Zionist Executive (later the Jewish Agency Executive), the local representative of the World Zionist Organization—elected by the World Zionist Congress; it was in charge of finance, including the mobilization of capital from abroad, immigration and settlement, labor and industry, representing the interests of the Jewish community before the mandatory government and, since 1930, defense.

The political center was a multiparty coalition, institutionalized in a parliamentary framework on the basis of proportional representation. From the early 1930s the political regime came to be characterized by a dominant party system in which one party, Mapai, became the major political power,[‡] and was clearly recognized as such by its followers and adversaries alike. Basically, this system has been maintained up to the present.

Although the political center of the Jewish community in Mandatory Palestine enjoyed a fair degree of autonomy, it was actually only a partial political system—with authority but not sovereignty. Lacking the force of sanctions available to a sovereign state, the national institutions had to base their power and authority on voluntary recognition by the political bodies and the community at large. They tried to achieve the widest possible consensus by forming a coalition regime that committed various parties to the national institutions. Thus, the political leadership consolidated its power by sharing it with the widest possible array of political bodies.

To elicit the cooperation of various political bodies, the political center was also obliged to concede several of its functions, thereby allowing these

---

*Preliminary attempts at political organization were made under Ottoman rule. However, only under the British mandate did the actual self-government of the yishuv take shape.

†Elected by the organized yishuv—known as Knesset Israel—in which some 95 percent of the Jews living in Palestine participated.

‡For a definition and analysis of this system, see Duverger (1964, pp. 308–09); Arian (1971); and Shapiro (1975, p. 12).

bodies to turn into what Horowitz and Lissak (1971) refer to as political subcenters. These subcenters (which included the parties, the Histadrut, the kibbutz and moshav movements, and some independent labor organizations) simultaneously participated in the coalitional national center and engaged independently in tasks parallel to those of the center.

They provided a wide array of economic, social, and cultural services that went far beyond political activity. Although they were differentiated by ideological cleavages, they did not confine themselves to debates; they organized immigration, colonization, health and welfare, housing projects, economic enterprises, and a host of other activities.

From the beginning, therefore, many functions usually fulfilled by the government bureaucracy were carried out by voluntary political bodies. This gave rise to a marked degree of politization, manifested in the pervasiveness of political criteria in all walks of life—a feature that still characterizes Israeli society to this day.

The political center also accumulated power by controlling the flow of resources into the yishuv: such as economic resources from the Zionist Organization in the Diaspora designed for colonizing and developing the yishuv; immigration certificates granted by the mandatory government; and positions in the administration of the national institutions themselves.

These resources were allocated to the parties that supported the national center according to the party political key; that is, in proportion to each party's strength in the most recent election. Their allocation served as an inducement for the political parties to share in the coalition, and to accede to the authority of the national institutions. Discrimination against dissenting groups in the matter of immigration certificates denied them reinforcements from the ranks of their followers abroad, hence served as one of the most effective sanctions at the command of the national institutions.

Over the years, the political center widened its control over the flow of these resources, thereby augmenting its power. This pattern tallied with the ideology and organizational structures of the labor movement, hence became particularly pronounced after the latter occupied the key position in the Zionist executive in the early 1930s; as noted, this pattern, too, has been maintained to this day.

Despite its growing power, and although the political center did its utmost to persuade the various political bodies to cooperate, not all of the bodies were willing. As noted, the right-wing Revisionist movement seceded from the organized yishuv; the more moderate right-wing parties also strove to reduce their dependency on the national center, although they did not go so far as to withdraw from its framework, which was thus maintained under the hegemony of the labor movement.

The most important of all subcenters was the Histadrut, which had established itself as a major locus of power in the yishuv. The stature of the national center depended, to a large extent, on its relations with this subcenter. In the 1920s the Histadrut maintained only weak ties with the national institutions, whose power was then rather limited. Things changed in the early 1930s, when the labor parties gained hegemony in the Zionist Executive. Once Mapai controlled both the Histadrut and the Zionist Executive, this party, (aided by the Histadrut) became a major factor in augmenting the executive's power, thus creating a two-branched conglomeration of power under its own control. The augmentation of the executive's power was further encouraged by political and military tensions with the Arabs and the British, which increased the importance of centralized coordination.

These tensions, which increased in the 1940s, finally led to the abdication of the mandatory power. By 1948, when the mandate ended and the State of Israel was proclaimed, the national institutions had developed sufficiently, and had accumulated enough power, to fill the political vacuum and to set up a full-fledged government within a short time.

THE POLITICAL FRAMEWORK OF ISRAEL

The Political Sectors

Several features of Israel's political system were handed down, with but minor modifications, from the prestate era. One such feature is the differentiation along the left-right and religious-nonreligious continua, and the consequent division into three major sectors: left, center-right, and religious.

The major parties that compose each sector are basically the same that existed in the yishuv era, although they have undergone various partitions, mergers, and alignments. The left-of-center labor movement is still headed by Mapai, which merged with some smaller parties to form the Israel Labor Party (ILP) and aligned itself with yet another party (Mapam) to form the Alignment.

The center-right is still composed mainly of the groups that united to form the General Zionists (later known as the Liberals) and Herut, which is the descendant of the Revisionists;* these two parties later aligned themselves with each other and joined forces with some smaller parties to form the Likud.

The religious sector is also composed of basically the same parties that prevailed in the yishuv era. Hamizrachi merged with Hapoel Hamizrachi (the

---

*Strictly speaking, Herut was the descendant of the Irgun Zvai Leumi that was part of the Revisionist movement. Subsequently, some of the Revisionist Party's leadership joined Herut.

religious labor party) to form the Mafdal, the National Religious Party. The more extreme orthodox sector still comprises Agudat Israel and Poalei Agudat Israel (the orthodox labor party). Thus, the religious front has both labor and nonlabor wings.*

Since the establishment of the state, the left has apparently been moving somewhat toward the center, or, at least, it has been less adamant in its leftist adherence. Therefore, it has been claimed, the cleavage between the two sectors is not as pronounced as it used to be. Nevertheless, some cardinal differences remain. The accepted ideological formulas of the labor movement are still those of egalitarian, collectivist socialism; the center-right still adheres to "liberalism." Both sectors adhere as a matter of course to the national ideology of Zionism, but the right emphasizes nationalism as an end in itself to a greater extent. These ideological differences have implications on the concrete policy level as well.

Both sectors advocate the welfare state, full employment, and minimum wages. Beyond this, however, the left gives preference to the public sector of the economy, while the center-right supports the private sector. The labor movement favors state planning and regulation of the economy, the center-right calls for the liberalization of the economy and sees itself as the champion and protector of unhampered free enterprise. While both sectors recognize the workers' right to strike, the center-right advocates compulsory arbitration when such strikes jeopardize essential services; the left, on the other hand, claims that the workers' right to strike is inalienable and is not to be curtailed except by the workers themselves.†

The labor sector, which holds hegemony in the Histadrut, is in favor of maintaining this organization in its present format: as a federation of trade unions, as the owner of major economic enterprises, and as the sponsor of Israel's major health services. The center-right (which is represented in the Histadrut but is in the minority) would prefer to confine the organization to its trade union function—having it relinquish ownership of economic enterprises and also nationalize the health services. Thus, the center-right would have the Histadrut's power severely curtailed.‡

The two sectors also differ on foreign policy: most center-right groups are generally more adamant toward the Arab states, while the left is more willing to compromise on territories.

---

*Only the major parties have been mentioned. For more details on mergers and alignments see Table 3.1.

†Hence, all attempts on the part of the right to enact compulsory arbitration have been defeated by the labor movement.

‡ These differences are evident in the platforms of the major parties in the two political sectors (Arian 1973). The characteristics of the religious sector are of less relevance for this discussion.

The Electoral System

Another feature continued from the yishuv era is the electoral and party system. It is based on countrywide proportional representation; each party that receives at least one percent of the total is represented in the Knesset (Israel's parliament) in direct proportion to its share of the votes.* This electoral system had been adopted in the prestate era because the absence of sovereignty made it necessary to gain the voluntary support of even minor parties. Since independence, various political personalities and groups have called for a change to personal-regional representation.

Israel has a multiparty system in which one party is dominant (alternatively referred to as a dominant-party system). No party has ever gained an absolute majority, so that the yishuv's coalitionary regime has been perpetuated. Also, basically the same party that established itself as dominant in the yishuv, the Israel Labor Party (formerly Mapai), has maintained its dominant position up to the present. The ILP has been the axis of all government coalitions (with the Mafdal as its minor partner),† and has always held the key ministries: prime minister, defense, foreign affairs, treasury, and education. As in the yishuv, the party's dominance is based not only on its control of the government, but on that of the Histadrut as well.

The continued dominance of practically the same political body for almost half a century is one of the most distinctive features of Israel's political system. It is the more remarkable in view of the fact the Jewish population has increased from less than 200,000 to nearly 3 million during this period, and its composition has undergone far-reaching changes. Part of our analysis is devoted to the devices used by the ruling elite to keep itself in power despite such changes.

The Role of Political Parties

Yet another feature originating in the yishuv is the great importance of political parties in spheres other than politics. The years 1948–51 saw mass immigration into the newly established state, and the major parties assumed the task of assisting in the absorption of immigrants. For this purpose, the party political key was reactivated: each party was allocated funds for the

---

*Elections are by secret ballot. There is universal suffrage for all citizens 18 years and over. All Jews who immigrate to Israel are automatically entitled to citizenship through the "law of return."

†The independent Liberals, a minor center party, also is a traditional coalition partner.

absorption of immigrants in proportion to its share of the vote in the national election.

Gradually, most absorption functions were transferred to the state. But most parties still maintain a network of economic facilities such as banks, housing projects, and loan funds. Some parties also maintain separate health funds. The Histadrut still holds onto the country's major health service, maintains a major bank, and owns some of Israel's largest economic concerns. The power amassed in this manner is used to benefit the labor movement—especially the ruling ILP.

As in the yishuv's national institutions, posts in the government bureaucracies are still frequently allocated according to political considerations. While regulations require that recruitment for all positions (except a few top ones) be based only on objective evaluation after public announcement of open positions, these regulations are at times circumvented (Etzioni 1966B). Although recruitment has been increasingly by merit lately, political affiliation of candidates is also taken into account (Eisenstadt 1967, p. 303). Consequently, the pervasiveness of political criteria in ostensibly nonpolitical spheres, a characteristic feature of the yishuv, has been perpetuated.

Centralization

Toward the end of the mandatory period, the power of the national institutions had increased; this process was greatly accelerated after independence. The new government took over the functions of the mandatory government as well as most of those of the Jewish Agency Executive and of the National Council.* This takeover was a landmark in the development of the political system: from then on there was a growing tendency towards the centralization of functions and power in the hands of the government and its administrative agencies.

Among the most crucial functions taken over by the state was the establishment and management of the unified Israel Defense Forces in place of the less centralized, voluntary prestate military organizations (the Haganah, its elite Palmach corps, and the dissident groups). Another was the establishment of a unified educational system to replace the yishuv's semiindependent educational frameworks. Educational policy, curricula, and teaching methods were now centrally devised and supervised by the Ministry of Education and Culture.

---

*The Jewish Agency continues to deal with mobilization of funds from the Jewish community abroad, with immigration, and with some aspects of absorption and settlement.

The structure of the political system itself was centralized as well. There is the traditional division into the executive, legislative, and judicial branches, but the executive branch (in conjunction with the center of the ruling party) actually wields the decisive political power and rules the country's sociopolitical life.

The president is elected by the Knesset (parliament) for a five-year term, but he is only the titular head of state; his functions are mainly ceremonial and symbolic. Officially, the president appoints the prime minister by charging a member of the Knesset with the formation of the government; however, he does so only after consultation with the major party leaders and, in fact, has little say in the matter. Thus, political power is concentrated at the governmental level rather than at the presidential level.

Israel has no formal constitution.* Ostensibly this fact enhances the importance of the Knesset—Israel's parliament—whose powers are not limited either by presidential veto or by the supreme court.† Moreover, the government is responsible to the Knesset and must resign when it fails to command its confidence. However, once a government coalition is formed with the blessing of the parties' leaders, usually the government will not fail to obtain a vote of confidence.

In fact, the power of the Knesset clearly falls below that of the government and the party centers (especially the dominant party's center). On almost all issues, MKs are obligated to vote in line with their parties' policies; in return, the coalition parties as a rule support the government's policy, which is usually precoordinated with the parties' centers.

This coordination is facilitated by the fact that the prime minister is usually the dominant party's leader, as well as by the fact that several government ministers also hold key positions in the dominant party's leadership. Thus, the government ministers and the dominant party's key functionaries (two groups that partly overlap) are the major wielders of centralized political power in Israel.

Special provision has been made for the scrutiny of government activities by Knesset committees. However, their effectiveness is limited by the fact that their members lack the technical knowledge (and the time) to check on government activities in detail (Weiss 1975).

Each party presents a slate of candidates for the Knesset. The candidates are selected by the parties' nominating committees and the public has no say

---

*However, there are basic laws generally considered to be components of a future constitution.

†Israel's Knesset is a one-chamber parliament consisting of 120 members elected for four-year terms.

in the matter. Since it is the party rather than the public that decides whether an MK will reappear on the list next term as a candidate for reelection, MKs subordinate themselves more to the party's leadership than they do to the public that supposedly elects them (Aronoff 1975).

There is similar centralization at the party level. In each of the larger parties an equilibrium is usually maintained among various factions and interest groups. Several factions coexist in the ILP—remnants of various independent parties that went into the making of this party. Also, there are representatives of other powerful interest groups, such as the kibbutz and moshav movements, affiliated with the party (Etzioni 1966A) as well as various powerful cliques. But within each of the major loci of power the structure is oligarchical. The parties hold internal elections for membership in party centers and for senior party posts. On the face of it, this should lend a certain amount of power to the parties' rank and file. In fact, however, the party bureaucracy has a great deal of control over these elections, which are not public or state controlled; furthermore, many of the positions (including the most powerful key positions) are usually appointive rather than elective.

The parties maintain permanent administrative machines that are active not only at election times but in interelectoral periods as well; the functionaries are salaried. As a consequence, lower-ranking functionaries are dependent on their superiors not only for promotion but also for their subsistence (Weiss 1971).

The tendency toward centralization is somewhat weaker in the center-right parties; still, in principle, the trend can be found among all well-established parties (Eisenstadt 1967, p. 305). The internal oligarchy of the Israeli parties carries special weight in view of the fact that there exist few independent voluntary organizations that could serve as alternative channels of upward communication from the rank and file of the public to the political elite (Fein 1962).

State Control of the Economy

The relationship between Israel's political system and the economy can be traced back to the yishuv era. The major ideological orientations in the economic field (as in most institutional fields) were shaped during the Second Aliya, when a collectivist-socialist ideology predominated. This ideology favored collective forms of social organization, and it emphasized the dominant role of the political system in all spheres of socioeconomic life. As Eisenstadt points out, the economy was not built up according to the ideological blueprint, but it was clearly influenced by it. This was evident in the control of economic resources and activities by political organizations; in the primacy accorded to sociopolitical considerations in regulating economic activities; in the stress put on economic activities that were important from the point of view of the collective (rather that on those that promised the greatest financial gain); in the great emphasis put on collective settlements and on cooperative forms of economic enterprise; and in the predominance of the public sector of the economy over the private sector. These patterns, which were prevalent in the preindependence period, have been perpetuated in Israel as well. Israel is first among modern non-Communist countries in the predominance of the public sector of the economy; the percentage of investment financed by the public sector is higher in Israel than it is in any Western country and is 3.5 times higher than in the United States (Barkai 1964, pp. 59–65).

The importance of political considerations in the economic system intensified even further after independence; this is reflected in the direct and indirect intervention of the government in all facets of economic life. Such intervention has been facilitated by the fact that the government concentrates enormous economic resources in its hands; because taxation in Israel is among the highest in the world, and because Israel, in view of its special position, absorbs large quantities of foreign aid. Capital from foreign sources constitutes some 60 percent of all capital allocated for development (Eshkol n.d.). The aid from abroad is naturally channeled through the government, and vastly increases the economic resources that it commands (Marx 1971).

It has been estimated that 45 percent of all financial resources at the disposal of the Israeli economy are, in one way or another, channeled through the government (Tal 1975). Also, the government's share in total investments in Israel has reached 80 percent, and recently has been estimated at more than 50 percent (Eisenstadt 1967, p. 82).

Government intervention in the economy is effected not only through direct ownership (or partial ownership) of economic enterprises, but mainly through the control of nongovernment enterprises. While the necessity of encouraging economic development (specifically, the import of capital from abroad) has brought the regime to reluctant concessions with private enterprise, it has seen to it that these remain directly or indirectly under the control of the government.

The control of such enterprises (and of the economy in general) is effected through monetary policy, in particular through credit policy (implemented mainly by the Bank of Israel); through the Treasury's fiscal policy concerned with the government's own budget and with various customs, duties, and taxes; through the regulation of production, consumption, and trade by means of import and export licenses, foreign currency allocations, and various tax exemptions, long-term loans, and subsidies; through wage policy;* and

---

*Officially, the wage policy is to be worked out by the Histadrut and the employers' association; in fact, however, it is greatly influenced by the government.

through development policy. Control of the economy is further facilitated by the close cooperation between the government and the Histadrut. By these means, the overriding importance of the government in the direction of the economy has become a permanent feature of the Israeli sociopolitical system. Although this system had its origin in the yishuv era, it has gained new significance in the state of Israel, where it is a major facet of the centralization of power in the hands of the political establishment.

Recently some complaints have been voiced in the Israeli press concerning an alleged "weakness" of the political leadership. This criticism, however, refers to the alleged reluctance of this leadership to work out a clearcut policy with regard to Israel's neighboring Arab countries and its inability to navigate the country with a surer hand toward some well-defined goal. On the other hand, the excessive power amassed by the establishment by virtue of its control of the economy is not in doubt.

The Role of Political Power

As a result of this economic control, large proportions of the Israeli population are directly or indirectly dependent for their subsistence on the government, various subsidiary public agencies, and the Histadrut. Some 40 percent of Israel's inhabitants are employed by the government and the Histadrut (Barkai 1964, p. 35), and most private concerns are dependent in one way or another on various benefits from the government. Hence various government and public officials are in a position to grant a wide variety of benefits to a large proportion of the population who are greatly dependent on these benefits (Etzioni-Halevy 1975C).

This great economic power amassed in the hands of the government, and the consequent dependence of large sectors of the population on government officials, has necessarily turned political power into a major criterion of status; it has also caused a gap to develop between those who wield such power and the rank and file of the population. This gap has been widened by the fact that the holders of political power have found ways to translate such power into economic benefits as well* (Etzioni-Halevy 1973).

---

*High-ranking government and public officials receive large expense allowances, some of them (and their families) receiving special health services beyond those offered by the sick funds; they also obtain special assistance in housing, car, and telephone allowances and the like. The more privileged parts of the population receive similar benefits from the organizations in which they are employed, but a sizable proportion of the population does not share them. In addition, some members of the political and administrative elites have been known to make use of their public office for their own pecuniary gain (see Israel State Comptrollers' Reports; see also Etzioni-Halevy 1975C).

This growing disparity between the political elite and most of the population is evident in the social sphere as well. The relatively close relations between the elite and nonelite groups that were prevalent in the yishuv weakened considerably after the establishment of the State. Members of the elite tended to detach themselves from the others, forming groups of their own; their whole pattern of life and association began to differ from that of the nonelite (Eisenstadt 1967, p. 304).

Thus, a major development that followed the establishment of the state "was the growing importance of political power as a social reward, a criterion of social status and position, and as a means of access to major occupational and economic positions" (Eisenstadt 1967, p. 155). This resulted in a growing gap between the political elite and the rank and file of the public.

CONCLUSION

The left-of-center labor movement (represented chiefly by immigrants of the Second and Third Aliyot) gained ascendancy in the yishuv, among other things, because its ideology and organizational patterns were the most successful in coping with the problems confronting the community. The basic features of this ideology were its collectivist-pioneering bent and the primacy it accorded to the collective (as represented by its political organizations) over all facets of socioeconomic life. Accordingly, the labor movement emphasized collective endeavors and organizational patterns in which political and economic activities intermingled, and political organizations that controlled economic resources as well. This ideology and these organizational patterns later layed the foundation for the concentration of economic power in the hands of Israel's political establishment.

Another source of this development lay in the features of the yishuv's political center: lacking sovereignty, it elicited the support of various political bodies by controlling the flow and allocation of the community's economic resources, a pattern that has been perpetuated by Israel's sovereign political center as well. This, in turn, led to the dependence of large segments of the population on the establishment and to an excessive power gulf between the political elite and the rank and file of the public.

As is well known, government intervention in the economy has been growing in all Western societies (Heilbroner 1972). But the control that the Israeli government wields over the economy, and the consequent dependence of various groups of the public on the political elite, is probably not equaled in many of these societies; although it is, of course, common in many non-Western, for example, Communist societies.

THE POLITICAL SIGNIFICANCE OF EXTRA POLITICAL PROCESSES

Some developments on the Israeli social scene that are not within the political realm proper are directly relevant to it. These include developments in Israel's ethnic relations and in its value patterns.

The Political Significance of Ethnic Relations

Besides the growing gap between the political elite and the public, there is another social gap that holds political significance: that between Jews of Western (European-American) origin, also known as Ashkenazim, and Jews of Oriental (Afro-Asian) origin. The basic patterns of the relations between these ethnicities were set shortly after the proclamation of the state, in the late 1940s and early 1950s. Before this, most of Palestine's Jewish inhabitants had been of European origin; the minority of Orientals living in the country belonged in part to the "Old Yishuv," and many of them remained outside the yishuv's sociopolitical system. Consequently, no marked problem of interethnic relations developed.

But with the establishment of the state and the abolishment of the restrictions set by the British mandate, large-scale immigration took place, and a sizable proportion of the immigrants came from the neighboring North African and Asian countries. As a result, Israel's two major Jewish ethnicities reached nearly equal numbers.* While Jews of Oriental origin had accounted for only 23 percent of the Jewish population in 1948, they comprised 45 percent in 1964 and 52 percent in 1970 (Eisenstadt 1967, p. 64; Smocha and Peres 1974, p. 39).

It soon became evident, however, that this numerical equality was not to be matched by socioeconomic equality. Originating from a more traditional society whose way of life, social organization, and value systems differed from those of European Jewry, the Orientals encountered serious difficulties in integrating into Israel's more modern economic, occupational, and educational structures, and they tended to gravitate into low-ranking, low-income occupations. In addition, they were regarded by many as somewhat lower in social status than Westerners.

---

*Arabs form another ethnicity. But their problems are of an entirely different order and will not be discussed in this study.

Major efforts were made to incorporate Orientals into the existing political frameworks. These attempts seem to have been successful, since Orientals have not established any separate, viable political organizations, and all attempts of would-be Oriental leaders to establish specifically Oriental political parties have been conspicuously unsuccessful.* There are some organizations of Orientals, but these have never been very active or fulfilled any important functions in Israel's public life.† But although they have been successfully absorbed into existing political frameworks, Orientals have not been accorded any major power positions.

These developments conflicted with Israel's generally accepted ideology of the unity of the Jewish people and the equality of its subgroups. Faced with a somewhat different reality, the government responded by maintaining that any differences, if they existed at all, were temporary, concerning only the first generation of immigrants; their children, born or raised in Israel, would all be equal and united.

It soon became clear, however, that the patterns established for the first generation were perpetuated for the second generation as well; that the gaps established in the early 1950s did not become perceptibly narrowed. In their encompassing analysis of the subject, Smocha and Peres (1974, p. 30) point out that in 1970 the average standard of living of the Western family was twice as high as that of the Oriental family; that Westerners were represented in the higher-status white-collar occupations twice as often as were Orientals; and that there were six to seven times as many Westerners in institutions of higher learning. In addition, Westerners were still greatly overrepresented in the political elite, and still dominated all national centers of power, although Orientals had made some headway into secondary power positions, especially on the municipal level. This situation, some observers claim, has been carrying the seeds of sociopolitical tensions and the disaffection of the disadvantaged ethnicity from Israel's sociopolitical system. These subjects will be dealt with in Chapters 6 and 9.

The Political Significance of Values

The ideology to which all major sectors of the yishuv adhered was that of the charismatic national movement of Zionism. It held that throughout

---

*As a rule, they have not been able to gain the one percent of the vote required to win a Knesset seat; at best, they have been able to form minor, insignificant splinter parties.

†It is doubtful whether they are, in fact, independent organizations. It is more likely that they are sponsored by (or under the influence of) some non-Oriental political bodies such as the ruling Labor Party.

2,000 years of exile the Jews had remained one nation; that the solution to the Jewish problem could therefore be found only in the reconstitution of a national home for the Jewish people in Palestine; that this national home would eventually take the form of an independent state; and that gradually there would be an ingathering of all exiles of the Jewish people to this state.

The building of the national home was set up as an ideal to which all Zionists were expected to subordinate their aspirations for individual gain, advancement, and a high standard of living—and for which, in many cases, they were expected to endanger their lives as well. While this national-collectivist ideology was accepted by all major sectors of the yishuv, the nationalist element was emphasized to a greater extent by the right-wing Revisionists. On the other hand, the subordination of individual advancement to collective goals fitted the pioneering ideology emphasized to a greater extent by the labor movement.

The intensity of the ideological commitment was relaxed somewhat by the establishment of the state, which was a partial realization of the Zionist ideal; by the consequent incorporation of some of the prestate voluntary organizations (such as the Haganah and the Palmach) into the state bureaucracy; by the institutionalization of some ideological precepts; and the general routinization of life. As Eisenstadt (1967, p. 385) points out, "the acceptance of these [the Zionist] values often created a lack of patience with fully crystallized ideological formulations which began to seem obvious and trite."

The collective Zionist commitment was by no means abandoned; although Zionism is now in the process of routinization, it shows great vitality and persistance. Israel's educational system is still geared to the inculcation of national-collectivist values more than to any other values (Adar and Adler 1965), and the general emphasis put on such values in Israel is doubtlessly greater than in most Western societies (see Chapter 9). Compared to the Yishuv period, however, there has been a certain dilution in collective commitments.

This dilution is not so much in collective-nationalist commitments—which have been kept in high gear by the continuous external threat, among other things. Rather, it is more evident in the slackening of pioneering fervor. Collective settlements, the epitome of pioneering in the yishuv, have not grown anywhere in proportion to the growth of the country's population; furthermore, although they still form one of the most dedicated sectors of Israeli society, the settlements have put growing emphasis on a rising standard of living.

What is true for collective settlements goes even more for the rest of Israeli society. Before independence, the dominant ideology of the labor movement held that economic and social activities were to be valued to the extent that they contributed to collective goals; after independence, a growing emphasis was put on individual achievement per se, and on economic rewards.

Professional and executive groups increasingly demanded that they be renumerated according to their education, responsibility, and expertise, rather than by the collective considerations of the prestate era (Medding 1972).

In many cases, proponents of the collective ideology were perceived as representing vested interests opposed to the aspirations and interests of others (Eisenstadt 1967, p. 385). Consequently, various groups came to feel that they were getting less than their fair share of the national cake, and increased their claims for resources and rewards. Thus there was an erosion in certain elements of the collective-pioneering ideology, with individualist orientations coming more and more to the fore. This, in turn, had significant implications for the development of Israel's political system. The topic will be dealt with in Chapters 2, 3, and 9.

CHAPTER

2

THE LEFT-RIGHT CONTINUUM: THE SIGNIFICANCE OF POLITICAL ORIENTATIONS

An important element of the relationship between the public and the political establishment is the ideological congruence or incongruence between the two. Following Duverger (1964, p. 307) and Arian (1975), we may say that when a period is characterized by a dominant doctrine—adhered to by the majority of the public—and the political establishment is identified with this doctrine, its rapport with the public is thereby facilitated and its position strengthened. But when the political orientations of the public undergo a shift while the establishment holds on to the erstwhile dominant doctrine, a certain cleavage develops between the public and the establishment that may be a source of political tension, and the establishment's position is thereby weakened.

We shall argue that such a cleavage has indeed developed between the Israeli public and the political establishment, and that it has found expression on the left-right continuum. It seems especially appropriate to analyze the possible cleavages on the left-right continuum since the Israeli political system has traditionally been variegated along this line (see Chapter 1). In Arian's words, "... the political system is historically, if not geographically, an extension of the continental European parliamentary tradition for which the left-right continuum has special relevance" (1968, p. 26).

Some observers, however, would probably take exception to this view, either because they belittle the significance of value orientations in general, including ideologies and political orientations, as an active, independent force in affecting sociopolitical reality, or because they belittle the significance of political orientations on the left-right continuum in particular for present-day Israeli sociopolitical reality. Hence we must first inquire into the significance of left- versus right-wing political orientations in present-day Israel (this chapter) before we inquire into the evolving center-periphery cleavage as manifested on this continuum (next chapter).

ANALYTICAL FRAMEWORK: THE SIGNIFICANCE OF POLITICAL ORIENTATIONS

In an argument over the merits of advertising, the sales manager of a well-known publishing firm said to the advertising director, "I defy you to show me one order that advertising ever put on our books." "I will," the latter promised, "as soon as you show me a single load of hay that the sun ever put in a barn." Whatever the validity of this retort as far as advertising is concerned, it has special relevance for values. It is our contention that value orientations (political orientations included) carry substantial weight in the framework of sociopolitical reality, more so perhaps than some recently fashionable theories are willing or able to grant; that, however, the most significant implications of values are not necessarily the most obvious ones, nor the ones that have been most commonly emphasized and debated. If social scientists had put more stress on the less obvious implications of value orientations for social action, and less stress on the more obvious implications, this would have taken much of the wind out of the debate on the role of values in society.*

Consider, for instance, the following statements. On one hand, Parsons and like-minded thinkers have assigned overwhelming importance to norms and values, to the extent of claiming "... that the relational patterns of social systems are normative, which is to say that they *consist* in institutionalized normative culture" (Parsons 1973, p. 75) or at least that "values *determine* the choice men make..." (Stein and Cloward 1958). In contrast, the "Power and Conflict" school sees values, in the words of Mills, as "master symbols of legitimation" whose "... social relevance lies in their use to justify or to oppose the arrangement of power..." (Mills 1959, p. 37). Or, in the even more radical statement by Dahrendorf: "The interests of the ruling group *are* the values that constitute the ideology of the legitimacy of its rule..." (Dahrendorf 1959, p. 176). (All emphasis supplied.)

Of course these statements reflect the most extremist versions of their author's views. Still, if such statements could be voiced by major sociologists, it is because the authors were primarily concerned with the direct and manifest relationship of values and norms to social practice. It may be argued, however, that the importance of values lies not only in that they serve as guidelines for action or conversely in that they lend legitimation to interests or power structures. Their additional (and, perhaps, even greater) importance lies in their *indirect* and *latent* implications for social practice—that is, in the implications they have for how people perceive social reality and what they want of it. For

---

*For a succinct overview of this controversy, see Eisenstadt (1968).

example: (1) It is well known that any perception of reality and any involvement in reality, social reality included, is selective. No one can be aware of, or interested in, all its aspects. Value orientations are apt to sensitize individuals or groups to certain aspects of reality, and ipso facto are apt to render them insensitive to other aspects. In this way, value orientations may foster people's awareness of, and involvement in, some social issues, and their apathy toward other issues.

(2) In recent years observers have increasingly emphasized the importance of the "definition of the situation" for social action (Thomas 1927; Blumer 1967). No unanimously agreed definition of the "definition of the situation" has been presented. Nevertheless, it seems that what the various observers have in mind is that individuals react not to social reality as such, but to social reality as they perceive it; actors work out certain conceptions or images of social phenomena, processes, or entities, and these prompt their response. It stands to reason that such definitions or images are based not only on an *analysis* to social reality but on its *evaluation* as well. Thus, the definition, whether of any specific situation or of broader social phenomena, is composed of both cognitive and evaluative processes, and there must be a constant interplay between the two to yield a coherent image of social reality. Evaluation, however, does not take place in a vacuum; it is based on certain value orientations that the actor has in stock, so to speak, and that he applies to the situation or phenomenon at hand. Consequently, we may say that the actors' conceptions and images of social processes or social entities are value-impregnated.

(3) Textbook sociology frequently invokes the impression that values serve as bases for social norms, that is, for certain rules that instruct people on what they ought or ought not to be doing. Individuals either follow these precepts and are rewarded, or else deviate from them at the risk of incurring social as well as self-imposed negative sanctions. Value orientations, however, are not only at the root of what people feel they *ought* to be doing; in addition, they have implications for what people feel they *want* to do, receive, or attain. This is apparently what Durkheim had in mind when he claimed that the disruption of values is apt to disorganize people's aspirations, and it is apparently what Merton referred to when he spoke of "cultural goals" as molding aspirations. In addition, value orientations are significant for what people wish to see realized in their community or society as well. In other words, people's aspirations and preferences are also value-impregnated.

This is not to say that there is a one-sided line of influence of value orientations on involvement, conceptions, and preferences. Apparently the channel of influence works in the opposite direction as well. With regard to the "definition of the situation," this claim has been concisely stated by Thomas: "It is in this connection that a moral code arises ... which is built up by successive definitions of the situation ..." (Thomas 1927, p. 43).

While value orientations have implications for people's perspectives on social reality, these perspectives, in turn, lend value orientations their concrete significance. Once one knows to which social perspectives certain value orientations are related, one is in a better position to tell what significance they hold for the people who adhere to them.

Political orientations may be considered as one type of value orientation.* Hence, what has been said for value orientations in general holds for political orientations as well. In fact, political value orientations should be especially significant, in Israel, from this point of view, because of the high degree of politization, that is, the pervasiveness of political criteria in all spheres of social life.†

Within the political realm we impute special significance to the left-right continuum that has traditionally held a wide range of connotations in the realm of both domestic and foreign affairs. On the domestic front the left has been associated with the labor movement, and with its socialist, relatively egalitarian ideology,‡ while the right has been associated with the ideology of "free enterprise" and the minimalization of political control over the economy. On the foreign front the right has been associated with activism—and the left, with a more restrained approach.

Since the present-day Israeli political system is still differentiated along the left-right continuum, we shall ask whether leftism vs. rightism does in fact hold some or all of these connotations for the present-day Israeli public—whether therefore this differentiation is still meaningful in Israeli society.

If this should be the case (and in view of the foregoing) we would expect: first, that Israelis with different (left versus right wing) political orientations be differentially sensitized to various socio-political issues; second, that they tend to differ in their conceptions and images of various aspects of the sociopolitical situation; and third, that they tend to emphasize different preferences as to how various aspects of Israel's sociopolitical life be shaped. Such differences may be expected both in the realm of domestic affairs (for example, with regard to socialism and egalitarianism) and in the sphere of foreign policy (with regard to activism).

---

*We refer to them as "orientations" rather than as "ideologies," because the latter term usually designates a set of interrelated orientations (see Plamenatz 1970, p. 27; Arian 1968, p. 14); whereas in this study we are dealing with orientations only on a single continuum.

†See Eisenstadt (1967, pp. 7–58); Deshen (1970, p. 46); see also Chapter 1.

‡On the egalitarian commitment of left-of-center socialist movements in general, see for instance, Laidler (1947, passim). Thus, summarizing the common features of all socialist movements up to his time, Laidler writes (p. 751): "All desire the elimination of . . . gross inequality of wealth which they insist (is) inherent in the present organization of society." On the egalitarian bent of leftist parties see also Lipset (1963), for instance, as cited below, Ch. 7. On the egalitarian commitment of the leftist labor movement in the yishuv and at the beginning of statehood in Israel, see Eisenstadt (1967, esp. p. 147).

Should these expectations be borne out even in part, there would be both theoretical and empirical ramifications. On the theoretical level this would lend indirect support to our contentions on the role of value orientations in the confrontation of social reality. On the empirical level we would then have learned something on the significance of a leftist or a rightist political bent in present day Israeli society. Should there be such a significance, it would then make sense to demonstrate that the political orientations of the public (as variegated on the left-right continuum) have undergone some shifts and are no longer congruent with the ideological position represented by the mainstream of the establishment.

Should our expectations *not* be realized, we would have to conclude that our theoretical conception is not corroborated by the data. On the empirical level we would have learned that left- versus right-wing political orientations are not (or no longer) meaningful in Israel today. It would then make little sense to demonstrate either an incongruence or a congruence between the political orientations of the public on the left-right continuum and the political doctrine of the establishment.

Empirical research in Israel has repeatedly focused on the political trend with which people identify: left, center, or right. However, the various studies did not, as a rule, probe any further; respondents were not asked what concrete content they imputed to their "leftism" or "rightism." Therefore, in the present (secondary) analysis, no a priori assumptions have been made as to the content of the orientations; and the terms "left-wing," "center," or "right-wing" orientations simply refer to such orientations *as conceived by the Israeli public itself.* On the basis of our general knowledge of Israel's political life, we felt justified in assuming that within the realm of domestic affairs a "leftist" orientation was akin to a socialist one, and that a "rightist" orientation was, in some way, its antonym. But no assumptions have been made as to the actual content of either. In order to assess the significance of these orientations in Israel, we thus had to explore the empirical relationship between them and a series of concrete sociopolitical perspectives of Israelis.

We did so mainly on the basis of the 1973 General and Panel study,* on a sample of 1,935 respondents[†] representing a cross section of the adult, Jewish, urban population of Israel. Where results of other studies are pertinent, they are also incorporated into the analysis.[‡]

---

*The data were collected for the Israel Elections Research Group in a survey conducted by the IIASR. The project was headed by Professor A. Arian and Dr. E. Torgovnik of the Department of Political Sciences, Tel Aviv University. The data have been made available to us by the generosity of these gentlemen.

†For technical reasons, cross tabulations included only 1,905 respondents.

‡Unless otherwise stated, all studies analyzed throughout this study are on cross sections of the adult, Jewish urban population of Israel.

THE SIGNIFICANCE OF POLITICAL ORIENTATIONS IN ISRAEL

Political Orientations and Political Involvement

As expected, political adherence was related to differential involvement in various aspects of Israel's sociopolitical life. This can be seen from Table 2.1, which gives the Percentage Difference Indexes (PDI) for involvement by political orientation.

Leftists professed more involvement than did rightists in politics in general, in problems of socioeconomic gaps among various strata, and even (to a slight extent) in security problems.* On this topic, the results of the General and Panel Study correspond to those of two previous studies. The first of these was done by Zloczower in 1964.[†] His results indicated that socialists[‡] were much more likely than were nonsocialists to be active in a party, and to be party members or sympathizers. They were thus more involved than others in political affairs (see Table 2.2).

The second study is that conducted by Arian in 1969. Asked what determined their voting decision, moderate leftists were more likely than rightists to name the party's platform as the determining factor, while rightists were more likely to name a candidate (Arian 1973, p. 100). Thus, once again, the leftists proved to be more sensitive to political issues.

A leftist or a socialist orientation, then, seems to sensitize individuals to some sociopolitical issues and enhances their involvement and/or participation in certain political spheres—or, conversely, the more involved are drawn towards the left—while a rightist political orientation spells comparatively less political interest but a stronger allegiance toward political leaders.

Political Orientations, Perceptions, and Images

Leftists professed a greater involvement with the problems of socioeconomic gaps in Israel; consequently, it was expected that they would be more likely than rightists to perceive such gaps as excessive, and that they would be more likely to define what the government was doing to close these gaps

---

*The centrists and the religious are dealt with separately, below.

[†]On a representative sample of male, Jewish residents of Haifa, aged 25–54. See Zloczower (1968 and 1972).

[‡]That is to say—persons who said they preferred "socialism" to "free enterprise" as a socioeconomic system.

TABLE 2.1

Political Involvement Percentage Difference Indexes (PDI)
By Political Orientation, in 1973

	N	PDI for Interest in Politics	PDI for Discussions of Politics with Friends	PDI for Interest in Problems of Socioeconomic Gaps	PDI for Interest in Security Problems
Left	422	6	1	14	37
Center	628	−5	−15	4	31
Right	441	−16	−19	4	32
Religious	135	−34	−50	−12	7
No response	279	−47	−51	−21	8

Explanatory Remarks:

1. A percentage difference index (PDI) value indicates the preponderance of one type of response over another for a single variable. For each variable, the PDI was computed by subtracting the percentage of the most negative responses from the percentage of the most positive responses. Resulting negative index values indicate a preponderance of negative responses over positive responses, while positive index values indicate the reverse. The possible range of PDI values is from +100 to −100. This method has been adopted from Miller (1974A, p. 954).

2. The central question on political adherence that recurs in this and many other tables was: "With what political trend do you identify? 1) Left 2) Moderate Left 3) Center 4) Right" (The categories of "left" and "moderate left" have been combined for this analysis). For the wording of the other questions throughout this study, see Appendix A.

3. Respondents were presented only with the left-center-right alternatives, but some respondents spontaneously identified their political orientations as "religious." This must be understood in the context of Israel's political scene that includes specifically religious parties.

Source: General and Panel Study (1973).

as inadequate. This, however, was not the case: in the General and Panel Study *no differences* among people of various political orientations on these counts were revealed.* Furthermore, when asked about existing salary differentials between themselves and people *below* them on the salary scale, and between themselves and people *above* them on the scale, leftists, centrists, and rightists *did not differ* in the extent to which they defined such differentials as excessive.† Thus, they resemble each other in their perceptions of socioeconomic gaps in Israeli society.

---

*In addition, the differences between rightists and leftists in the extent to which they thought problems of economic gaps would influence their voting, were negligible. (More on this below).
†The last two questions were addressed to employees only.

TABLE 2.2
Participation and Involvement According to Political Adherence in Haifa, 1964
(in percentages)

	N	Party Actives, Members, or Sympathizers	Non-partisan, Anti-partisan, or no Response
Pro-Socialism and Pro-Histadrut*	175	65	35
Pro-Socialism and not Pro-Histadrut	127	58	42
Pro-Histadrut and not Pro-Socialism	121	52	48
Favor Free Enterprise and not Pro-Histadrut	148	32	68
Have no Ideology and not Pro-Histadrut	72	20	80

*The Histadrut is Israel's central federation of labor unions.
Source: Zloczower (1968, p. 124).

We asked whether this could be attributed to the fact that egalitarian orientations have been widely accepted by *all* parts of the Israeli public. In fact, the great majority of the respondents thought that socioeconomic gaps in Israel were excessive, and that the government's remedies were inadequate.* However, with regard to topics that personally concerned the respondents, quite a different picture emerged: the great majority of the respondents of all political orientations (employees only) thought that salary differentials between themselves and those above them on the scale and between themselves and those below them on the scale were just about as they should be.† Thus, while most respondents were ready to pay lip service to equality in the abstract, their readiness to adhere to equality shrank perceptibly where their own salaries were concerned.

---

*These opinions were held by 83 percent and 59 percent of the respondents respectively. In addition, 78 percent thought that the government should spend "a lot" of money to aid the disadvantaged.

†Only fewer than a quarter of the respondents thought that salary differentials between themselves and those above them on the scale were excessive and fewer than a fifth held this opinion with regard to differentials between themselves and those below them on the scale.

While persons of various political trends did not differ in their views on equality, they diverged to some extent in their conceptions of democratic procedures. The Percentage Difference Indexes in Table 2.3 show that leftists hold a somewhat more favorable image of elections, while rightists tend to be more suspicious.

TABLE 2.3

Election Image Percentage Difference Indexes (PDI) by Political Orientation, in 1973

	N	PDI for Images of Elections as Impairing Nation's Unity	PDI for Images of Politicians as Utilizing Citizens through Elections
Left	422	27	−1
Center	628	17	−6
Right	441	9	−9
Religious	135	15	−16
No response	279	0	−3

Note: Negative values of the percentage difference index (PDI) indicate a preponderance of negative images of elections or politicians over positive ones and vice versa.
Source: General and Panel Study (1973).

Political Orientations and Sociopolitical Preferences

The left-right cleavage is conspicuously reflected in preferences on both foreign and domestic affairs. This becomes evident from Arian's study of 1969:* 80 percent of the rightists in Arian's sample expressed a preference for an aggressive policy toward the Arab countries compared to 62–63 percent of the leftists. At the same time 77 percent of the leftists favored a socialist (rather than a capitalist) pattern of economic life, compared to 52 percent of the rightists. It is of special interest, however, that even among the leftists more than 60 percent favored an aggressive policy, and even among the rightists, more than 50 percent favored socialism. Evidently for many respondents, left- versus right-wing orientations structured sociopolitical reality *either* in the area of foreign policy *or* in the domestic sphere. Alternatively, many respondents based their leftist adherence on their stand on either foreign policy or domestic affairs. This point is further clarified by Table 2.4.

---

*Arian 1973, p. 122.

TABLE 2.4

Political Orientations by Preferences on Stand vis-a-vis the Arab Countries and on Economic Patterns, in 1969
(in percentages)

	Left	Center	Right	Religious	No Orientation
Percentage who favor Socialism and Nonaggressive Policy	30	15	10	9	12
Percentage who favor Socialism and Aggressive Policy	47	40	40	50	41
Percentage who favor Capitalism and Nonaggressive Policy	6	9	7	6	6
Percentage who favor Capitalism and Aggressive Policy	14	30	35	18	24
No Response	3	6	8	17	17
N	451	403	303	152	375

$p < 0.01$*

*In cross tabulations throughout this study, whenever relevant, the x^2 test of significance is used.

Source: Data supplied on the basis of Arian (1973). The study was conducted in three stages, each with a different sample. The data in this table are from the third stage.

It can be seen that leftists and rightists differed significantly on both ends of the spectrum: only a small minority of leftists favored both capitalism and an aggressive foreign policy, and only a small minority of rightists opted for the opposite views. However, a significantly larger minority of both leftists and rightists favored socialism combined with an aggressive policy toward Arab countries. The leftists who favored such a constellation, apparently saw their leftist adherences as relevant mainly in the context of domestic affairs, while the rightists who expressed a similar preference apparently viewed their rightist commitment as relevant chiefly in the sphere of foreign policy.

The relevance of left- versus right-wing orientations for preferences on both foreign and domestic affairs is also evident from the General and Panel Study, as shown by the Percentage Difference Indexes in Table 2.5.

TABLE 2.5

Percentage Difference Indexes (PDI) for Preferences on Territories and on Two Domestic Issues, by Political Orientations, in 1973

	N	PDI for Preference on Withdrawal from Territories in Return for Peace	PDI for Preference of Laws and Discussions over Strong Leaders	PDI for Preference of Ideal Party as Representing the Working Class (Rather than the Middle Class)
Left	422	4	2	39
Center	628	−14	−5	10
Right	441	−35	−18	6
Religious	135	−42	1	3
No response	279	−32	−10	0

Note: Positive PDI values indicate a preponderance of preferences in favor of withdrawal from territories, laws, and discussions (over strong leaders) and an ideal party as representing the working class. Negative PDI values indicate a preponderance of obverse preferences.

Source: General and Panel Study (1973).

To use popular terms, leftists are more frequently "doves," rightists are more frequently "hawks." At the same time, most adherents of *all* political orientations favor an aggressive policy toward the Arab countries and do not favor withdrawal from the major part of the held territories; a sizable minority favors withdrawal from no territories whatsoever.* At least this was the case in 1973, before the Yom Kippur War.

On domestic affairs rightists are less favorably oriented toward democratic procedures ("laws, discussions") and tend to favor "strong leaders" more frequently than do leftists. All in all, then, leftists tend to adhere more closely to what some observers consider a political culture appropriate for a democracy (Almond and Verba 1965; Pateman 1970): they are more frequently involved in politics and more frequently favor democratic procedures. The rightists are somewhat less involved in politics and tend somewhat more frequently toward "authoritarian" images and preferences. However, the differences are by no means large enough to justify labeling the former as "democrats" and the latter as "authoritarians."

---

*52 percent and 31 percent respectively, according to the General and Panel Study.

The cleavages in preferences of an ideal party are in line with what could have been expected. Indirectly, we learn that leftists identify more frequently with the working class; rightists with the middle class. This, however, does not imply different preferences with regard to economic gaps. According to the General and Panel Study, respondents of various political orientations do not differ in their opinions on whether the government should spend "a lot" of money to aid the disadvantaged.

In all, the evidence indicates that leftists are more interested than are rightists in the problems of socioeconomic gaps, just as they are more interested in other sociopolitical topics. But leftists and rightists do not differ on a variety of other items pertaining to equality. They do not differ in the extent to which they regard socioeconomic gaps as excessive (either on the abstract or on the concrete level) and in what they think should be done about such gaps. Thus on the whole, people of various political orientations *do not differ significantly in the degree of their egalitarianism.*

Since our concern is with a left-right *continuum* (not merely with a dichotomy), it is of interest how centrists align themselves. A general overview of the tables indicates that they are usually closer to the right than they are to the left. This fits in with the structure of Israel's party system, in which the major cleavage is between the left-of-center and the center-right, and in which center and right-wing parties are not clearly differentiated (see Chapters 1 and 3).

The religious, too, resemble the right on most counts, but cannot be clearly placed with regard to their affinity to democratic procedures. Some 90 percent of the religious oppose withdrawal from any substantial part of the occupied territories.* This seems to follow from a certain widespread interpretation of the "Halacha," the Jewish religious law. According to this interpretation, Jews are forbidden to give up any part of the Land of Israel to foreign hands. Not unexpectedly, the religious evince the most adamant position where religion is (indirectly) concerned.† This ties in with the fact that Israel's religious parties are composed of both left- and right-of-center factions, and, hence, usually take a clear stand only on religious or semireligious issues.

The question was raised whether the divergence among adherents of various political orientations in involvement, images, and preferences may not be a product of differences in their SES‡ or social origins. This, however, was not the case: when each background factor (including age and country of

---

*This datum is from the General and Panel Study.
†The recent demonstrations against withdrawal from territories were led and manned in great part by religious youth.
‡Socioeconomic status

origin), was controlled for, the disparities among adherents of diverse political orientations still persisted. In some instances, the differences were smaller for some categories and larger for others (more on this below). But in no case did the differences disappear when background factors were controlled. We attribute special importance to this finding, for it indicates that the relationship between political orientations and attitudes is not spurious—thus lending support to our line of argument.

In summation, the items analyzed may be divided into those concerned with foreign and those concerned with domestic affairs. The latter may be subdivided into those concerned with politics proper, and those concerned with socioeconomic patterns. Political orientations, as differentiated on the left-right continuum, have clear implications for stands on foreign affairs; on the domestic front, they have clear relevance for politics proper (involvement in politics and stands vis-à-vis democratic procedures). The situation is less clearcut for socioeconomic issues. On one issue (equality) the left-right cleavage has no clear implications, while on another (preference of socialism) the implications, though not as definitive as could have been expected, are strong and significant.

Social Groupings and the Significance of Political Orientations

A well-known professor in the social sciences who had developed close ties with Israel as well as with the United States stated, in one of his public lectures in Israel, that he saw no difference between socialism and liberalism. "When I am in the U.S.," he said, "I call myself a liberal. When I am in Israel, I call myself a socialist." One of his listeners then retorted: "If it is indeed as you say, that there is no difference between socialism and liberalism, then why don't you call yourself a liberal when you are in Israel and a socialist when you are in the U.S.?"* The reply of the professor, unfortunately, was not recorded for posterity. At any rate, this true little anecdote exemplifies that similarly tagged political orientations may mean different things in different societies. Can they also mean different things to different groups of people in the same society? And is this, in fact, the case, in Israel?

So far we saw that the left-right cleavage is of significance when the public as a whole is treated as an entity. It was reasoned, however, that the left-right division should be of a different and greater significance for the elderly and the oldtimers (especially those raised in the prestate era when ideological issues

---

*In Israel the "liberal" parties are to the center-right rather than to the left of the political spectrum.

might have held greater salience than they do today) and that it should be of a different and greater significance for persons of higher education, who would show more of a tendency to relate to social reality in terms of abstract ideas. Since the left-right cleavage is originally a European cultural product, it was also expected that it would be of lesser significance for persons of Oriental extraction.

On the basis of the General and Panel Study no consistent differences were revealed according to age, length of stay in the country, and, on most counts, according to education. With regard to country of origin, however, our expectation was borne out: on most items the left-right differences were greater among Westerners than they were among Orientals. This is shown in Table 2.6.

TABLE 2.6

Differences among Left, Center, and Right-Wing Adherents, by Country of Origin, in 1973
(in percentages)

	Very or Fairly Interested in Politics			Very or Fairly Interested in Socioeconomic Gaps			Think Ideal Party Should Represent Middle Class		
	1	2	3	1	2	3	1	2	3
Left	68	55	63	79	70	77	26	21	14
Center	52	47	57	73	69	72	33	30	38
Right	67	50	45	71	60	60	67	32	40
Religious	43	13	33	43	41	60	43	11	39
No response	22	27	25	22	37	46	11	25	18
Total	55	43	52	66	58	66	39	27	30
N	92	574	1,209	92	574	1,209	92	574	1,209

Explanatory Remarks:

1) 1 = third generation Israelis; 2 = Orientals; 3 = Westerners.

2) Persons of Afro-Asian origin (Orientals) constitute slightly more than half of the Jewish population in Israel. Hence it can be seen that persons of European-American origin (Westerners) are greatly overrepresented in this sample. A similar overrepresentation of Westerners is to be found in the sample of the Arian study (Arian 1973, pp. 238-39). Since the field work for both the Arian study and the General and Panel Study was carried out by the Israel Institute of Applied Social Research, the source of overrepresentation must lie in the Institute's sampling procedures. According to Arian, Orientals are underrepresented because a relatively lower proportion of this group is found in the (urban) survey areas and they constitute a higher proportion of illiterates.

3) In all three subtables: for Westerners, the differences among leftists, centrists, and rightists were significant at the 0.05 level; for Orientals they were not.

Source: General and Panel Study (1973).

While the left-right cleavage is not meaningless for Orientals either, its significance is clearly greater for Westerners. Interestingly, in one respect, the left-right cleavage seems to hold antithetical meanings for different groups of people, as can be seen from Table 2.7.

The table shows that among the less educated and among Orientals, rightists are more frequently influenced by socioeconomic gaps in their voting intentions; among the highly educated and among Westerners, the opposite is the case. Thus, among the less-favored groups, *rightism* more frequently spells concern with inequality; among the more-favored groups, *leftism* more often has this connotation.

Since (by definition) the less-favored groups are adversely affected by socioeconomic gaps, it seems that those among them who turn to the *right* thereby frequently protest *their own* and their peers' disadvantaged position. Since (by definition) the more-favored groups benefit from inequality, it seems that those among them who turn to the *left* thereby frequently register protest against the disadvantaged position *of others*.

Higher-status leftists who are concerned with inequality while (perhaps inadvertently) enjoying its benefits are sometimes dubbed by Israeli rightists

TABLE 2.7

Percentages of Leftists, Centrists, and Rightists Who Think Problems of Socioeconomic Gaps Will Influence Their Voting, by Education and by Country of Origin, in 1973

	Education			Country of Origin		
	Low	Medium	High*	Third Generation Israelis	Orientals	Westerners
Left	36	47	59	58	42	49
Center	36	41	44	30	51	37
Right	44	43	39	50	48	38
Religious	22	22	23	29	26	21
No response	13	28	23	0	22	20
Total	31	40	44	38	41	37
N	588	887	419	92	574	1,209
	$p < 0.01$			$p < 0.0$		

*Low = elementary education or less.
Medium = full or partial high school education.
High = full or partial higher education.
Source: General and Panel Study (1973).

as "beautiful souls."* This epithet, however, is merely part of the left-right controversy in Israel. In actual fact, there is no indication that the higher-status leftists' concern with inequality is any less genuine than the higher-status rightists' (*less* frequent) concern with this problem.

CONCLUSION

Traditionally, leftism in Israel has been associated with egalitarianism and with socialism; rightism has been associated with activism in foreign policy. At present, the former is apparently no longer the case and, in the mind of the Israeli public, association of "left" with "equality" no longer holds. On the other hand, association of leftism with socialism and of rightism with activism, does seem to hold in present-day Israel, at least for a considerable part of the public.

Since leftism is still clearly associated with socialism, why is it not, or no longer, associated with egalitarianism? Partly, this probably stems from the fact that not all leftists express a preference for socialism while some rightists do (see above). However, in view of the strong positive relationship between leftism and socialism, this may account for the phenomenon only in part.

Perhaps an additional explanation for the lack, or loss, of egalitarian connotations of leftist orientations in the mind of the Israeli public lies in the traditional tendency of the socialist ideology and left-of-center socialist movements (in Israel as well as abroad) to concern themselves mainly with the inequality of "workers" vis-à-vis "employers"; with the subordination of the "working class" by "capitalists." Yet they had little to say concerning the problems of ethnic discrimination, poverty, and the culturally disadvantaged, or even on differentials of political power. Gradually, however, the workers' conditions improved; certain groups of employees in Israel, and probably elsewhere as well, joined the ranks of the advantaged (rather than the disadvantaged); the Israeli central organization of labor, the Histadrut, became one of the country's major loci of power; and, finally, the public sector of the Israeli economy has long been clearly predominant, whereas private employers are in the minority as well as being highly dependent on the government and the Histadrut. As a result of these various factors and developments the entire problem of the cleavage between employers and employees faded into the background.

On the other hand, other types of inequality, such as the disparities between ethnicities, the income differentials among various groups of em-

---

*The equivalent of this idiom in English would be "bleeding hearts."

ployees, or the gaps between members of the political elite and the rank and file (see Chapter 1) became increasingly prominent. Since the leftist ideology had little to offer on any of these issues, it became less and less relevant in this context. This in turn may explain the loss of egalitarian connotations of the leftist adherence.

In contrast, another issue on which the left and right traditionally diverged, that of activism in foreign policy, has become increasingly prominent and increasingly controversial between the two political blocs in recent years, especially since the Six-Day War. Even before that there were, of course, activists and nonactivists in Israel. But since the Six-Day War, which resulted in the conquest of what is known in Israel as "the territories," the issue of "how much to relinquish in return for what" became increasingly salient, and the controversy between the "doves" and the "hawks" increasingly sharpened. In fact, to a large extent, Israel's political life and its constellation of parties came to be crystallized around this issue, and the left-right division came to coincide largely with the "dove"-"hawk" cleavage. Thus, Achdut Ha'avoda, traditionally a leftist and activist party, which joined the left-of-center alignment, became rather moderate in its foreign policy orientation.* Conversely, the "Labor Movement for a Greater Israel," which was leftist on domestic affairs, but "hawkish" as far as the territories were concerned, joined the center-rightist Likud. In this context it is not surprising that the left-right cleavage is highly relevant for the Israelis' stand vis-à-vis the Arabs.

This raises the question of whether the controversy concerning this topic is merely a matter of strategy in foreign policy or whether it assumes broader sociocultural significance. To put it differently, is this strictly an instrumental issue of how best to cope with a difficult situation, or does it have to do with the basic problems of sociopolitical identity within Israeli society, specifically with Israeli nationalism.

Two points seem to be indicative. First, it must be noted, that there is a broad consensus in Israel concerning basic national identification (see Chapter 8), a consensus shared by all political trends with the exception of a few minute marginal groups. Hence the controversy concerning the manner of confronting the Arabs cannot be seen as one between Israeli "nationalists" and opponents of such nationalism.

Second, however, it must be kept in mind that the dilemma of the territories and the manner of dealing with the Israeli-Arab conflict are core issues on which Israel's very existence, or at least the lives of a great many Israelis, may depend. Hence it was to be expected that the controversy on this topic would assume such a central position in Israel's political life. Hence, too, it

---

*For details on parties, see next chapter.

is not surprising that the controversy has not been confined to the expediency of various alternative policies but has assumed emotional overtones as well. The "doves" have been accusing the "hawks" of adherence to the myth of the "fatherland" (Nachlat-Avot) and of chauvinism, while the "hawks" have presented themselves as the true defenders of the values of Zionist nationalism, accusing the "doves" of defeatism. Thus the left-right cleavage is of relevance for a central, emotionally laden controversy in which the Israeli public has been embroiled.

Furthermore, it could be seen above that the left-right cleavage is of relevance not only for possible withdrawal from territories, but also for attitudes toward an overall "aggressive" versus "nonaggressive" policy toward the Arab countries that is a much more encompassing and diffuse controversy, with even clearer sociocultural significance.

To conclude, while the controversy between "doves" and "hawks" is not one between "nationalists" and "cosmopolitans," neither does it revolve around a purely instrumental issue of expediency. It has, rather, to do with the emphasis put on nationalism (some would say chauvinism) and with the manner in which nationalism is perceived and presented. For this cardinal issue, then, the left-right cleavage is highly relevant.

We can now relate the analysis back to our theoretical concern, and to the main theme of this study. The contention proposed was that value orientations are of greater (albeit indirect) relevance for the manner in which men confront social reality than emerges from some theories that have recently become fashionable. We argued that his relevance is manifested by the implications that value orientations have for individuals' sensitivity to various aspects of this reality; for the manner in which they perceive and interpret this reality; and for what they wish to see realized in it. Applying this contention to political value orientations as differentiated on the left-right continuum, it was, at least in part, corroborated. As expected, left- versus right-wing political orientations have implications for involvement, perceptions, and preferences of Israelis with regard to various (though not all) facets of Israel's sociopolitical reality. Alternatively, we may say that Israelis tend to structure several of their perspectives on sociopolitical reality in terms of their orientations on the left-right continuum.

It is noteworthy that similar research on the liberal-conservative cleavage in the United States has come up with two sided results.* On one hand, "repeated samples of the national electorate by the Survey Research Center (Campbell et al. 1960; Converse 1964) have convincingly demonstrated that

---

*Such research, however, has mostly been based on various scales of liberalism versus conservatism, rather than on respondents' own self-identification.

no such organizing dimension or ideological structure exists for most citizens" (Robinson et al. 1968, p. 79). On the other hand, Free and Cantril (1967) have found the liberal-conservative continuum to be highly significant in structuring various concrete attitudes of the American public in both the political and the socioeconomic realm. This despite the fact that sizeable proportions of the public hold to a conservative ideology while at the same time qualifying as operational liberals. In Israel, too, it has sometimes been argued that the traditional left-right cleavage is no longer relevant for the public today. In contrast to the United States, however, the empirical evidence all points in the same direction, indicating, as we have seen, that this is not so.

In view of the pervasiveness of the left-right continuum in structuring political reality for Israeli citizens, we would be justified in claiming that a possible incongruence between the political establishment and the public with regard to their location on this continuum may serve as a major point of stress on the Israeli political scene that might weaken the position of the political establishment. In the next chapter we shall argue that recent shifts in the political orientations of the Israeli public have in fact resulted in such an incongruence.

CHAPTER 3

CHANGES IN POLITICAL ORIENTATIONS AND IDEOLOGICAL INCONGRUENCE

In the yishuv era and at the beginning of statehood there was, in the Jewish community, a dominant political doctrine, that of collectivist socialism;* there also was a dominant party (Mapai) that identified itself with this doctrine and whose policies were, by and large, in line with it. There was thus a basic congruence between the ideological configuration to which the public adhered and the political structure: the dominant party derived additional power from the left-of-center ideology that legitimated political control of economic concerns and the leftist ideology was strengthened by the hegemony of the labor movement and its consequent dominance over the systems of political socialization (see Chapter 1). Is such a congruence still evident today?

The same left-of-center party (the Israel Labor Party—formerly Mapai)† is still dominant.‡ Although it has recently been putting less emphasis on its adherence to a leftist ideology, it has by no means abandoned it. Nominally it still pledges allegiance to socialism, and it still maintains some basic left-of-center affinities de facto as well (see below). But is the left-of-center socialist orientation still the dominant political doctrine of the community? We shall argue that recently the orientations of the public have undergone some changes with which the doctrine of the establishment (as represented by the dominant party) has not kept pace.

---

*See Duverger (1964, p. 307) and Arian (1975).
†See explanatory remarks on Table 3.1.
‡It has been noted that Mapai/Labor Party has always been a rather moderate, as well as pragmatic, socialist party. So much so that it has sometimes been characterized as a "center party" (Etzioni 1966B, p. 714). However, as Arian (1971, p. 265) points out, this refers to a mathematical and not to an ideological center. The Labor Party's basic commitment to a socialist ideology (albeit a moderate one) has not been at issue.

CHANGES IN POLITICAL ORIENTATIONS: AN EMPIRICAL ANALYSIS

There are various ways of inquiring into possible changes in the political orientations of the public. The first, and ostensibly the most obvious one, is an examination of election results, comparing how socialist (left-of-center) and nonsocialist (center-rightist) parties have fared against each other throughout the years. We shall see, however, that the interpretation of such results is far from simple and that changing election results, although they are apparently affected by changes in political orientations, are by no means identical with such changes.

Election Results and Changes in Political Orientations

To permit an overview of Israeli election results over the years, it must be noted that the socialist parties have undergone various splits, mergers, and alignments. The end result of these is the present-day Alignment that encompasses them all.* These various processes, somewhat reminiscent of family quarrels and reconciliations, seem to attest to the basic affinities among these parties.

The center-right-wing parties (the General Zionists, later known as the Liberals, and Herut being most prominent among these) have also undergone various splits, mergers, and alignments not unlike those of the socialist parties, the end result of which, is the present-day Likud. Here too these processes have attested to the fact that although not in complete agreement, these parties are basically akin to one another.

The third major political bloc is that of the religious parties. These include labor as well as nonlabor sections, yet the major commitments of the former as well as the latter have been on the religious front. All other parties have usually been minor splinter parties. Table 3.1 presents the three major blocs in separate groupings.†

Despite the various partitions, mergers, and alignments, election results were basically stable from 1949 until 1965.‡ This holds for socialist parties, which (no matter how their inner partitions may have changed) have usually totaled 48 to 50 percent of the votes. Disregarding the first election in 1949, center and rightist parties have also secured a rather stable percentage of the vote, ranging from 24 to 27 percent. Similarly, support for the religious parties has not varied by more than 3 percent.

---

*See remarks on Table 3.1.
†For a glossary and translation of the major parties' names, see Appendix C.
‡This point has been made by Smith (1971, pp. 244–45).

TABLE 3.1

Distribution of Votes among Parties and Blocs in Knesset Elections, 1949–73
(in percentages)

Party and Group	1st Knesset (1949)	2nd Knesset (1951)	3rd Knesset (1955)	4th Knesset (1959)	5th Knesset (1961)	6th Knesset (1965)	7th Knesset (1969)	8th Knesset (1973)
(1) *Communists*								
Maki	3.5	4.0	4.5	2.8	4.2	1.1	1.1	—
Rakach	—	—	—	—	—	2.3	2.8	3.4
Moked	—	—	—	—	—	—	—	1.4
Total Communists	3.5	4.0	4.5	2.8	4.2	3.4	3.9	4.8
(2) *Labor Parties*								
Mapam	14.7	12.5	7.3	7.2	7.5	6.6	—	—
Achdut Ha'avoda			8.2	6.0	6.6	—	—	—
Mapai	35.7	37.3	32.2	38.2	34.7	—	—	—
Alignment Mapai-Achdut Ha'avoda	—	—	—	—	—	36.7	—	—
Rafi	—	—	—	—	—	7.9	—	—
Alignment Labor Party-Mapam	—	—	—	—	—	—	46.2	39.6
Total Labor Parties	50.4	49.8	47.7	51.4	48.8	51.2	46.2	39.6
(3) *Total Minorities' Parties*	3.0	4.7	4.9	4.7	3.9	3.8	3.5	3.3
(4) *Center and Right Wing Parties*								
Ind. Liberals (Progressives)	4.1	3.2	4.4	4.6	13.6	3.8	3.2	3.6
General Zionists (Liberals)	5.2	16.2	10.2	6.2		—	—	—
Herut	11.5	6.6	12.6	13.5	13.8	—	—	—
Gachal	—	—	—	—	—	21.3	21.7	—
Hareshima Hamamlachtit	—	—	—	—	—	—	3.1	—
Hamerkaz Hachofshi	—	—	—	—	—	—	1.2	—
Likud	—	—	—	—	—	—	—	30.2
Total Center and Right Wing Parties	20.8	26.0	27.2	24.3	27.4	25.0	29.2	33.8
(5) *Religious Parties*								
National Religious Party	12.2	8.3	9.1	9.9	9.8	8.9	9.7	8.3
Agudat Israel		2.0	4.7	4.7	3.7	3.3	3.2	3.8
Poalei Agudat Israel		1.6			1.9	1.8	1.8	
Total Religious Parties	12.2	11.9	13.8	14.6	15.4	14.0	14.7	12.1
(6) *Others*	10.1	3.6	1.9	2.2	0.3	2.5	2.5	6.4

Explanatory Remarks:

1) *The Communist Parties:* For many years Maki was the only communist party in Israel. In 1965, when its mainstream declared allegiance to Zionism and the Jewish State, a more extremist group (Rakach) splintered off from it. In 1973 a new party (Moked) came into existence, which merged with Maki.

The communist parties are grouped separately from socialist labor parties, because they are very different in character and, as a rule, attract a very different kind of voter: Rakach, for instance, attracts mostly marginal Jews, or Arabs in search of a channel of protest against the Jewish regime.

2) *The Labor-left-wing (Socialist) Parties:* As noted, the history of the Israeli labor parties is wrought with splits, mergers, and alignments. By 1954, Mapam, the more extreme leftist party, was divided; a more moderate leftist party (Achdut Ha'avoda), more activist in foreign affairs, split off from it. In 1965, Achdut Ha'avoda formed an alignment with Mapai, the most moderate of Israel's socialist parties and the key partner in all government coalitions. At that time, another moderately socialist party, Rafi, split off from Mapai. In 1968, Mapai, Achdut Ha'avoda, and Rafi merged to form the Israel Labor Party. For the 1969 election this party formed an alignment with Mapam that was retained for the 1973 election as well. (It should be noted that the Achdut Ha'avoda party which existed from 1954 to 1968 is not identical with the Achdut Ha'avoda of the yishuv era.)

3) *The Minorities' Parties:* These are various Arab and Druze parties, usually affiliated with the Israel Labor Party (formerly Mapai). Because of their small size they are not reported on separately.

4) *The Center and Right-Wing Parties:* These have been included in the same group since the demarcation line between center and right-wing parties in Israel is rather unclear (see text). The Independent Liberals were formerly known as the Progressives. The General Zionists came to be known as the Liberals. In 1965 this Liberal Party joined with Herut, at that time Israel's most rightist party and the most activist in its foreign policy, to form Gachal. By 1969 an even more extremist party, Hamerkaz Hachofshi had splintered off from Gachal while at the same time Hareshima Hamamlachtit splintered off from Rafi as the latter merged with Mapai. In 1973 all center and right-wing parties except the Independent Liberals aligned themselves to form the Likud.

5) *The Religious Parties:* The National Religious Party (formerly the National Religious Front) is composed of the Mizrachi, a center religious party, and Hapoel Hamizrachi, a labor religious party. Agudat Israel and Poalei Agudat Israel are more extremist orthodox parties; the former is a labor party, while the latter is not. Sometimes the last two parties joined forces.

6) While all these splits, alignments, and mergers are rather complicated, it is not necessary to be cognizant of all details in order to follow the overall picture that emerges when only the total in each group of parties is considered.

Sources: (1) H. Smith (1971)
(2) Central Bureau of Statistics (July 1974)

In 1969, however, a new trend became apparent. Electoral support for socialist parties started to decline perceptibly, while support for center and rightist parties increased. While the socialist parties as a group netted as much as 51.2 percent in 1965, they could secure only 39.6 percent in 1973. In the same time span the center and rightist parties were able to work themselves up from 25 percent to 33.8 percent.*

Is this recent electoral decline of the left peculiar to Israel or is it a more general phenomenon? An overview of election results in Western democracies shows that in some countries left-of-center parties gained strength in recent years; in others they gradually lost support, and in still others no clear trends are visible. Since there seems to be no overall pattern to which the Israeli trend could be compared, the latter may best be interpreted in the context of Israel's own sociopolitical developments.

There is some difficulty in this, however, since it is well known that election results present a rather complex code that is not easy to decipher. A party's ideology is obviously but one of the elements on which its electoral support is based. This point is well illustrated by data from the Arian study of 1969. When asked what determined their voting decision, only 37 percent of the respondents named the party's platform as the determining factor, and only 40 percent stated that they would change their vote if the party of their choice changed its stand on the most crucial political issues (Arian 1973, p. 99).† Other observers found that various types of individuals differed in the significance they attributed to the party's political stand. Thus Hendles (1975),‡ applying a model of path analysis, shows that various background factors affect political involvement that, in turn, affect voting decisions: people who are greatly involved in politics are less likely than others to change their vote if the party of their choice alters its stand on crucial political issues. Similarly, Yatsiv (1974, p. 198) reports that for class-conscious respondents there is frequently no consistency between their own orientation and that of the party they support, while respondents who are not class-conscious tend to be more

---

*Reviewing these results, the question arose whether the decline in adherence to socialist parties was primarily related to population turnover, or whether the *same* persons had changed their voting patterns throughout the years. While this question cannot be answered for the population at large, it has been tackled by research projects on samples or groups of the population. Tracing the voting patterns of the same respondents in two or more elections, these projects indicated that some personal shifts in voting allegiance did occur and that these were in favor of the Likud more frequently than in favor of the Alignment (see Ben Sira and Winter 1973A, 1973B, and 1974; Keydar 1972, p. 40).

†Other factors mentioned included the party's candidates (21 percent), and loyalty to the party itself (17 percent).

‡In a secondary analysis of data from the Arian study.

consistent.* These findings illustrate the point that some types of voters, at any rate, base their party choice on factors other than the party's orientation.

This being the case, it is not clear to what extent the voters' own political orientation affects their party choice. For instance, where the ruling party is concerned, voters' decisions may be prompted by their views on the government's concrete policies as well as by their general political orientation. Since the two are most likely to be interrelated, one would wish to inquire into the independent effect of each on voting decisions.

For this purpose a multiple regression analysis was employed, based on the IIASR survey of February-April 1973 (Levy and Guttman, August 1973)† in which voting decision served as the dependent variable;‡ while political orientation (on the left-right continuum),** opinions on domestic policy (government aid to the disadvantaged, government handling of economic affairs), and opinions on foreign policy (withdrawal from territories, government handling of Arab terrorism) served as independent variables.†† Table 3.2 gives the net effects (normalized regression coefficients) for that equation.

It is evident that generalized political orientation carries more weight than does opinion on each concrete policy issue in affecting the probability that a person will vote for the Alignment rather than for other parties. But all factors combined account for only a small proportion of the variance in intended voting. Since voting decisions thus remain partly unexplained, there remains the difficulty in interpreting the recent decline in electoral support for the left-of-center Alignment. This difficulty holds especially for the last election (December 1973). Since it took place shortly after the Yom Kippur War,

---

*In a study of 520 respondents drawn from four residential districts in Jerusalem.

†This survey was on 1,935 respondents. The General and Panel study was carried out as part of this project (see Chapter 2).

‡The question was: "For which party do you intend to vote in the coming election?" Replies were recoded into two categories: 1) Alignment, 2) All other parties. The statistical shortcomings of regression analysis with dichotomous independent variables are well known (cf. Goldberger 1964, pp. 251–55). Nevertheless, this method is being employed by political sociologists whenever it seems to be preferable to alternative available techniques for estimating relations with limited or qualitative dependent variables, for instance for reasons of data management (see House and Mason 1975).

**For the wording of this question, see Table 3.3.

††For the formulation of all other questions, see Appendix A. The question on withdrawal from territories did not pertain directly to government policy. But the government's policy concerning territorial compromise is well known; hence it was to be expected that views on this issue would affect voting decisions. Since practically none of the respondents expressed an intention to vote left of the Alignment it was reasonable to presume that the less adamant on the issue of territories would be more likely to opt for the Alignment, while the more adamant would be more likely to prefer center-right and religious parties.

TABLE 3.2

Net Effect (Standardized Regression Coefficients) on Voting Decision of Political Orientation and of Opinion on Concrete Policy Issues, in 1973

	Beta
A. Political orientation (from left to right)	.28*
B. Policy issues	
Government handling of economic problems	.18*
Withdrawal from territories	13*
Government handling of terrorism	08*
Government aid to the disadvantaged	05

$N = 1,935 \qquad R^2 = .16$

*Significant $p < 0.01$.
Source: Supplied by the IIASR on the basis of data from the survey of March-April, 1973 (Levy and Guttman, August 1973A).

it is commonly felt that the results of this election indicate the voters' disappointment with the government's handling of the war (independently of their political orientations). But the fact that decline in support for the Alignment had begun several years before, indicates at the very least that the war was not the only factor in this decline. In fact, Peres, Yuchtman, and Shafat (1975) demonstrate, on the basis of a survey shortly before the war (August 1973),* that the election results could have been predicted quite accurately at that time. Hence, they conclude, the weakening of the Alignment and the strengthening of the Likud *does not* emanate from the war. Interpreting this decline, Peres and his colleagues suggest that it stems from the toughening of public sentiment with regard to foreign policy and security after the Six-Day War (a shift that is in line with the Likud's position); from a gradual process of legitimation of the right-wing opposition (furthered especially by its participation in the national-unity government from 1967 to 1970); and from the growing disaffection of Orientals, who have recently become increasingly conscious of and resentful of their disadvantaged position.

Interestingly, these interpretations clearly tie in with the left-right continuum. Thus, it will be recalled that an adamant position on foreign policy was positively related to a rightist political orientation, and that, for Orientals, concern with socioeconomic gaps was also related positively to a rightist bent (see Chapter 2). Hence one may infer from this analysis that the decline in

---

*On a representative sample of 1,910 Israelis.

electoral support for the left-of-center Alignment has resulted, at least in part, from an apparent shift toward the center/right among the Israeli public.* *However, this, as well as our foregoing analysis, suggests that the decline in electoral support for the Alignment is by no means identical with such a shift.* Therefore, to see whether a shift away from the left and toward the center/right has indeed occurred among the public, it was necessary to consult data of various surveys, pertaining directly to the avowed political orientations of the public, to compare such orientations by age, ethnic origin, and length of stay in the country, and to trace their development over time.†

Age Differences and Changes in Political Orientations

One of the most notable facts of Israel's culture is that the younger generation tends to favor center and rightist parties, and that the support for leftist parties is consequently disproportionately recruited from the older generation.

Thus Arian (1973, p. 42) reports, on the basis of his 1969 study, that among people whose age was 50 or more, 61–68 percent had voted for the left-of-center Alignment; among those aged 18–24, only 38–49 percent had voted for this party. Similar results were obtained in the study by Peres et al. (1975).‡

Why is it that the younger generation is disproportionately drawn towards the rightist party and away from the Alignment? Is it merely that they are less satisfied than their elders with the manner in which the affairs of state have been run, or are these tendencies the result of ideological preferences as well? To answer this question, it is necessary to go beyond voting analyses and to examine the political orientations of the various age groups directly. Such an examination shows that members of the younger generation as a rule evince a right-wing bent more frequently and a leftist bent less frequently than do their elders.

---

*As noted, the Labor Party-Alignment itself has been moving somewhat toward the center but has still retained its leftist adherence. The analysis suggests that the public has been moving toward the center-right to an even greater extent.

†The relevance of these comparisons for the analysis of change should become evident below.

‡Of those aged 36 or more, 48 percent declared their intention to vote for the Alignment, as against 30 percent of those aged 18–35. The converse was true for the Likud: 18 percent of the former as against 43 percent of the latter age group declared their intention to vote for that party. Practically identical results were reported in the Ben Sira and Winter surveys (1973A, 1973B, and 1974) on samples of 642, 530, and 1,066 respectively. Hereafter, these will be referred to as the Ben Sira surveys.

Thus, Shapira and Etzioni-Halevy (1973, p. 97), in their study of Tel Aviv University students and faculty* found that among faculty members aged 40 and over, 29 percent identified with a *pronounced* leftist bent. Among faculty members aged 40 and under, 12 percent identified with this bent, whereas among students only 6 percent did so. Similar results were obtained by Arian (1971, pp. 257–86) in his research project of 233 elite members (legislators, senior government officials, and university students).†

Such cleavages are to be found among the general population as well. This is evident from various public opinion studies conducted in 1973. In these surveys, an identical question on political orientation was posed to three cross sections of the adult population and to one representative sample of youngsters aged 17–20. A comparison of the results is presented in Table 3.3.

Youngsters exhibit a lesser tendency towards the left and a greater tendency towards the right than do adults.‡ In addition, respondents to the General and Panel Study and to the Youth Survey were asked how they visualized an ideal party that they would like to see in office.** The results showed that 48 percent of the adults and 54 percent of the youngsters visualized an ideal party as right of center.†† Thus, the differences between adults and youngsters on the basis of voting studies are as anticipated, but are not great. This may be due to the fact that in adult studies, various age groups that include young adults are part of the sample. This problem was overcome in the General and Panel Study (1973) where various age groups within the adult population could be compared.

The comparison shows that young adults tend more towards the right than do their elders: 33 percent of the youngest age group (20–34) against only 17 percent of the oldest group (50+) identified with the right.

When asked about the ideal party they would like to see in office, 39 percent of the oldest age group as against 59 percent of the youngest group visualized such an ideal party as a rightist one.

---

*A sample of 560 students and 179 faculty members.

†Among those aged 56 and over, as many as 66 percent adhered to a prosocialist ideology in the economic realm; only 33 percent of those aged 18–21 adhered to this ideology.

‡Another survey on youngsters aged 17–20 was done in 1973. Here, sons of respondents of the General and Panel Study were interviewed. The results concerning political orientations were as follows: left and moderate left: 24 percent; center: 25 percent; right: 27 percent. However, this survey (to which we refer as "Accompanying Survey") was made on 120 respondents only, and these did not constitute a representative sample.

**This question was not included in the other adult surveys.

††57 percent of the respondents to the Accompanying Survey made such a choice.

TABLE 3.3

Political Orientations of Adults and Youngsters,
as Revealed by Various Surveys, in 1973
(in percentages)*

	Adult Survey General and Panel Study Spring 1973 (1)	Adult Survey Panel Survey Sept. 1973 (1)	Adult Survey Voter Questionnaire Nov. 1973 (2)	Youth Survey Youth Questionnaire Spring 1973 (3)
Left	22	22	25	15
Center	33	33	27	25
Right	23	20	28	36
Religious	7	5	9	12
No response	15	20	11	12
N	1,939	523	587	823

*The question posed in all surveys was: "With which political trend do you identify?" For details see Chapter 2.

Sources: (1) The General and Panel Study. This project was carried out on a cross section of the adult, Jewish, urban population. For more details, see Chapter 2. This study had a sequel in the form of the Panel Survey, carried out in September 1973 on a subsample of the previous sample (column 2). (2) Voter Questionnaire, November 1973. This survey was carried out by the Society of Sociological Services on a cross section of the adult Jewish population in towns and cities of 5,000 inhabitants or over (N = 437) and on a group of randomly selected enlisted men (N = 150). (3) Youth Questionnaire, Spring 1973. This survey was carried out by the Society for Sociological Services on a representative sample of Jewish-Israeli youngsters aged 17—20. It should be noted that the adult studies are on samples of the urban population whereas the Youth Survey is on a sample of the entire population. However, since the overwhelming majority of the Jewish-Israeli population is urban, this is not a decisive difference.

Parallel results are reported in a research project done by Shapira et al. (1975) on a representative sample of 2,500 recent high school students and graduates.* It was found that the percentage of these young adults professing a rightist orientation was significantly higher than that adhering to the left. This, of course, is in contrast to what was found among the the general adult population (see Table 3.3) where the percentages of those adhering to the left and of those adhering to the right were approximately equal. It was further revealed that as age decreased, so did the leftist orientation, while rightist adherence was inversely related to age.

---

*1,387 were high school graduates; the rest were eighth-grade high school students.

All these data lead to the conclusion that part of the younger generation tends to move towards right-wing political allegiance.* In a way, this seems to be a rather unusual pattern. Even though there are no overall patterns of voting differences by age in Western-style democracies (Rose 1974), it is well known that in many Western countries at least the politically active part of youth has tended toward the left. In Israel, on the other hand, both elite and rank-and-file youngsters tend disproportionately toward the right. In many Western countries, of course, leftism has spelled radicalism, to which politically active youth has been disproportionately attracted. Not so in Israel, where the left is associated with the establishment. In a sense then, Israeli youngsters, by showing a disproportionate preference for the *right,* disassociate themselves from the establishment just as many of their Western co-peers have been doing by turning to the *left* or "the new left." However, the Israeli establishment is conspicuously *moderate* in its leftist adherence. Hence, youthful disaffection might well have found expression in an *extreme* leftist bent The fact that Israeli youngsters tend to the right rather than to leftist extremism seems to indicate that, although they tend to dissociate themselves from the establishment, they do so in a nonradical manner. This, in turn, corresponds to the findings of various studies that, in Israel, a pronounced generation gap is not evident and that intergenerational differences, where they exist, are gradual and rather mild.†

The tendency to refrain from marked radicalism, exhibited by Israeli youth, may be explained by the fact that they themselves grew up within the folds of what was at one time a radical, charismatic, ideological movement: Zionism, which once implied severance with the customary way of life and the establishment of an entirely new social reality. Present day Israeli youngsters are the second or third generation of this one-time rebellious movement that still is in the process of institutionalization. Hence the impetus for further radicalism seems to be greatly attenuated.

Does the disproportionate tendency of Israeli youth to favor the right indicate an overall shift over time in that direction? Basing conclusions concerning trends of change on age differences is a somewhat tricky business. It is hard to tell whether the young display a distinctive political bent as representatives of a certain age group or as representatives of a certain generation. Do the youngsters, upon advancing in age, adopt the political tendencies of their erstwhile elders, or do they hold on to their own? In some Western countries the following saying used to be prevalent: "He who has reached the age of twenty and is not a socialist, has no heart. He who has reached the age of forty

---

*The data are not systematic enough to enable one to assess how pronounced this tendency may be; but the tendency, as such, is clearly visible.
†See, for instance, Shapira and Etzioni-Halevy (1973); Katz and Gurevitz (1973).

and is *still* a socialist, has no head." Conceivably, what we perceive in Israel may be a realization of this slogan, albeit in a reverse fashion: as Israeli youngsters grow older, they may return to the fold of the established socialist tradition. If this should be the case, then age differences would have little significance as far as change over time is concerned. On the other hand, it is quite possible that their first political frame of reference may remain in force for the rest of their lives—in which case intergenerational differences would be evident and temporal change toward the right would be indicated.*

It seems to us that in Israel at least some of the differences may be taken to indicate change over time. This because of changes that have recently occurred in the Israeli frameworks of political socialization. Before the establishment of the state and immediately after, the Israeli educational system was divided into subsystems—by political trends. A formidable part of the youth was educated in schools sponsored by the left-of-center labor movement. This arrangement was abolished shortly after the establishment of the state, so that none of the present-day youngsters are graduates of such schools. Moreover, left-of-center, pioneering youth movements, which once played a major role in youngsters' political socialization, have become less influential. Hence another source of political socialization toward the left has become attenuated. It thus seems that the generation factor (indicating temporal change) is at least partly responsible for the reported differences in political orientations. Unfortunately, however, the available data do not enable one to disentangle the two factors from each other. Therefore, yet another set of data has been considered.

Ethnic Background and Changes in Political Orientations

Of Israel's two major Jewish ethnicities, Westerners and Orientals, the latter have had a higher birth rate and their proportion in the population has been steadily increasing (see Chapter 1). Consequently, a comparison of Orientals with Westerners can supply some indirect indications as to possible shifts in political tendencies over recent years. Such a comparison shows that, in general, Orientals tend to support left-of-center parties less, and rightist parties more, than do Westerners.

Thus, Kies (1969), who analyzed the 1959, 1961, and 1965 election results in Jerusalem, reports (p. 202) that the major center-right-wing party—Gachal (later to become the Likud)—found considerably more support in precincts

---

*For a discussion of this topic in the framework of other political systems, see Lipset 1963; see also Peres et al. (1975).

inhabited chiefly by Oriental Jews than it did in precincts predominated by Ashkenazi inhabitants. Significantly, Kies also reports that the center-right achieved best results where second generation Orientals concentrated. Another study conducted in Jerusalem (Yatsiv 1970),* reports basically the same results: Oriental respondents disproportionately tend to commit their vote to Gachal.

This pattern is by no means unique to Jerusalem. Parallel results are reported by Peres et al. (1975): for the population at large, from among persons of European-American background, 47 percent intended to vote Alignment and only 20 percent Likud. Among persons of Afro-Asian origin the percentages were 32 percent and 43 percent respectively.† Orientals also evince leftist political orientations less frequently than do Westerners, as shown by Table 3.4.

Possibly, the disproportionate tendency of Orientals to disassociate themselves from the Alignment (the epitome of the establishment) presents a channel (albeit mild) of social protest.

It is especially significant that the differences between second generation Westerners and Orientals are greater than those found in the first generation. It follows that the higher birthrate among Orientals in Israel must indeed have resulted in a decreasing leftist adherence among the Israeli population. It should be noted, however, that this does not necessarily indicate similar trends for the future, since it is not clear whether the proportion of Orientals in the Israeli population will continue to increase. There are some indications, in fact, that differences in birthrates are slowly decreasing, although it will probably take quite some time before they disappear altogether.‡ In addition, the pool of potential Western immigrants is much larger than that of Oriental Jews. But the differences between Westerners and Orientals are certainly of significance for understanding the dynamics of change to date.

Because of differential birthrates the Oriental population is on the average younger than the Western population. Hence it is conceivable that the relationship between age and political orientation, or that between country of origin and political orientation, might be spurious. The cross tabulation in Table 3.5 shows that this is not the case.

Within each ethnic group, the young show more of a *rightist* tendency than do their elders. Within each age group, Westerners show more of a *leftist*

---

*On 520 respondents drawn from four residential districts.

†Similar differences are reported by Arian (1973, p. 42); in the General and Panel Study (1973); in the Voter Questionnaire (1973); and in the Ben Sira Survey (1973A).

‡See Central Bureau of Statistics (1974D, p. 81).

TABLE 3.4
Political Orientations by Country of Origin, in 1973
(in percentages)

	Country of Origin					
	Born Israel Father born Israel	Born Israel Father born Asia-Africa	Born Israel Father born Europe-America	Born Asia-Africa	Born Europe-America	Total Population
Political Orientation						
Left	21	15	29	17	24	22
Center	36	26	27	29	36	33
Right	26	33	30	24	20	23
Religious	8	9	7	8	7	7
No response	9	17	7	22	13	15
N	92	115	220	459	989	1,939*

$p < 0.005$

*In this and the following table the total number of respondents is somewhat greater than the sum of partial n's. This is so because for a small part of the population, age and country of origin could not be ascertained.

Source: General and Panel Study (1973).

tendency than do Orientals. So both age and country of origin are independently related to political orientation, a fact that further strengthens our presumption on trends of change.

Immigration and Changes in Political Orientations

Additional support for our thesis is afforded by the fact that the old-timers in Israel tend to support the left, and that the later people immigrated, the stronger their tendency toward the right. Thus, Antonovsky (1963A) reports that persons born in Israel and persons who had immigrated before 1948 were more leftist in their orientation than later immigrants.* In addition, a survey of new immigrants conducted in 1973 indicates that the newcomers identify

---

*On the basis of his 1962 study on 1,170 respondents (see Table 3.4).

TABLE 3.5

Political Orientations by Age and Country of Origin, in 1973
(in percentages)

	Country of Origin									Total Population
	Israel			Asia-Africa			Europe-America			
Age Group	20–34	35–49	50+	20–34	35–49	50+	20–34	35–49	50+	
Political Orientation										
Left	15	26	26	15	20	13	25	25	25	22
Center	32	33	48	28	27	30	26	37	37	33
Right	36	22	9	30	29	13	35	21	17	23
Religious	7	11	4	6	4	19	6	7	7	7
No response	10	8	13	21	20	25	8	10	14	15
N	41	27	23	236	212	119	250	306	643	1,939
	$p < 0.05$			$p < 0.005$			$p < 0.005$			

Source: General and Panel Study (1973).

somewhat less with the left than does the Israeli population at large:* against 22–25 percent of the general population 17 percent of the new immigrants report a leftist commitment.[†]

Similar results emerge from the General and Panel Study when political orientations are broken down according to length of stay in the country. Twenty-nine percent of those who reached the country before 1948 express a leftist allegiance, as opposed to 17–20 percent of the later immigrants. We conclude that the mass immigration after the establishment of the state, as well as recent immigration, must have resulted in a gradual decrease in the proportion of leftist adherents among the Israeli population.

Comparison Over Time

Tentative conclusions on changes in political orientations of the Israeli public may also be reached by comparing such orientations at different time

---

*The New Immigrants' survey was conducted by the Society of Sociological Services on a random sample of 650 persons who had immigrated to Israel within the last five years.
†See Table 3.3

periods. Unfortunately, research projects on this subject have been few and far between.* Nevertheless, the results of the comparison do seem to indicate an unmistakable trend, as shown in Table 3.6.

In general, the later the survey, the smaller the adherence to the left. The differences are not large, and they are somewhat blurred by the fact that in the last survey conducted in 1973 leftist adherence was slightly greater than in the first 1973 surveys. Nevertheless, the differences are clearly there and cannot be disregarded. The support of a centrist orientation generally increased with each subsequent survey; the differences are approximately the same (although in the opposite direction) as those concerning adherence to a leftist bent.

TABLE 3.6

Political Orientations of Israelis at Various Time Periods
(in percentages)

	1962 Antonovsky Project (1)	1969 Arian Project (2)	Spring 1973 General Panel Study (3)	Sept. 1973 Panel Survey (3)	Nov. 1973 Voter Questionnaire (4)
Left and Moderate Left*	31	28	22	22	25
Center	23	24	33	33	27
Right	8†	19	23	20	28
Religious	5	9	7	5	9
No response	33‡	19	15	20	11
N	1,170	1,351	1,939	523	587

*For wording of question (identical in all surveys), see Table 3.3.

†In the Antonovsky project, the choice presented was not "right" but "Herut," which, at that time, was Israel's right-wing party. Possibly, if the choice were "right" without any party being mentioned, adherence to this bent might have been somewhat greater.

‡For the Antonovsky sample, this category includes 25 percent who declared themselves not interested in politics and an additional 8 percent who were defined as "others." See also, Antonovsky 1963B, p. 25.

Sources: (1) Antonovsky (1963A). This project was conducted on a representative sample of the Jewish population outside of kibbutzim. (2) Arian (1973). This project was conducted on a cross section of the adult, Jewish, urban population in three phases. The data are from the second phase. (3) General and Panel Study. For details, see Table 3.3. (4) Voter questionnaire. For details, see Table 3.3.

---

*Moreover, only one pertinent question recurred in all of these studies, so the analysis must necessarily be based on this question alone. At the same time, it must be considered fortunate that even one such recurrent question could be located, so that we at least know that differences revealed cannot be due to differences in the wording of the questions.

Commitment to the right has increased, too, but the differences are difficult to gauge (see explanatory remarks on Table 3.6).

Keeping in mind the noted qualifications, it seems that the surveys showing differences over time, although they do not constitute conclusive evidence, are sufficiently consistent, and the differences among them sufficiently pronounced, to indicate some recent changes in political adherence. These changes, though small, are especially noteworthy since they cover a time span of only 11 years. This, by the way, is also approximately the period during which the leftist parties lost electoral support, whereas the center and rightist parties gained. It seems, then, that the changes in electoral support are at least partly related to changes in political orientations.

It is sometimes asked whether war experiences may have affected the Israelis' political orientations. Most of the available data, having been collected at long time intervals, are not specifically geared to answer this question. In 1973, however, surveys were carried out before (May, September) and immediately after (November) the Yom Kippur War. A comparison of these surveys leads to the tentative conclusion that, if there was any change in the wake of the war, it was towards increased adherence to both leftist and rightist orientations and a decrease in the center-oriented political bent. Thus, to the extent that the war had any effect, it was one of polarization and a weakening of the middle path. To reach more positive conclusions on the impact of the war, more extensive data would have been required. Until such data become available, the present evidence enables us to conclude, at any rate, that the decline in support for the left-wing bent cannot be attributed to the war experience. This conclusion ties in with that stated by Peres and his associates (see above) that the loss of electoral support for the Alignment did not stem from the war experience either.

TRENDS OF CHANGE—AN INTERPRETATION

The central question posed was whether the traditionally dominant left-of-center socialist orientation, which is still represented by the Israeli establishment, is still as prevalent as it had been before among the public, or whether some recent changes are discernable. We saw that socialist parties lost electoral support in the last two elections, while center and rightist parties gained; that youngsters tend to the right more frequently than do their elders; that Orientals (who comprise a growing percentage of the Israeli population) tend to the left less frequently than do Westerners; that newcomers tend to the left less frequently than do old-timers; and that, in general, the later the survey conducted, the smaller the support for the left and the greater the support for the center-right. Each type of data had some shortcomings, so that each of these results separately may be inconclusive; however, when taken in conjunction, they cannot but lead to the tentative conclusion that, in the last decade or so, some changes in orientations have indeed been taking place in Israel, notably a certain decline in support for the left, paralleled by an increase in support for the right.

This does not signify, of course, that the leftist orientation is on the point of disappearing, or even that the rightist bent is now dominant among the Israeli public. Rather, it seems that the dominance of the leftist orientation has given way to a situation in which various orientations compete for support; and the outcome of this competition is by no means a foregone conclusion. It is not clear whether the weakening of leftist orientations and the strengthening of center and rightist ones will continue. The trend to date, however, calls for an interpretation.*

It will be recalled that some of the major implications of the left-right cleavage today are in the realm of foreign policy: rightists favor an adamant position vis-à-vis the Arabs more frequently than leftists (see Chapter 2). Hence, it is reasonable to presume that the shift towards the right was related to an increasing prevalence of this position.† This supposition is supported by various IIASR studies. Asked whether they supported an aggressive policy towards the Arab countries, 42 percent of the respondents replied in the affirmative in 1962—compared with 61 percent in 1966 and 1969, and 70 percent in 1970.‡ This shift may have been related to the constant military threats and actual wars to which Israel was exposed. Thus Peres (1971) reports

---

*As noted (Chapter 1) socialism was first and foremost the ideological commitment of the veterans of the second and third waves of immigration who had reached the country at the beginning of the century. This commitment apparently was not shared to the same extent by subsequent immigrants or by subsequent generations of native-born Israelis. Hence the diminishing adherence to a leftist ideology may partly reflect the decline in the number of the still surviving old-timers: as these diminish, adherents of socialism diminish as well. The reported differences in leftist adherence by age and time of arrival in Israel seem to support this interpretation. But this is certainly not the whole story, since various surveys have shown shifts towards the right in the party allegiance of the *same* individuals. Furthermore, if latecomers and the younger generation have not been committed to leftism quite so strongly as these old-timers, this itself calls for an explanation.

†Also it may have been related to disillusionment with the Soviet regime, the major example of socialism in action. For instance, the shrinking support for Mapam (see Table 2.1), the party that has traditionally harbored a strong commitment to the Soviet Union, is almost certainly related to this disillusionment. But not too much weight should be accorded to this explanation, since the mainstream of the Israeli-brand socialism has always been consciously and deliberately noncommunist.

‡See Adi and Froelich (1970A).

that following the Six-Day War there was a perceptible increase in hostility toward the Arab minority in Israel.* However, following the Yom Kippur War, the trend toward an increasingly adamant position vis-à-vis the Arab countries was halted (at least temporarily).† Until then, at any rate, the decline in adherence to the left was accompanied by (and presumably related to) a shift towards increasingly unyielding (and even hostile) attitudes towards Israel's Arab neighbor/enemies. Since an adamant position vis-à-vis national enemies indicates an emphasis on certain patterns of nationalism or perhaps even chauvinism (see Chapter 2) we may say that the shifts in political orientations were related to an increase in this emphasis among the Israeli public.

Congruent Changes: Political Orientations and Inequaltity

Diminishing emphasis on leftism in Israel can also be understood in the context of some internal sociocultural developments, most notably, the transition from collectivist, egalitarian, pioneering ideologies, and social patterns to greater emphasis on individual achievements and differential rewards. Before and immediately after the establishment of the state, an egalitarian ideology was prevalent, paralleled, on the structural level, by a relatively egalitarian income and salary scale‡ (Chanoch 1961); by a tendency to separate economic potential from opportunities for achievement; and by a typically imbalanced or inconsistent status profile whereby many individuals ascended the occupational and prestige ladder by relinquishing economic benefits, or vice versa. Although Orientals tended to occupy balanced lower positions, they were a relatively small group at that time—so their predicament had little effect on the mainstream of society (Lissak 1970).

Shortly after the establishment of the state, the narrow gap in income distribution began to widen. According to Chanoch's analysis, the proportion of the total income earned by families in the lowest decile dropped, while the

---

*In his study of a representative sample of 450 Tel Aviv residents, Peres found that in 1967, before the war, 80 percent of the respondents thought "It would be better if there were fewer Arabs." After the war, in 1968, 91 percent held this opinion. Before the war, 73 percent of the respondents were convinced that "every Arab hates Jews"; after the war, 80 percent held this conviction.

†In the prewar General and Panel study (Spring 1973), only 22 percent of the respondents declared that Israel should be willing to relinquish most territories in return for a peace treaty. In the postwar Ben Sira survey (January 1974), 45 percent of the respondents expressed this view.

‡Some observers claim that in the 1920s and 1930s income differentials were similar to those in the 1960s; but all agree that shortly before and after the establishment of the state they were significantly smaller than they are today.

proportion of those in the highest decile rose perceptibly. According to Yuchtman and Fishelson (1970), the Lorenz coefficient of inequality for urban employees grew from 100 to 213 between 1950 and 1967.* From 1967 to 1973 the income inequalities decreased slightly, but were still perceptibly greater than in 1948.† A concomitant process was the partial institutionalization of congruence among level of education, economic rewards, and occupational achievements. Furthermore, the mass influx of immigrants from Oriental countries, and the resultant increase of the Oriental sector of the Jewish population (from around 15 percent in the 1930s to more than 50 percent at present) without any marked improvement in its social position, made the near-congruence between class and ethnic division more salient (Lissak 1970). Thus, there are definite signs of crystallization–if not of full-fledged separate social strata, at least of clearcut, across-the-board vertical differentiations as bases of social separation.

Just as the one-time egalitarian patterns were congruent with an egalitarian ideology, so these changes toward greater differentiation are in line with changes in ideologies and orientations of the Israeli public. The official egalitarian ideology has not been manifestly abandoned either by the establishment or by the public; but in practice egalitarianism has been losing its appeal for large sectors of that public, and today the idea of income equality is far less prevalent than it used to be (Derber 1970). In fact, as Derber points out, a competing ideology has come to be increasingly prominent in Israel. This ideology holds that each should be rewarded in proportion to his training, his efforts, his initiative, and the responsibility he shoulders; in short, in proportion to his overall contribution. Clearly this ideology serves as a rationale for differential allocation of rewards. It is increasingly referred to by various advantaged groups of employees to justify demands for further salary increases, demands to which the government has not been impervious. The trend towards increasing differentials in the salary scale is thus related to the receding of the ideology of *equality* and the advancement and increasing prominence of the *ideology* of *equity*.

Is this dual development in ideology and in actual vertical differentiation related to the shift in Israelis' political orientations? It is commonly thought that in the past, egalitarianism was rooted in the ideologies of pioneering and national unity as well as that of socialism. In the previous chapter we saw, however, that leftism is no longer disproportionately associated with egalitarianism. Therefore it would seem, prima facie, that Israel's decrease in egalitari-

---

*These figures refer to gross income; the growth of inequality in net income was smaller, because of the redistributive effect of the income tax.
†See Central Bureau of Statistics (1974, p. 273).

anism is related not so much to the mild shift from left to center-right as to the erosion of the egalitarian connotations of the left-wing adherence itself.

But although there may be no direct relationship between declining egalitarianism and diminishing adherence to the left, *we maintain that the two trends are indirectly related;* the intervening link is the decreasing emphasis on certain types of collectivism and the concomitantly greater emphasis on individual achievement (see Chapter 1). The pronounced collectivist tendencies in the yishuv and at the beginning of statehood derived not only from the Zionist ideology, with its emphasis on common national ideals, but also from the leftist-socialist ideology, with its emphasis on new patterns of collective life. Also, in the yishuv, collectivism was intertwined with egalitarianism;* according to the collectivist values† of the labor movement the highest prestige was accorded to those groups and individuals who made the greatest contribution to collective goals, that is, to persons who devoted themselves to various pioneering tasks (Lissak 1970). Thus, in effect, the highest esteem went to those who did the least to accumulate private economic benefits for themselves. Clearly, then, collectivism entailed a de-emphasis on individual economic achievements and, hence, to a certain extent discouraged economic inequality.

After the establishment of the state, there was a gradual decrease in the emphasis on collectivism: less importance came to be attached to pioneering and to some of the new patterns of collective life. Concomitantly, the emphasis shifted increasingly towards individual rewards for individual efforts, a shift that necessitated an increasingly competitive struggle for these rewards, *and resulted in increasing differentiation in their attainment* (Lissak 1970; Eisenstadt 1967, pp. 153–55). Thus, the strengthening of individualist, achievement-oriented tendencies, and the growing prevalence of non- (or less than) egalitarian tendencies, were merely different aspects of the same process.

We may now draw together the lines of the argument. Since certain types of collectivism were anchored in the socialist ideology, the Israeli public's partial shift from left to center-right may be viewed as related to a de-emphasis on these patterns of collectivism and to an increased stress on individual achievement. Since the latter trend, in turn, is connected with changes toward greater inequality, the shift in political orientations and the growing inequality may be seen as clearly (albeit indirectly) interrelated. Thus we reach what, on the face of it, might look like a paradoxical conclusion, namely, that the partial shifts away from equality and the partial shift away from the left are intercon-

---

*This is not to say that collectivism necessarily implies egalitarianism, but only that this was the case here.

†These collectivist values were not accepted by the "citizens" group, but were clearly part of the dominant ideology of the Yishuv.

nected, even though today the leftist adherence seems to hold none of its traditional egalitarian connotations.

Incongruent Changes: The Public and the Establishment

While changes in political orientations and changes in patterns of stratification were basically congruent with each other, it seems that an incongruence has been developing in the political sphere itself: left-of-center, socialist party still dominates the political establishment; at the same time leftist political orientations, though still widespread, are no longer dominant among the public.

Conceivably, the dominant labor party might have been alert to this, adapting its own official ideology to the public's changing orientations. However, Arian (1972) demonstrates that this is not so. In a study of three elite groups* carried out in 1964, Arian found that 75 percent of the Mapai representatives in the elite identified with the moderate left, while only 21 percent of all elite members expressed such a preference. Comparing the official ideologies of Israel's major parties to the orientations of the public at large[†] and to those of the three elite groups, Arian revealed another discrepancy: the political orientations of individuals who supported left-of-center parties—and mainly Mapai—were frequently to the right of the party's official position. Which means that although the dominant party may have become less adamant in its socialist adherence since the yishuv era, it clearly has not kept pace with the changing orientations of its potential supporters.

Since 1964 (when Arian's study was conducted) Mapai has merged with Achdut Ha'avoda, becoming the Israel Labor Party and subsequently has entered into an alignment with Mapam. But Achdut Ha'avoda was even somewhat to the left of Mapai; and Mapam is even more leftist than Achdut Ha'avoda. Certainly, therefore, the merger and the alignment have not weakened the party's leftist adherence. As there are no indications that the Labor Party's ideology has undergone any significant changes since then, and as the shift toward the right among the public has been continuing, it may be concluded that the incongruence between the party and the voting public at the very least has not decreased in recent years.

The ideological incongruence between the public and the establishment, as represented by the dominant party, has not been confined to the realm of political slogans but has apparently found expression on the concrete policy

---

*A sample of 233 Knesset members, senior officials, and students.
†On the basis of Antonovsky's study of 1962.

level as well. While the dominant party has kept in line with the changing orientations of the public by being less adamant on the issue of equality (see above) and by allowing marked income differentials to develop in Israel; and while the dominant party no longer appears to be the champion of "laborers" in their "class struggle" against "capitalists," it has consistently perpetuated a socialist-oriented policy by fostering the public sector of the economy as over the private one and by maintaining tight government control of the economy as a whole (see Chapter 1). As Eisenstadt points out, "The government saw itself, in principle, as the supreme economic agent, both in planning, encouraging and supervising economic life. . . . By a series of acts and decrees, the government regulated production, consumption, and most other economic activities" (Eisenstadt 1967, p. 82). This political control of the economy, which has its origins in the prestate era, has not been loosened to this day. While some degree of state intervention in the economy is standard procedure in modern Western societies, the degree of political regulation of the Israeli economy, and the resultant dependence of economic enterprises on the political establishment, is clearly above and beyond what is common in these countries.

This state of affairs is due to a variety of factors that are beyond the scope of this study. It is clear, however, that, *inter alia,* the establishment's socialist-oriented tradition is highly significant. This pattern is especially congruent with the collectivist-socialist ideology; it has repeatedly been criticized by the center-right in the name of "free enterprise" (see Chapter 1). Consequently, it seems that with the gradual enhancement of individualism and the mild shift toward the center-right, a certain degree of incongruence has been developing between this politicoeconomic pattern and the orientations of an increasing part of the public. The present pattern of political regulation of the economy affords the political elite a great deal of control over the allocation of rewards, and thus greatly enhances its power. Paradoxically, however, it may well boomerang, if the trend of change from left to center-right continues.

In summation, it seems that a discrepancy has been developing between the official ideology of the dominant party and some socioeconomic patterns devised by it on the one hand, and the public's changing political orientations on the other hand. It is difficult to foretell, at this point, how far-reaching and decisive this discrepancy may turn out to be in the long run. It makes sense, however, that if this growing incongruence is indeed significant, it should have resulted in growing dissatisfaction and withdrawal of support from the political center. This topic will be tackled in Chapter 5. First, however, we would like to call attention to yet another discrepancy on the Israeli political scene: that between high political involvement and low political efficacy, which may also be referred to as the blocking of political involvement.

CHAPTER

4

THE BLOCKING OF POLITICAL INVOLVEMENT

The manner in which the rank-and-file citizens confront politics—their political involvement, participation, and sense of efficacy—is an important element in a society's political balance. Not all societies encourage their members to take an active stand in the political arena. Despite Aristotle's famous dictum that "Man is by nature a political animal," observation has shown that this is not invariably the case. Societies vary a great deal in the degree to which their members are "political animals"; some people in some societies are actually quite apolitical; that is, passive, apathetic, and incompetent as far as politics is concerned. Moreover, observers are at odds with each other concerning the degree to which people in a given society are indeed "political animals."

It has been suggested, for instance, that contemporary society is characterized by a massive and growing involvement of people in the political life of their country. Eisenstadt (1966, pp. 15–16), for instance, writes: "The broader strata of society tend more and more to impinge on its central institutions, not only in making various demands on it but also in the sense of developing the aspirations to participate in the very crystallization of the center, its symbols and institutional contours. . . . The growing participation of broader strata in the center of society and in the civil order can be seen as two basic attributes of modern nation building, of the establishment of new, broader, political and social entities." (See also Almond and Verba 1965.)

Conversely, we are sometimes told that modern societies (and especially American society) are characterized by increasingly widespread political apathy and impotence among the masses. Mills (1956, p. 324) writes: ". . . in many countries . . . they lose their will for rationally considered decision and action; they lose their sense of political belonging because they do not belong; they lose their political will because they see no way to realize it." (See also Marcuse 1964.)

It is intriguing that such antithetical conceptions could have been formulated to characterize the same reality, and that they coexist peacefully in modern sociology. Perhaps this is partly due to the inclusiveness of these theories, in which objective processes and subjective perspectives—the public's political participation, involvement and efficacy—are treated merely as different aspects of one entity. However, it seems more fruitful to treat them as independent ways in which citizens impinge on (or withdraw from) the political arena.* Although they may be empirically related, this is not necessarily so; moreover, incongruencies among involvement, participation, and efficacy are highly significant, since they may result from and breed political discontent. In this chapter we argue that such incongruencies have been evident on the Israeli political scene, and that they have indeed been related to political discontent.

HOW ISRAELIS CONFRONT POLITICS

Until recently, pertinent empirical data have been sparse in Israel. A study tapping political participation, involvement, and efficacy was carried out in 1960 (Fein 1962), but it was on a rather small sample and concerned only the Jerusalem population. Only from 1969 onwards did various studies repeatedly address themselves to these aspects. To utilize their findings for our analysis, we review involvement, participation, and efficacy separately; then we explore their joint constellation.†

Political Involvement

How involved are the Israelis in the political life of their country? Recent studies have tackled this problem with a variety of questions. Israelis have been requested to state how interested they are in "politics," in socioeconomic problems, in security problems, and in a variety of other issues. The percent-

---

*This is how they have been treated on the empirical level. Most empirical analyses treat involvement, participation, and efficacy as independent variables, although they report positive interrelations among them. See Campbell et al. (1960); Almond and Verba (1965); Milbrath (1965); DiPalma (1970); Verba and Nie (1972), and others.

†In this chapter we explore how things look from the vantage point of the public, that is, from a subjective point of view. In Chapter 6 we explore what impact various groups of citizens have actually been able to make on the sociopolitical system.

ages of people who declared themselves as "very" or "fairly" interested in such issues are presented in Table 4.1.*

A majority of the public professes a high or fairly high involvement in public (that is, political) affairs. This picture is complemented by the Katz and Gurevitz study.[†] Asked what importance they imputed to various needs, 87 percent of the respondents gave "understanding what is going on in the country and the world" and 60 percent gave "tracing how the government fulfills its task" as very important.[‡]

In evaluating data such as these there are at least two schools of thought. Some researchers accept such results at face value, and focus on their interpretation. Fein, for instance, writes (1967, p. 141): ". . . the civic culture of Israel places high value upon political interest and participation. In addition to the conventional association of these perceptions and behavior with democratic theory, they also flow directly from the Yishuv tradition with its great emphasis on self-help, communal responsibility and the utility of personal commitment." Arian (1973, pp. 24–25) furnishes an additional interpretation: "These formidable rates of interest and discussion also reflect the very smallness of the country. A family feeling is pervasive, especially during a time of crisis or tragedy. Few public issues do not directly relate to the individual or to someone he knows. . . . The alertness and sensitivity of the public and the small size and integrated character of the society facilitate the rapid circulation of news, political gossip and rumors."

A second approach holds that results such as these are not very meaningful, for two reasons. First, the marginal distribution of responses to the pertinent questions are an artifact of the formulation of these questions; if the questions had been formulated in a different manner, different distributions of replies would have been obtained. Second, there is a "social desirability effect" that is apt to bias the results; when asked if they are interested in public affairs, respondents are apt to reply that they are (even if they are not) because they think that this is what is socially expected from them.

While marginal distributions of replies are probably influenced by the formulation of questions, it is noteworthy that in our case a great variety of

---

*All items reported in Table 4.1 presented respondents with four precoded response categories, two positive and two negative. (The percentages reported in the tables are of respondents who chose one of the positive categories.) Questions in which any other number of precoded alternative responses were presented are not included in the table, nor are questions in which one of the responses was neither clearly positive nor clearly negative.

†Carried out in 1970 on a cross-section of the Jewish population of Israel, with 3,697 respondents.

‡The results of this survey were not included in Table 4.1 because respondents were presented with three (rather than four) alternatives, as follows: 1) very important, 2) somewhat important, and 3) of no importance (see Katz and Gurevitz 1973, p. 276 and Appendix B, pp. 19 and 45).

TABLE 4.1

Political Involvement and Political Efficacy among the Israeli Public, 1960–73
(in percentages)

Date Project N	1960 Fein Project 165	1969 Arian Project See Remarks	March 1972 Peled Survey	Spring 1973 General & Panel Study 1,939	Sept. 1973 Panel Survey 523	Dec. 1973 Ben Sira Survey 530
Political Involvement						
Very interested or fairly interested in foreign defense and security problems		86		84		
Very interested or fairly interested in economic or social policy (or gaps)		66–67		64		
Very interested or fairly interested in election results		76		74	80	79
Very important or important to vote						
Very important or important to criticize government when its actions are unjust			67			
Definitely wish or wish to influence government policy					47	65
Very important or important to learn more about political life in Israel					73	
Very interested or fairly interested in politics	39			48	47	
Very important or important to understand how democracy works					77	
Very important or important to have a say on which party will be in office					71	
Political Efficacy						
Think that they or people like them (or they and their friends) can influence policy	25	See Text		28	45	33

Explanatory Remarks: A) The Arian project was carried out in three phases. Phase one was on a sample of 380 respondents; phase two was on 1,315 respondents and phase three was on 1,825 respondents. All were cross sections of the Israeli Jewish urban population. The questions on interest in economic, social, and defense policy were included in the first phase; the question on interest in election results was part of the third phase; and the question on efficacy was asked in the second phase. B) For wording of questions, see Appendix A.
Sources: Fein (1962); Arian (1973); IIASR Survey; Peled (March 1972A); General and Panel Study (1973); Panel Survey (1973) and IIASR Survey; Ben Sira and Winter (1973B).

questions, formulated in different manners, administered to different cross sections of the population at different times, evinced similar results. It is questionable whether such coinciding results can be attributed to item formulation.

In addition, cleavages in political involvement among various categories of the Israeli population are just as might have been expected. The General and Panel Study, for instance, indicates that the poorly educated, the newcomers, and those born in Asia-Africa profess significantly less political interest than do the highly educated, the veteran residents, and the Westerners. Since there is no reason to presume that the former group would be less anxious than the latter to appear in a socially favorable light (in fact, the opposite would make more sense), these differences lead one to the notion that the "social desirability effect" is not as great as might have been suspected.

Moreover, differences in the extent of involvement in various public spheres are also as could have been expected. In view of Israel's situation, it is not surprising that interest is highest in defense and security matters—which, indeed, must be perceived by individuals as being of personal as well as of public importance. It also makes sense that interest in "politics" should be professed by a significantly smaller percentage of the public than interest in various specific public (political) affairs. "Politics" or "political affairs" are frequently associated with partisan affairs, which have less-than-positive connotations for many Israelis. In sum, then, although the various cleavages and differences do not prove anything, they all make sense in the light of Israel's sociopolitical life, and thus increase the credibility of the results.

In any case, as we see it, the question is not whether Israeli citizens are indeed as widely interested in public/political affairs as they profess to be, or whether they merely say so to please the interviewer. Given Israel's special situation and the direct implications that political decisions have on the lives of individual citizens in the security and economic spheres, it would be surprising if most citizens did not have some political awareness. The question is rather what political involvement actually means to those who profess it; specifically, what degree of commitment it implies. Thus, we must ask to what extent Israelis are willing to back up their political interest by political participation.

Political Participation

One important measure of political participation is election turnout. This measure, although admittedly crude, is highly reliable and especially appropriate for tracing developments over time. As can be seen from the following list, voting turnout in Israel has oscillated around 80 percent, with small deviations in one direction or the other.

Election Turnouts in Israel 1949–73

1949 – 86.9 percent	1961 – 81.6 percent
1951 – 75.1 percent	1965 – 83.0 percent
1955 – 82.2 percent	1969 – 81.7 percent
1959 – 81.6 percent	1973 – 78.6 percent

What significance can we attribute to these data? Do they indicate widespread political participation on the part of Israeli citizens? On the face of it, it would seem that such data could best be evaluated by a comparative perspective. In fact, however, such a comparison is highly problematic. In some countries, voting turnout is lowered by extraneous factors such as preelection registration requirements (in most states of the United States, for example); in others, the turnout is artificially raised by fines for nonvoting (Australia and Belgium, for instance; see Lane 1959, p. 350). Therefore, no conclusion can be based on systematic cross-cultural comparison.*

What is significant about election turnouts in Israel is that the percentage of those who express commitment to the act of voting or interest in election results (see Table 4.1) is surprisingly close to the percentage of those who actually turn up at the polls to cast their votes. In other words, the expressed interest in elections found by public opinion research is in fact backed up by the act of voting.

Data on elections, however, are merely a first approximation. Other facets or political participation have been dealt with by various research projects, as can be seen from Table 4.2.

On many items, the various studies coincide quite closely, so that a rather clear-cut picture of the political participation of the Israeli public emerges. The great majority reports reading daily newspapers and doing so daily; a similarly great majority reports listening to the radio primarily for news or information. A somewhat smaller percentage, but still the majority of the public, reports following election campaigns on television (see lower part of the table).

In general, the percentage of those who report following public affairs in the various media and discussing them with their friends is not perceptibly

---

*Just for the record, it is worth noting that voting turnout in Israel is on an intermediate level in comparison with Western-type democracies. It is clearly much higher than in the United States where, in recent years, turnout has oscillated around 60 percent; it is somewhat higher than in Switzerland, Canada, Britain, and Ireland; about as high as in Norway, Finland, and France; and somewhat lower than in Australia, Austria, Belgium, Holland, Denmark, Sweden, West Germany, and Italy (see Urwin n.d.). But, in view of the above, these data are not very significant.

Table 4.2

Political Participation among the Israeli Public, 1960–73 (in percentages)

	1960 Fein Project	1969 Arian Project	1970 Katz-Gurevitz Project	Spring 1973 General & Panel Study	Sept. 1973 Panel Study	Nov. 1973 Voter Questionnaire	Dec. 1973 Ben Sira Survey
N	165	see remarks	3,697	1,939	548	437	530
Partisan Activity							
Party member holding paid posts		1		1	0		1
Party member holding unpaid posts		1		2	2		3
Party member holding no posts		2		13	12		8
Party sympathizer		41		39	34		39
Not party supporter		41		40	52		49
N.R.		4		5			
Active in election campaign	20				5		6
Member of political organization (or party)		18	12				

(continued)

(Table 4.2 continued)

Frequently attends lectures on political subjects		5		
Frequently attends party-sponsored lectures in preelection periods			7	
Frequently attends party meetings	4	8-10		
Reads party-sponsored advertisements in newspaper			31	
Listens to election campaigning on radio			45	
Watches election campaigning on T.V.		57	68	44
Discusses politics with friends frequently or sometimes	61		44	75	54

Discusses topics of foreign policy and security often or sometimes	84	
Discusses social and economic topics often or sometimes	63–65	
Reads at least one daily newspaper		86
Reads a newspaper every day	63	77
Listens to radio primarily for news and information	84	

Note: The Arian project was carried out in three phases (see note A to Table 4.1). The questions on discussion of various public matters were included in the first phase; the question on radio listening was administered to the total sample. The question on party meetings was included in the first and second phases; the question on watching T.V. was included in the second and third phase. The question on political lectures was included in the first phase.

Sources: Fein (1962); Arian (1973); Katz and Gurevitz (1973); General and Panel Study (1973); Panel Survey (1973); Voter Survey (1973) and IIASR Survey; Ben Sira and Winter (1973B).

smaller then the percentage of those who profess involvement in such affairs.*
Thus, we may say that Israelis do back up their professed political involvement
by equally extensive political participation.†

However, the political participation that the majority of the Israeli public
reports is of a special type, namely that which Milbrath (1965, p. 20) termed
"spectator" activity. That is to say, most Israelis engage in activities that
consist of following attentively what *others* are doing in the political arena. In
contrast, only a small minority is engaged in what Milbrath termed "gladiatorial" political activities; that is, only a few are willing to enter the political
arena and themselves participate in the political contest. The various studies
indicate that only up to 6 percent hold party posts and the percentage who take
the trouble to attend political meetings or are active in election campaigns is
usually not much larger (see Table 4.2, upper part).

Furthermore, a study of Israeli students (Shapira and Etzioni-Halevy
1973)‡ found that these potential elite members (who in many countries evince
special political alertness) did not show more of a tendency to engage in
"gladiatorial" activities than did the public at large.

Although no detailed comparisons are possible,** one gains the impression (Almond and Verba 1965, esp. pp. 54 and 79) that in professed involvement and in "spectator" activities Israelis compare favorably with citizens of
Western-type democracies (including the United States). In contrast, it seems
(Milbrath 1965) that relatively more Americans than Israelis are engaged in
"gladiatorial" political activities.

Why is it that so many Israelis actively follow public affairs and profess
to be involved in them, yet so few are willing to do their share in shaping or
influencing such affairs? Is it that Israelis are so content with the existing state
of affairs that they feel that nothing is left to be done? In the following chapter
we shall see that this is not so.

It must be surmised, then, that this has to do with the character (rather
than with the breadth) of Israelis' involvement in political life. Although
widespread, this involvement is possibly not sufficiently intense to prompt the

---

*It is possible, of course, that respondents could be exaggerating their participation as well
as their involvement. But since concrete activities are tapped, it would be more difficult for the
respondents to do so without committing themselves to a deliberate untruth. Hence, the fact that
data on participation coincide so closely with those on involvement adds to the latter's credibility.

†For instance, the percentage discussing politics with their friends is not smaller than the
percentage professing interest in politics.

‡Conducted on 560 students who formed a representative sample of a class of Tel Aviv
University students.

**Among other reasons, because of differences in the formulation of questions. Also, see
below p. 82.

majority of Israelis to invest the time and effort required for participating in the political struggle. Alternatively, this may be due to the patterns of political efficacy of the Israeli public.

Political Efficacy

Israel's well-known satirist Ephraim Kishon once noted that the law guarantees that anybody may say whatever he pleases about the government; on the other hand, continued Kishon, *there is no law that says anybody has to listen!* In this succinct observation Kishon gives vent to the feeling that Israel's freedom of speech has not served as an effective channel of influence on the government. How widespread are such feelings of low political efficacy among the Israel public?

A general overview of the evidence indicates that a sense of low political efficacy has been rather widespread. This is indicated first by the results of the Fein Survey carried out in 1960. Only 25 percent of the respondents agreed with the statement that people like them could have an influence on the government (Fein 1962, p. 72; see Table 4.1). This, as Fein points out, is a drastically lower sense of efficacy than found among a comparative sample of the population in the United States (Campbell 1960, p. 479).

On this point, the results of the Arian study (although obtained almost a decade later) are generally in line with those of the Fein project. When asked whether they (or people like them) could influence policy, only 15 percent of Arian's respondents stated that they could do so a very great deal, or a great deal. Roughly similar results were obtained a year later in an IIASR survey.* When asked whether they (or people like them) could generally influence government decisions, only 21 percent replied "definitely yes" or "yes" (Adi and Froelich 1970A).†

The question on political efficacy was presented in three 1973 surveys (see Table 4.1). In two of these (May and December), only one-third or fewer expressed confidence in their ability to influence government policy. In the third survey (September), the sense of efficacy was found to be somewhat more

---

*On a cross section of the Israeli Jewish, adult, urban population (N=3,507).

†The results of the last two projects mentioned are not listed in Table 4.1 because the response categories do not parallel the categories in projects that are listed. The former have five categories; the latter four. The Fein project has been listed in the table despite the fact that five response categories were presented, because only two respondents opted for the middle category of "undecided."

widespread, but, even here, less than half of the respondents were confident of their ability to influence government policy.*

A majority of the respondents in many of the surveys (usually some two-thirds) think that their votes have an impact on election results, and approximately the same proportion think that election results have an impact on government policy. These, however, are replies to roundabout questions that do not enable us to reach any clear-cut conclusions. We would have to know what percentage of the public feel that through their vote they are actually capable of influencing policy; this cannot be established on the basis of these two separate items. Thus, we remain with the result that the majority of Israelis feel that there is little they can do to influence government policy.

In practically all surveys the percentage of those professing high political efficacy is perceptibly smaller than the percentage of those professing high political interest. Even when extensiveness of interest in "politics" is compared to confidence in ability to influence policy, political interest *still* clearly exceeds political efficacy (Table 4.1).† Only in the September 1973 panel survey was this difference found to have shrunk to some extent. Thus, most surveys indicate that a clear discrepancy has developed among the Israeli public between declared political involvement (which is rather widespread) and confidence in political efficacy (which is much less so).

In some ways this is rather surprising. The yishuv tradition of independent initiative under foreign rule may have been expected to have encouraged not only political interest, but political efficacy as well. Efficacy may have been encouraged, especially by the transition from colonial rule to independence. The shift from life under a foreign government (whose policies were dictated by anything but the preferences of the Jewish population) to a rule of this population's "own" government, manned by its "own" representatives, might have been expected to have led to a high sensitivity to citizens' demands on part of the political elite and a widespread sense of having a say in policy on part of the public. Furthermore, the smallness of the country and the consequent intimacy of its public life would have led one to harbor similar expectations.

On the other hand, the modest extent of political efficacy actually found among the Israeli public seems to fit in rather well with certain features of the

---

*Unfortunately, only one question that clearly pertains to political efficacy was included. At the same time, confidence in the results based on this question is strengthened by the fact that it recurs in several studies.

†For the Arian survey this gap between political interest and efficacy is not evident from the table itself, but it *is* evident from the data (see above).

political regime. In a democracy, the choice among alternative ruling elites (as crystallized in parties) by means of free elections may be perceived as one major mechanism by which the rank and file can press its mark on the political process. Hence, the Israelis' relatively low sense of political efficacy may well be related to Israel's party and electoral system. As noted, Israel is characterized by a multiparty system coupled with proportional representation, and Israel's dominant party has, until recently, secured about twice as many votes as the next strongest party. As a consequence of this constellation, Israel's ruling elite has remained in office despite electoral shifts that, in a biparty system, would have resulted in its replacement (see Chapter 3). In Arian's words: "Israel provides a fascinating example of a political system . . . in which changes in public opinion are not reflected in the voting results" (Arian 1972, p. 202). It is therefore possible that the Israelis' relatively low sense of efficacy partly reflects the fact that the country's electoral system is not a sufficiently sensitive mechanism for registering the voters' wishes.

Yet the majority of the public expressed the feeling that election results *do* make a difference and that their own votes *do* affect election results. It is possible that Israel's electoral system is an objective factor working for low political efficacy, even if it is not subjectively recognized as such. Nevertheless, the fact that most Israelis are not consciously dissatisfied with their electoral system indicates that an additional explanation should be looked for.

Perhaps many Israelis sense themselves to be politically impotent not on election day but in interelectoral periods (which, after all, cover the vast majority of the time). Possibly they may feel that there are no adequate extraelectoral channels through which they can express their demands. This, in turn, may be related to the growing centralization of power in the hands of the political establishment and the growing gulf that has thus developed between this establishment and the rank and file of the citizens (see Chapter 1). It may also be related to the fact that except for the multiple parties and the Histadrut, Israel is characterized by a relative paucity of voluntary organizations that could serve as channels of upward political communication. In Fein's words (1962, p. 86), there "is an almost total absence of organizations with quasi-political interests and other similar groups, which occupy so important a position in American group life." Thus, it seems that the discrepancy between involvement and efficacy is due, in part, to an inconsistency between certain aspects of Israel's culture (which have encouraged political involvement) and certain structural features of the political system (which have discouraged efficacy).

The widespread feeling of low political efficacy, in turn, may explain the tendency of most Israelis to refrain from "gladiatorial" political activities. Since so many Israelis feel that they cannot really make a difference at the central level of policy decisions, this may discourage them from even trying.

Stability or Change—The Impact of the Yom Kippur War

Have there been any recent changes in the manner in which the Israeli public has confronted the political scene? The data on election turnout suggest that the level of political participation, at any rate, has remained quite steady. Research data on both political participation and political interest from 1969 onwards also show that the same steady level of political participation and interest was maintained (see Tables 4.1 and 4.2). As for political efficacy, certain methodological problems prevent us from tracing its development throughout these years (see above, pp. 77–78).

It would be of interest to know how the recent wars have affected the Israelis' political interest and efficacy. For the Six-Day War no pertinent data are available. On the other hand, a number of surveys were conducted shortly before and after the Yom Kippur War, and these enable us to reach some tentative conclusions on short-term changes that took place in the wake of this war.*

Referring once more to Table 4.1, it may be seen that the Yom Kippur War did not effect any clear-cut changes in political activity; the percentage of those active in parties or in election campaigns was about equal before (September) and after (December) the war. Changes in other items of participation seem to have balanced each other: while the percentage watching the election campaigns on television decreased following the war, the percentage of those discussing politics increased significantly (compare the results of September with those of November). This result, by the way, cannot be surprising to anyone familiar with the heated controversy in which the Israeli public was embroiled following the war.

As for political involvement, it is apparent (Table 4.1) that the Yom Kippur War did not bring in its wake an increased involvement in voting, although the elections took place only two months after the war—a few days after the Ben Sira Survey (1973B). This conclusion is in line with the actual election turnout as well: the percentage of those participating in the December 1973 election was not any greater than the percentage participating in previous elections (see p. 72).

In contrast, we perceive a definite heightening in the public's wish to influence government policy. Shortly before the war (September), less than half of the respondents expressed a wish to do so; immediately after the war (December), almost two-thirds expressed this wish. Again, this could have

---

*We cannot tell with certainty that they occurred *because* of the war, although this seems plausible.

been expected—and may be explained by data (Ben Sira 1973A)* showing that 70 percent of the respondents felt that Israel's situation had deteriorated as a result of the war, and that 88 percent of all respondents held the government responsible for the change in Israel's situation. This being so, it is only natural that an increased number of persons should wish to influence government policy, ostensibly in order to prevent such lapses in the future. It is of interest, however, that in spite of the various dilemmas that Israel faced as a result of the war, dilemmas that to many may seem insoluble, the public did not succumb to feelings of utter confusion and helplessness. On the contrary: more people seemed to feel confident that they knew what should be done, as evidenced by the wish to influence government policy.

The Yom Kippur War does not seem to have effected any obvious changes in political efficacy; immediately after the war, political efficacy resumed its dimensions of half a year before (see Table 4.1). Immediately preceding the war (in September 1973), efficacy was somewhat more widespread. Possibly this was because the September survey took place on the eve of the supposedly imminent election in October and people suddenly felt more effective politically. But if this is so, why was no such heightening of political efficacy evident in the December Ben Sira survey (1973B) that took place a few days before the rescheduled election?

Since data are sparse, one can only speculate. Possibly the war experience brought about the feeling that even elections do not open up an avenue of political influence for the rank and file, for neither of the two major parties held great attraction for the voters. The image of the incumbent Labor Party was damaged because of the alleged war failures. On the other hand, the Likud, the major alternative, was not excessively attractive to a large part of the public because the hawkish policy it advocated was thought by many to encourage the advent of yet another war. Quite possibly then, many postwar Israeli voters, faced with two major alternatives they could not whole-heartedly endorse, did not feel that their votes could really bring about the state of affairs they wished to see realized on the political scene.

Thus, the Yom Kippur War was followed by a perceptible increase in the proportion of those who wished to influence government policy—but apparently did not bring an increase in those who felt that this could be achieved through elections, or in those who felt that this could be achieved at all by whatever means. Thus, while the public's wish to influence policy was heightened after the war, its confidence in being able to do so was not. Consequently, the war seems to have led to a further widening of the existent discrepancy

---

*These data do not appear in Tables 4.1 and 4.2, where only the second Ben Sira survey (1973B) is cited.

between relatively widespread political involvement and much less widespread political efficacy.

This discrepancy is by no means self-evident, as may be seen from Almond and Verba's five-country survey. By comparing these countries among themselves,* it may be seen that where relatively many citizens are active and involved in politics, relatively many feel politically efficacious as well. Conversely, where the percentages expressing involvement are lower, so are the percentages expressing efficacy. Thus, in the U.S. and the United Kingdom both percentages are *relatively* high; in Italy and Mexico both are perceptibly lower. Only Germany resembles the U.S. and the U.K. in political involvement and Mexico and Italy in efficacy, and even here the discrepancy is by no means as clear-cut as it is in Israel (Almond and Verba 1965, pp. 54, 79, 142, and 188).

This, at any rate, was the situation in the early 1960s. Since then, however, some changes have apparently occurred in the United States. As Converse (1972, p. 334) put it: "Indicators of political attentiveness and activism appear to have edged forward over the past two decades . . . and these trends stand in rather marked contrast to the evolution of feelings of political efficacy in the population. . . . It has shown a marked regression during the middle 1960s." (See also Miller 1974A and 1974B; House and Mason 1975.) Thus, a certain similarity may have developed between the Israeli and American patterns. Since the Israeli and American political cultures differ so greatly in other respects (for instance, in the prevalence of voluntary organizations as channels of upward political communication), the question is whether this ostensibly similar discrepancy between political involvement and efficacy carries similar meanings in the two cultures. This, however, must be left as an open question pending further investigation.

CONFRONTATION OF POLITICS AND CONFIDENCE IN THE ISRAELI ESTABLISHMENT

What is the significance of the Israelis' high political involvement coupled with a widespread feeling of political futility? It is our contention that it both reflects and precipitates political discontent.

---

*No detailed comparisons with Israel are possible because the questions employed in Almond and Verba's survey are not identical to those employed in the Israeli surveys. This problem does not arise when the countries surveyed by Almond and Verba are compared among themselves. Even when identical questions are employed, however, the comparison is not unproblematic: there remains the problem of equivalence. It has been pointed out, for instance, that identical questions may carry different meanings in different cultures. Moreover, even if this is not the case, the patterns revealed by the questions may fit very differently into the wider context of the respective cultures. (On this, see, for instance, MacIntyre 1971; Rosenbaum 1975, p. 30.)

We could not supply direct proof for this contention, but we did so indirectly by comparing citizens with various degrees of political involvement and efficacy according to their confidence in the government. On the basis of the 1973 General and Panel Study we constructed a scale of political involvement composed of the following items: professed interest in political, socioeconomic, and security affairs, and reported discussions of politics.* Respondents were scored as high, medium, or low on this scale. We had only one item of political efficacy to work with; respondents were scaled as high or low on this count.†

We first examined the relationship between political involvement and confidence in the government and the relationship between political efficacy and confidence, separately.‡ Almond and Verba (1965), in their survey of five countries, concluded that the citizen who is politically involved or politically confident is also more likely to be proud and satisfied with the performance of his political system. Surprisingly, however, no similar conclusion emerges from the Israeli data; we found only slight relations between political involvement and efficacy on one hand and confidence in the government on the other.

We next sought to explore the implications of the *joint* constellation of political involvement and political efficacy on confidence in the political establishment, by cross-tabulating political involvement with political efficacy, a procedure that yielded the typology shown in Figure 4.1.

The first type may be termed the "politically integrated" citizen, since he feels that he shares in the political life of his country by being involved in it and by being confident in his ability to help shape it. This type of citizen fits in with the image of the involved and self-confident citizen as presented by Almond and Verba, and with the conception of the modern citizen as visualized by Eisenstadt, for instance.

---

*We felt justified in combining political involvement and political discussions into one scale, since the latter item was positively correlated with the former. Moreover, the correlations between political discussions and various items of political involvement were no lower (and even somewhat higher) than the correlation among the various items of political involvement. The Pearson correlation coefficients among the various items were as follows:

	1	2	3	4
1. Interest in "politics"		.37	.33	.67
2. Interest in socioeconomic affairs			.34	.40
3. Interest in security problems				.30
4. Discussion of politics				

†For this item see Table 4.1.
‡Respondents were requested to state what the country's two most urgent problems were. They were then asked if they thought the government capable of solving these problems. For full wording of the questions, see Appendix A.

FIGURE 4.1
Typology of Citizens

	Political Efficacy	
Political Involvement	High	Low
High	A) The politically integrated citizen	A) The politically blocked citizen
Medium	C) Intermediate type	D) Intermediate type
Low	E) The politically withdrawn citizen	F) The politically alienated citizen

The last type may be characterized as the "politically alienated" citizen. The term "political alienation" is used in the sense in which it was used by Neuman (1957, p. 290); that is, estrangement from and powerlessness vis-à-vis the political system. This type fits in with the image of the member of the mass society as visualized by Mills.

The second type of citizen has been termed the "politically blocked" citizen; he is politically involved and therefore (presumably) would like to press his mark on the political life of his country, but feels incapable of doing so; thus his involvement is blocked by his sense of political futility. Finally, there is the "politically withdrawn" citizen; although he is efficacious, he is content to leave the management of the affairs of state in the hands of the political elite, and thus withdraws voluntarily, so to speak, from the political arena. (The remaining two types of citizen are of an intermediary character.)

Ostensibly, the integrated type of citizen should be the most favorable, while the alienated type should be the least favorable in his orientation to the political establishment. Following our previous analysis, however, we harbored an alternative expectation: we reasoned that high involvement and low efficacy should be related to a certain type of strain, or even to political frustration. Hence the politically blocked citizen is apt to respond by disparaging the political establishment, which he may view as the cause of his frustration. The data pertaining to this expectation are presented in Table 4.3, which compares the various types of citizens with regard to their confidence in the government.

In line with our expectation, the politically blocked citizen was the least likely to express confidence in the government; unexpectedly, the politically withdrawn citizen was the most likely to do so. Possibly, this citizen's greater

TABLE 4.3

Types of Citizens Who Do Not Express Confidence in the Government, in 1973
(in percentages)

	Political Efficacy	
Political Involvement Scale	High	Low
High	Politically integrated citizen 52 (n = 322)	Politically blocked citizen 63 (n = 513)
Medium	Intermediate type 54 (n = 105)	Intermediate type 54 (n = 329)
Low	Politically withdrawn citizen 43 (n = 74)	Politically alienated citizen 53 (n = 332)

$p < 0.01$

Source: General and Panel Study (1973).

confidence in the government's ability to cope with the country's problems explains his voluntary withdrawal from the political arena, or else he may simply justify his political withdrawal by approving of what is being done in any case. The politically integrated and the politically alienated types were both intermediate in their stand toward the system.

Presumably, the relatively negative stand toward the establishment of the politically blocked citizens ensued from having their desire to influence policy blocked by their perceived inability to do so. This presumption is corroborated by data from the Panel Survey.* Here, respondents were asked directly whether they wished to influence policy decisions and whether they thought they would be able to exert such an influence. Those who wished to influence policy but felt unable to do so were indeed the most negatively disposed toward the government. Thus 70 percent of the politically blocked citizens thought the government would not be able to solve the country's most urgent problems—as against only 56 percent of the politically integrated citizens, 57 percent of the politically alienated, and 52 percent of the politically withdrawn.

Much has been written concerning the implications of political involvement for the democratic regime, but no unanimity prevails as to the nature of

---

*The Panel Survey was a follow-up to the General and Panel Study. A subsample of 523 respondents was reinterviewed a few months later.

these implications. Traditionally, the theory of democracy has stressed the crucial importance of citizens' involvement in politics for the maintenance of stable democracy. Lately, however, several political theorists have pointed to the dangers inherent in *excessive* involvement on the part of the citizens—which may curtail a democratic government's freedom of action and thus incapacitate it.*

In this context the present analysis takes on added significance. It leads to the suggestion that what is significant for the regime is not only (and perhaps not even chiefly) the extent of political involvement as such, but the joint constellation of political involvement and political efficacy. For if the recent theories of democracy are to the point, and high involvement may indeed lead to excessive interference, then it may be reasoned that *blocked* involvement with its attendant stress and negation of the regime may, under certain conditions, lead to a hostile type of interference.

CONCLUSION

We asked how Israelis shape up as political animals. We found that most of them profess high political involvement and engage in "spectator" political participation; but most also profess low political efficacy and refrain from "gladiatorial" participation.

This brings us back to the two theories cited at the opening of the discussion: the "optimistic" conception that stresses the wide and growing participation of the citizens in the political center of contemporary societies, and the "pessimistic" conception that stresses the growing alienation of the masses from the center.

We conclude that as far as Israel is concerned both conceptions have some empirical support, since both involvement and disaffection are evident. But neither of these contentions is fully corroborated by the data. Perhaps the state of affairs in Israel is most nearly in line with Shils' perceptive analysis of the contemporary political scene:

> To a greater extent than ever before in history the mass of the population ... feel themselves to be "part" of their society. ... They have ceased to be primarily objects of authoritative decisions by others; they have become, to a much greater extent, acting and feeling subjects with wills of their own which they assert with self confidence. ... Men have become citizens in larger proportions than ever before. ... Nonetheless this greater incorpora-

---

*For an excellent overview of both theories, see Pateman (1970).

tion carries with it also an inherent tension. Those who participate in the central institutional and value systems, who feel sufficiently closer to the center—also feel their position as outsiders, their remoteness from the center in a way in which their forebears probably did not feel it. (Shils 1975, p. 14).

We suggested that such a discrepancy between affinity with the center and remoteness from it, as has been found on the Israeli political scene, may well serve as a disgruntling political experience that may reflect and affect a tendency to disparage the political establishment. We found that citizens who embodied this disparity were indeed less confident in the government compared with all other types of citizens, a fact that lends indirect support to this conception.

If disparity between affinity with the center and remoteness from it predisposes citizens to political discontent, we would expect the general support of the Israeli public for the political establishment to have been low or declining in recent years. Has this actually been the case? This topic is examined in the next chapter.

CHAPTER 5

THE DECLINE OF CONSENT?

The idea that government is to rest on the consent of the governed has had a wide currency in Western thought, both in social philosophy and in the ideology of democracy.* Indeed, the principle of "consent by the people" seems to be so widely accepted in the Western world, that to oppose it would be about as popular as opposing motherhood (before women's lib, at any rate). Yet "consent" is a vague term whose essence has not been clearly established, and we only have limited knowledge on the factors that promote "consent by the people" or detract from it. While most contemporary observers would probably agree that "consent" is, in some manner, an outgrowth of the interaction between the people and the government, there is no unanimity on the manner in which this interaction affects consent; and it is not clear which partner to the interaction has a greater effect on it. Although some conceptions concerning this effect have been worked out, its concrete manifestations have not been widely explored.

CONSENT AND THE ESTABLISHMENT

The Impact of the Establishment on Consent

Traditionally, the prevalent idea in social philosophy has been that the people extend their consent to the government, which thereby becomes autho-

---

*For a concise overview of the development of this idea in Western thought, see Partridge (1971); Pitkin (1965 and 1966).

rized to act in their name. Lately, however, another view has become predominant. The claim is that it is actually the government or, to use a more fashionable word, the political establishment that, to some extent, molds the people's consent to itself and its own policies. According to this view, consent is taken as descending from the top, no less (and perhaps more) than ascending from the bottom.

This view has been expressed, for instance, by Walter Lippman (1961, p. 248) who writes: "That the manufacture of consent is capable of great refinement, no one, I think, denies... the opportunities open to anyone who understands the process are plain enough. The creation of consent is not a new art. ... It has ... improved enormously in technic because it is now based on analysis. ... Within the life of the generation now in control of affairs, persuasion has become a self conscious art and regular organ of popular government."

More recently it has been argued that the establishment may promote consent by distributing information selectively (Partridge 1971, p. 41);* by emitting symbolic cues that define or interpret states of affairs for the public (Edelman 1971);† and by means of ritualistic, evocative, rhetoric-and-emotion-laden linguistic symbols that, in themselves, contain predefinitions of the situation (Mueller 1973).

With regard to these conceptions, several points of interest emerge. First, as so often happens when social scientists attempt to make their point forcefully, some of these authors have greatly overstated their case. Evidently a major part of the interaction between the public and the establishment takes place on the symbolic level. Granting that definitions of situations are important in such an interaction, it should be evident to any unbiased observer that these authors have underemphasized the limits of what such definitions can accomplish; that there are exigencies that simply cannot be defined away, or alternatively, be defined into existence.‡

Second, some of these conceptions emphasize symbolic means to the deprecation or partial neglect of a great variety of nonsymbolic devices that may similarly be employed by an establishment in the struggle to obtain the people's consent. We would like to argue that, at least in the case here analyzed, the establishment's ability to encourage consent through the manipulation of symbols is more limited, while its ability to do so by nonsymbolic means is more extensive than emerges from these conceptions.

---

*See also p. 118.
†Edelman claims that the potency of these cues is augmented by the fact that they often encounter no competing cues from other sources.
‡Furthermore, some of these authors have evidently underplayed the importance of alternative definitions of the situation that, in Western type democracies, are supplied to the public by agencies other than the government.

Finally, it should be evident, that "consent by the people" is the outgrowth of an intricate and *manifold* interaction between the political establishment and the rank and file of the public, of which conscious manipulation of the former by the latter is only one facet. We would like to argue that a *generally* successful interaction is apt to be reflected in high or rising consent, while discrepancies or tensions between the government and those it governs are apt to find expression in relatively low or declining consent. Hence various "devices" (symbolic or nonsymbolic), deliberately employed by the establishment in order to manipulate the public, may mitigate such a decline, but their effectiveness has its limitations, especially when overall discrepancies between the public and the establishment become paramount. This, we claim, has in fact been the case in Israel in recent years.

Forms and Expressions of Consent

At this point we can no longer evade the question: What is consent? How do we know whether a government in fact enjoys the consent of the governed? For it is one thing to extoll "consent by the people" in abstract terms, or even to discuss the measures that may be employed for encouraging it. It is quite another matter to pin it down and establish the extent of such consent empirically. Lacking unanimously-agreed-upon definitions, the term "consent," as here employed, refers to approval or support of a political elite or a government, its composition, program, and course of action.*

This, of course, raises the problem of how such support may be expressed and, hence, recognized. It is sometimes assumed that free elections give citizens an opportunity to express the degree of their consent. To examine it, therefore, all that one must do is to read the election results. But is this in fact so?

Obviously, election results must indeed be regarded as the sole valid basis of democratic government. For sociological analysis, on the other hand, it would be less than satisfactory to rely on election results alone. For one thing, elections occur periodically; it is not clear to what extent they reflect consent during interelectoral periods. Moreover, voting can be a matter of habit or even of perceived self-interest, rather than of deliberate approval. Also, elections offer a choice only between existing alternatives; therefore, many may feel constrained to endorse the lesser of two (or more) evils, thus voting into office a government that has not truly enlisted their support.† For these reasons (as

---

*For a somewhat different definition, see Plamenatz (1968, p. 18).
†On this topic see also Duverger (1964, p. 347); Arian (1973).

well as others), we are using here an additional measure of consent: declared approval of government policy, as revealed by public opinion studies.

This measure, of course, has its own disadvantages: responding to a questionnaire does not entail the same degree of commitment as does the casting of a ballot; also, public opinion studies pertain to cross sections of the population rather than to the population as a whole. On the other hand, such studies have several advantages not inherent in election returns. They are, for instance, not beset by the "one vote—many issues" dilemma, as a variety of questions on a variety of issues can be included in the study.*

All things considered, it seems that the optimal procedure is to establish consent on the basis both of election results and of public opinion surveys; this is the procedure we have, in fact, adopted for exploring recent trends in consent on the Israeli political scene. Although it cannot be expected to yield the whole unvarnished truth, it has the advantage of combining two partial truths and thus approximates a more balanced view of the situation.

The Impact of Consent on the Establishment

Once a method for operationalizing consent has been decided upon, it is possible to trace not only the impact of the establishment on consent, but the converse line of influence as well. Does consent, or lack thereof, have any clear implications for the establishment? Assuming that certain cleavages have developed between the public and the establishment, and that these have found expression in a declining level of consent—how significant is this for the viability and stability of the establishment?

Little has been written that could serve as a guideline. Following the Weber tradition, a certain degree of legitimation has been considered as a sine qua non of the stability of a political regime (see, for instance, Eisenstadt 1956, p. 9; Mueller 1973, pp. 127–77). However, legitimation (although it is a related concept) obviously cannot be equated with consent; while legitimation (in the spirit of the Weber tradition) refers to the recognition that a government holds its position by rightful claims, consent, as here defined, has to do with support of that government.

On the face of it, it would seem that the impact of consent (versus dissent) on the establishment does not pose much of a problem for sociological analysis, at least where the regime is democratic. Ostensibly, in such a regime, when the

---

*Further, such studies can pinpoint the opinions of various subgroups in the public—a task which can be accomplished only in part, and only by employing devious methods, when dealing with election results.

government no longer enjoys the consent of the majority of the governed, it is simply replaced by a government that does.

However, the question remains of how a ruling elite is affected when electoral consent for itself declines considerably but not to the extent of making it lose its ascendancy over the opposition. In a dominant party system such as Israel, where for many years one party has usually netted at least twice as many votes as the second largest party, this constitutes a very real problem. Moreover, the question arises of how the establishment may be affected by a waning of consent, as expressed by public opinion that for one reason or another, is not fully translated into election results; or else by such decline in interelectoral periods.

Recently it has been claimed that the effectiveness of democratic leadership depends not only on legitimation but also on actual, diffuse support by the public; when such consent is low, or waning, this is apt to jeopardize the stability of the regime (Easton 1965, p. 273; Gamson 1968, pp. 43–46; Miller 1974). However, little has been said on how declining consent is supposed to evince this result. As we shall see that consent has recently declined in Israel, the question is: does this conception fit the Israeli case? Lacking clear theoretical guidelines we shall attempt only a preliminary exploration of this subject.

In sum, three topics will be explored: the impact that the Israeli establishment has made on consent for itself* as well as the limitations of this impact; the trends of decline in consent in recent years; and, finally, the effects of such decline on the establishment.

CONSENT AND THE ISRAELI ESTABLISHMENT

The Impact of the Israeli Establishment on Consent

The Israeli political elite has made abundant use of both symbolic and nonsymbolic mechanisms of fostering consent. Thus, it has been pointed out (Boim 1971–72) that relatively more funds are expended for election campaigns (that is, for symbolic persuasion) in Israel than in any other country in the world and the quantity of verbal messages that emanate almost daily from high-ranking government officials, labor leaders, and military commanders is proverbial.† A systematic analysis of the symbolic content of various

---

*By means of nonsymbolic mechanisms of eliciting consent.

†Such messages gain added significance in view of the high exposure of the Israeli public to the various media that relay such messages (see Chapter 4).

political messages, and of the utilization of verbal symbols to foster consent, would thus make a fascinating study.*

Our present concern, however, is to understand how nonsymbolic means of eliciting consent have been working. To do so, it is necessarry to bear in mind that the Israeli government and the Histadrut largely control the economy and that, consequently, large parts of the population are directly or indirectly dependent on the establishment for their subsistence. Further, it will be recalled that in the prestate era, in the absence of a full-fledged Jewish government, political organizations, especially the Histadrut and the political parties, assumed various encompassing tasks such as channeling and absorbing immigration and providing employment and health services. With the founding of the state, part of these functions were gradually transferred to the government, but part of them were maintained by the parties and the Histadrut. In general, these bodies maintained their erstwhile powerful positions and continued to play prominent roles in Israel's political life (see Chapter 1).

From this point of view, the Israel Labor Party (formerly Mapai) has traditionally been the most prominent. Therefore, and in view of its longtime hegemony in both the government and the Histadrut, this party (more than any other) has come to be identified with the political establishment. It will be seen that the various nonsymbolic mechanisms employed for eliciting consent have worked predominantly in its favor and, to a lesser extent, in favor of its traditional coalition partners, thus, strengthening the status quo.

One type of such device concerns the molding of policies in response to the perceived wishes of the electorate, especially in regard to resources and rewards. Devices of this type may be ordered on a continuum from the general, national (macro) level to the specific, local, or even individual (micro) level. On the macrolevel this device concerns the creation of overall national (for instance, economic) policies. On the intermediate level it has to do with the molding of policies in line with the demands of various countrywide interest groups. On the microlevel it entails benefits to various communities, subcommunities, or certain interest groups within communities—or, finally, to families and individuals, As one moves from the macro to the microlevel, this device turns into an exchange of benefits for votes.

While it may have been to the advantage of all parties to utilize this device at the microlevel, not all of them have been in a position to do so. Since most potential benefits accrue from the state, or the Histadrut, or else are channeled through the state via the various ministries, the parties whose representatives

---

*On the utilization of religious and other symbols for election campaigns see Deshen (1970, 1972).

in the cabinet control these ministries (that is, the dominant party, followed by the other coalition parties) are in the best position to grant such benefits.

There is, in fact, considerable evidence on the employment of this device, especially in smaller localities. Cohen et al. (1962) report the following on the basis of their research in a small town in the late 1950s: "There is a tendency, especially among newcomers, to turn any social framework in the town into a device for gaining concrete benefits. . . . The parties and their leaders utilized this tendency before the election in order to secure the inhabitants' votes and presented the parties as instrumental in providing such benefits. Phenomena such as promises of work, housing, etc., in exchange for a vote were mentioned many times by the respondents" (p. 101).

In his study of the 1965 and 1969 election campaigns in another small town, Deshen (1970 and 1972) tells of an intricate combination of symbolic devices and concrete benefits employed (especially by coalition parties and their affiliated political bodies) as a means of increasing electoral support. The benefits consisted of religious articles promised and donated to the several congregations in the community and also of more tangible benefits such as loans for public projects or housing, financial aid, and employment for individuals. Similar conclusions are reached by Aronoff. Referring to a senior official in the Labor Party-Alignment, he writes: "From his dominant position he ran the 1969 election very much like a classic political boss, offering manifold resources to those who would comply to his dictates and threatening sanctions to those who would not. The object was victory for the party in the election" (Aronoff 1972, p. 161). And further on: "A telephone call of a top [party] leader . . . is still quite sufficient to get the Ministry of Housing to allocate twenty living units in a development town . . . This process of using influence is known in Israel as "proteksia" or using vitamin P—and there is no institution in the country with more proteksia than the Labor Party. In fact, it is the main manufacturer and distributor of Vitamin P in Israel" (p. 165).

At a certain point, substantive devices shade over into organizational devices of enhancing consent. By organizational devices we mean utilizing the structures of political or nonpolitical organizations (or introducing changes into such structures) for the purposes of eliciting consent.

One such device may be viewed as an elaboration of the exchange of benefits for votes. This is the device of cooptation especially of leaders of ethnic or occupational groups.* In its rudimentary phase, this mechanism utilizes local leaders as middlemen in the bargaining process, turning it into a three-way exchange: the leaders elicit the support of their respective groups for the

---

*This device has been reported by Zamir (1964) in her study of a small town, and by Deshen (1972) in his study of another small town.

party, in return for various benefits for the rank and file—and thereby enhance their own leadership positions. Further elaboration of this device incorporates the local leaders into the party's own hierarchy and grants local power positions to them; in return, they mobilize the support of their followers for the party (see Zamir 1964, pp. 10 and 51; Medding 1972, pp. 69–71). Since this device is related to the granting of benefits it, too, has worked predominantly in favor of the ruling party.

All this evidence on the use of nonsymbolic devices of eliciting consent comes from nonurban areas, where they have been most conspicuous. However, the majority of the Israeli population resides in urban areas; hence it would be surprising if the parties had not made attempts to employ similar devices in these areas as well as on the general population. There is some evidence that they have, in fact, done so. Kies (1969), analyzing the 1959, 1961, and 1965 election returns in Jerusalem, reports that although the demographic composition of a neighborhood could serve as a fairly good predictor of electoral results in that neighborhood, *changes* in such composition did not result in parallel changes in electoral results. In other words, a neighborhood remained a certain party's neighborhood even when the demographic composition changed (p. 294). Interpreting these patterns, Kies maintains that they are the result of the traditional strength of political party organizations that seem to maintain a grip on communities and subcommunities (pp. 224, 288).

Kies' analysis, though instructive, does not enlighten us as to the specific organizational devices used by the various parties in mobilizing the vote. More detailed analyses (albeit only on the dominant party) may be found in Medding's study (1972). The most important mechanism on which Medding reports is that of "organizational penetration." While the mechanism of cooptation, described above, entails the incorporation of various groups' leaders into the party's organization, "organizational penetration" may be viewed as the obverse of this mechanism; it entails the incorporation of party activists and supporters into the leadership of various groups: "Assured support for Mapai* among organized interest groups was sought by capturing control of their executive bodies and then coordinating their policies with those of the party. On occasion, Mapai even organized the interest group's institutions in order to benefit from its support" (p. 19). Medding then goes on to describe how Mapai employed this device with a variety of groups such as industiral workers, artisans, professionals, immigrants, ethnic groups, women, and the like (pp. 19–85). He concludes by saying: "Mapai stood at the apex of a whole interconnected network of organizations and institutions which it controlled and directed from within. Thus it not only controlled the key governmental

---

*Later, the Israel Labor Party.

structures but many of the secondary associations that filled the social space between individuals and their government. . . . In every instance, it brought their organizational strength to bear in support of the party and its policies" (p. 305). This is not to say that this party was the only one to employ such devices; but it outranked other parties both in resources and in resourcefulness.

Activities such as these, as well as election campaigns, require financing that, thus, forms an additional though indirect method of fostering consent. The 1969 law regulating elections to the Knesset and the municipalities provides that the elections be financed by the state, and that each existing party receive a sum proportional to the number of MKs it had in the Knesset (Boim 1971–72). Thus, each existing party receives according to what it has. Understandably, this law was viewed by the opposition as a "total freezing of the existing establishment" (p. 31).*

The organizational devices mentioned thus far have been employed *separately* by the various parties. There are some devices, however, that have to do with *interparty* politics—namely, mergers and alignments. To appreciate the crucial significance of mergers and alignments for the Labor Party, it is necessary to trace the electoral fate of this Party through the years (Table 3.1). It can be seen that Mapai (later the Labor Party) faced the electorate as a separate party for five consecutive elections, in which it usually secured around a third of the votes. After that, it entered into various mergers and alignments whose end result is the present Alignment. In the 1969 election the Alignment received fewer votes than its component parties had received separately in previous elections, but more than Mapai had secured by itself. In 1973 the Alignment lost six percentage points, almost reverting to the percentage that Mapai formerly had been able to obtain on its own.

It follows that it is only by means of various mergers and alignments that the Mapai/Labor Party has been able to counteract (in part) its shrinking electoral support and to maintain a sufficiently wide electoral basis to ensure its continued hegemony in all government coalitions.

Nonsymbolic mechanisms of enhancing consent have thus permeated all layers of Israel's political life. How has the public responded to such devices? To answer this, we must first review some recent developments in various forms of consent.

Consent in Israel: Some Recent Developments

The most notable facts about electoral consent in Israel are that, time and again, the Labor Party-Alignment has been voted into office; (although it has

---

*Radio and TV electioneering time is allocated on the same principle.

never gained an absolute majority) that its electoral support has been decreasing in recent years,* but that it is still ahead of its adversaries (see Table 3.1).

As for consent to the government as a whole, it is notable that in its 28 years of existence the State of Israel has been ruled by no less than 20 successive governments (see Appendix D). At the same time, the composition of each successive government has been quite similar (and sometimes identical) to that of the previous one: the Religious Party and the Independent Liberals have been the Mapai/Labor Party's more or less permanent coalition partners. Thus, it may be said, ever since 1948, basically the same government has enjoyed uninterrupted electoral consent. If, however, only the last eight years are considered, it can be seen that the electoral support for the government has been diminishing (see Figure 5.2), as has the support for the Labor Party-Alignment†

Consent for the government's policy (as examined by public opinion research) was measured by the following three items: approval versus disapproval of the government's policy in general, its defense policy, and its economic policy. These items have recurred periodically in the public opinion surveys conducted by the IIASR (in conjunction with the Communications Institute of the Hebrew University) beginning in June 1967. The percentage of the respondents who have approved of government policy on these counts from June 1967 through September 1975 are presented in Figure 5.1.‡

The extent of support for government policy has been in continuous flux, and the range of its variation has been exceedingly large. Nevertheless, when opinion on overall government policy (the most continuously recurrent item) is considered, gradually decreasing support is clearly evident.** In fact, roughly three periods can be distinguished: 1967–70, when support for government policy is (comparatively speaking) highest; 1970–73, when it is intermediate, and from the end of 1973 onward, when it is lowest. After the Yom Kippur War a decline in support for the government's economic policy and its defense policy, is similarly evident. Thus we witness a combination of short-term

---

*We do not claim that this decline in consent is necessarily a long-term trend, but merely that it is perceivable in recent years.

†The decline in these two forms of electoral consent was interrelated since the narrowing down of electoral support for the Alignment, and especially the reduced margin between the Alignment and its major adversary, the Likud, was thought to increase the former's vulnerability, hence made it more difficult for this party to engage the support of its traditional coalition partners and to form a broadly based government (see below).

‡For a list of the surveys on the basis of which the figure was plotted, see the bibliography at the end of this book. These surveys were all conducted on representative samples of the adult, Jewish urban population of Israel, which is the great majority of the population.

**As noted, data are available only from June 1967. It is possible, and even likely, that before the Six-Day War consent for government policy was lower, so the trends analyzed pertain only to the period following this war.

Figure 5.1

Consent for Government Policy, 1967–75
(in percentages)

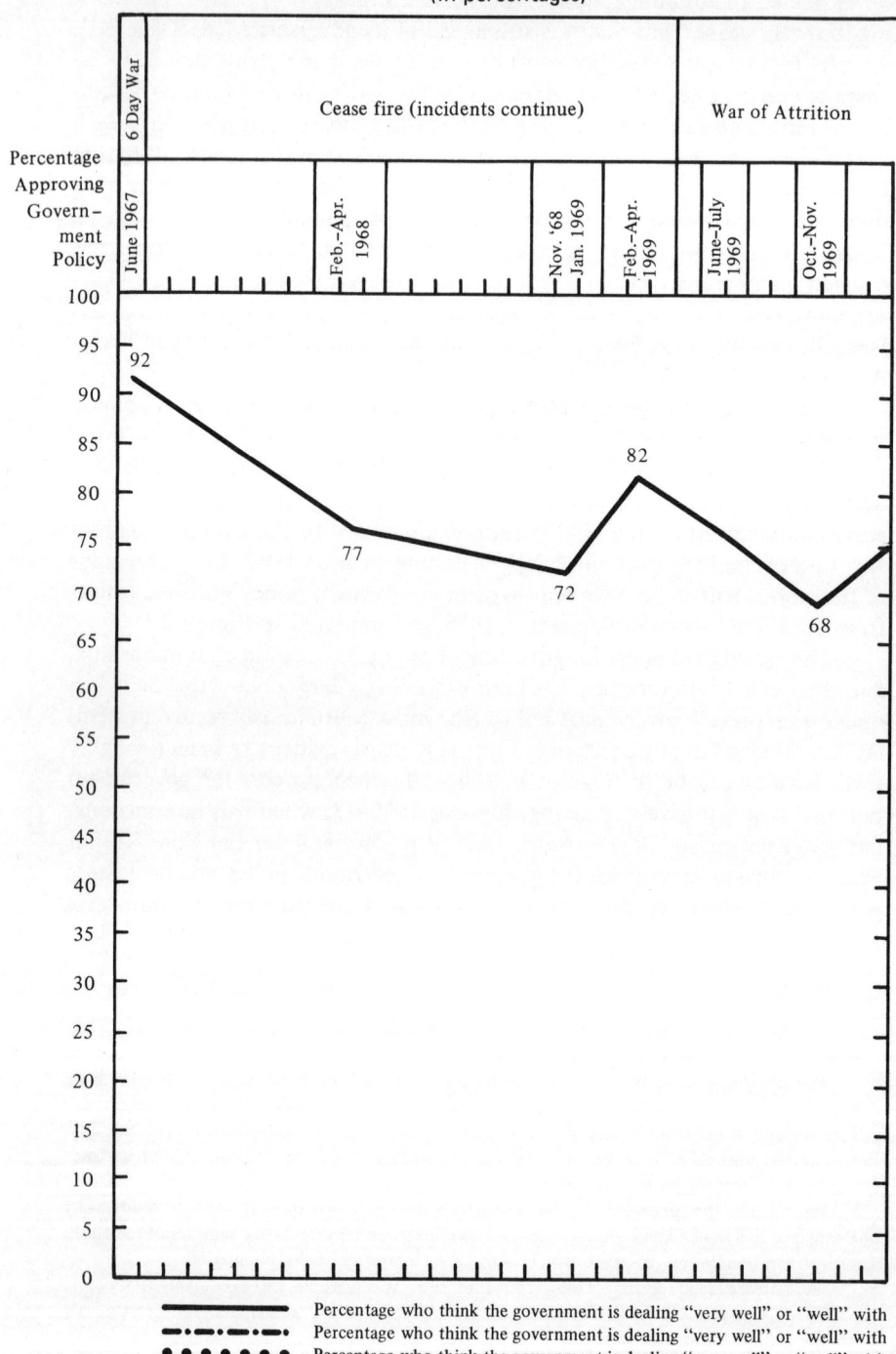

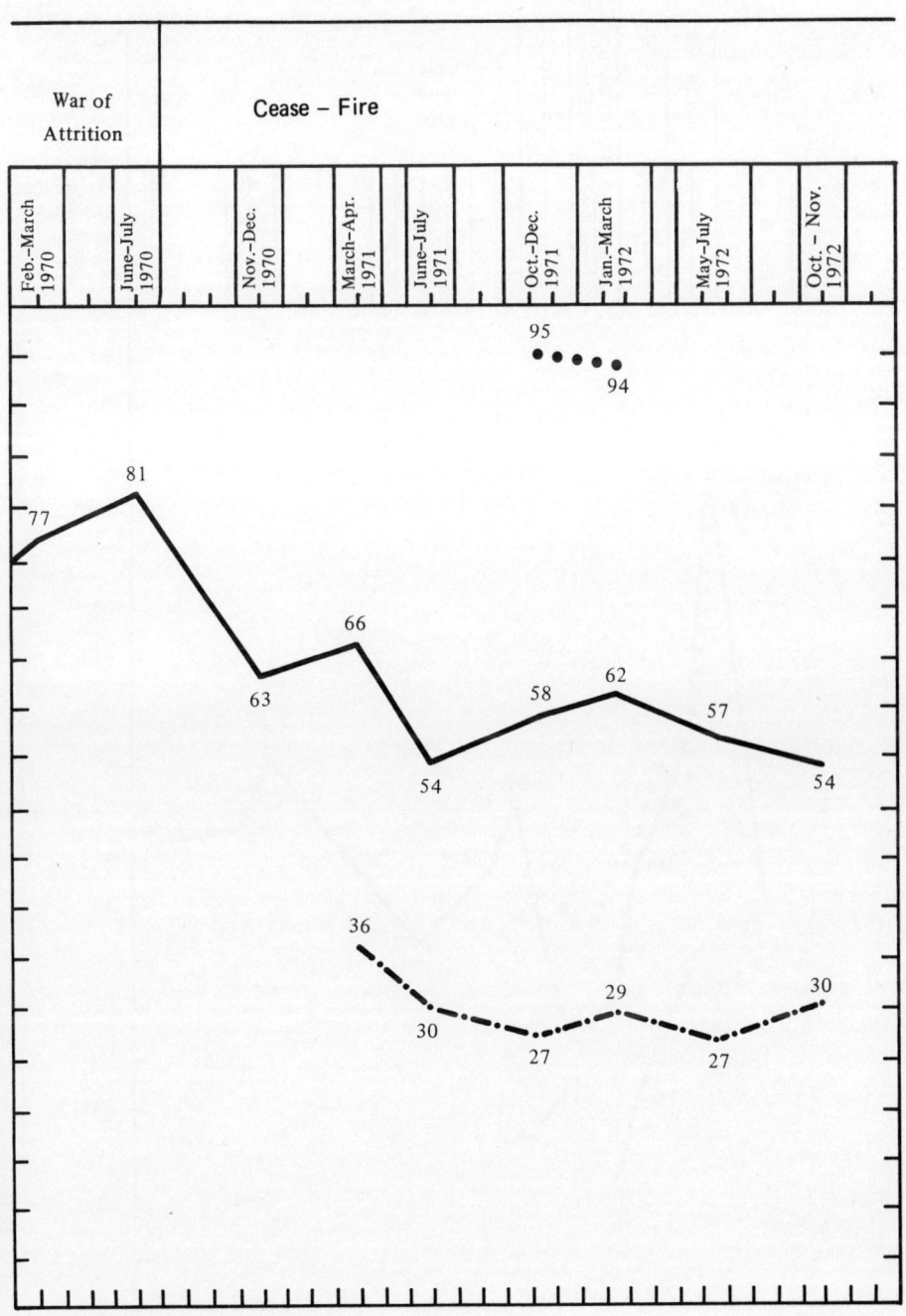

the problems of the present situation.
the country's security problems.
the country's economic problems.

(continued)

Figure 5.1 (continued)

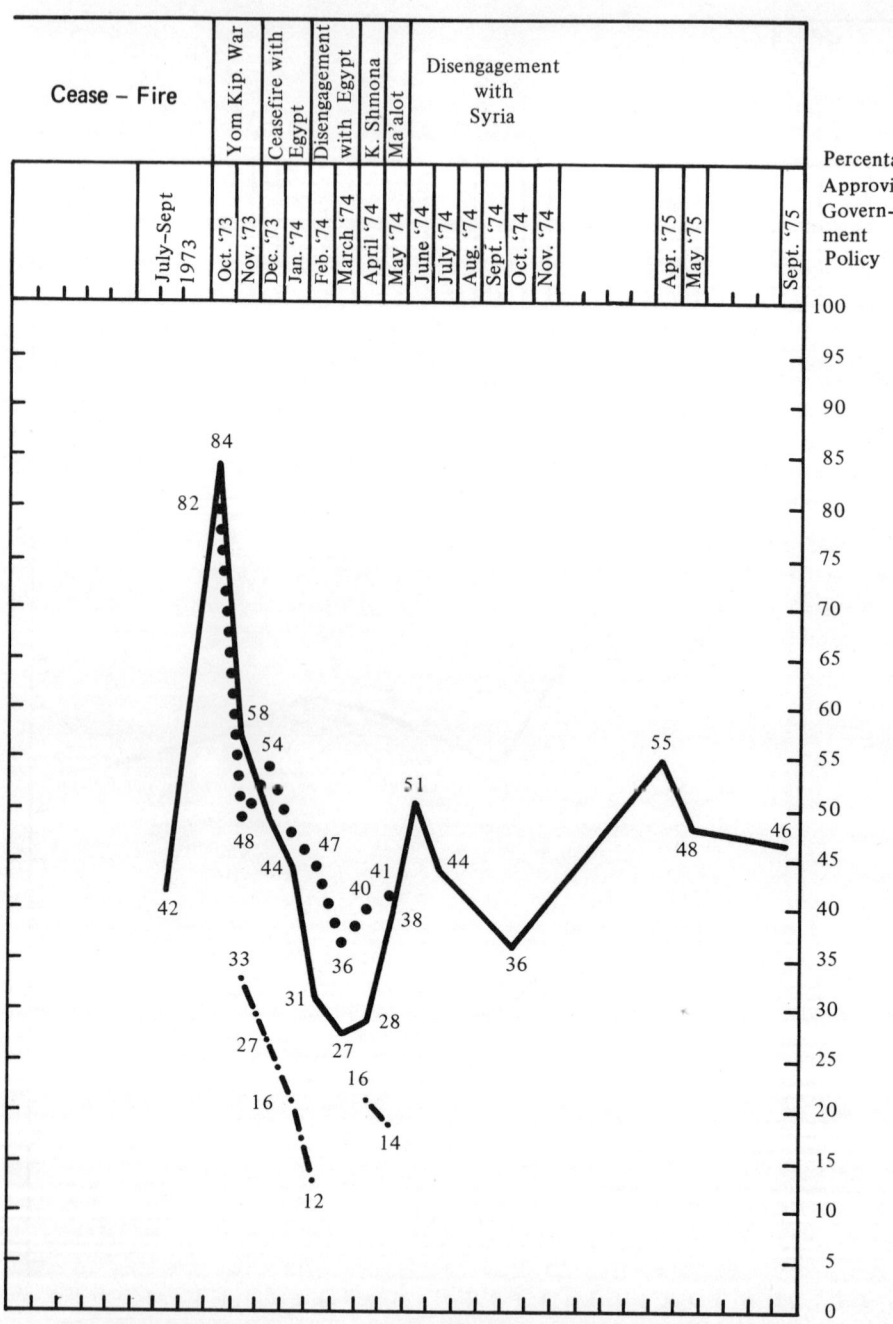

Note: Each 5mm symbolizes one month. Spaces left blank are months in which no surveys were carried out or in which the item of consent was not included. For wording of questions, see Appendix A.

fluctuations with some more-encompassing trends: in all three periods the level of consent for government policy continues to fluctuate. But in each successive period these fluctuations revolve, so to speak, around a progressively lower axis.

Figure 5.2 indicates that from 1969 until the end of 1974 all three forms of consent are on the decline. The correspondence in the development of the various types and subtypes of consent from 1969 onward points to a certain (not necessarily complete) consistency between the public's attitudes toward the ruling party and its attitudes toward the government headed by this party.* Hence their simultaneous decline in recent years leads to the claim that a certain overall disaffection of the public from the establishment has occurred during those years.

This raises the question how this disaffection and the resultant decline in consent may be interpreted. We have no hard-core data that could supply a direct answer to this question; indirectly we may learn something on this from data on various factors affecting consent at a given point in time. Thus, we may learn something on electoral consent from Table 3.2, which gives the effect of various attitudes on voting decisions. It shows that political orientations have a significant effect on intended voting and that they affect it more than do opinions on various concrete policy issues: a left-of-center political orientation is conducive to electoral support of the ruling Alignment, while center-rightist and religious orientations are conducive to support for all other major parties. Since certain shifts away from the left have recently occurred in the political orientations of the public, we may surmise that the ideological cleavage that has thus developed between parts of the public and the dominant party helps explain the recent decline in electoral consent for this party.

Among concrete policy issues, opinion on economic policy was the most influential in affecting electoral consent for the dominant party. Declared consent for the government as a whole, was also affected by opinions on domestic policy. This may be learned from the IIASR survey of March-April 1971. A multiple regression analysis was employed, in which the independent variables consisted of opinions on two items of policy with regard to the Israeli-Arab conflict (preference of a more- or less-adamant policy than the one adopted by the government, and opinion on the government's handling of terrorism) and two items of domestic policy (opinion on the government's

---

*Also this correspondence may be due to the fact that when a certain party is included in the government coalition its wishes are (to some extent) incorporated in the government policy, and therefore, the supporters of that party are more likely to be satisfied with the government's policy. Hence, the fewer parties included, and the smaller the electoral consent for these parties, the less widespread was the declared approval of the government's policy.

Figure 5.2
Three types of Consent, 1967-75

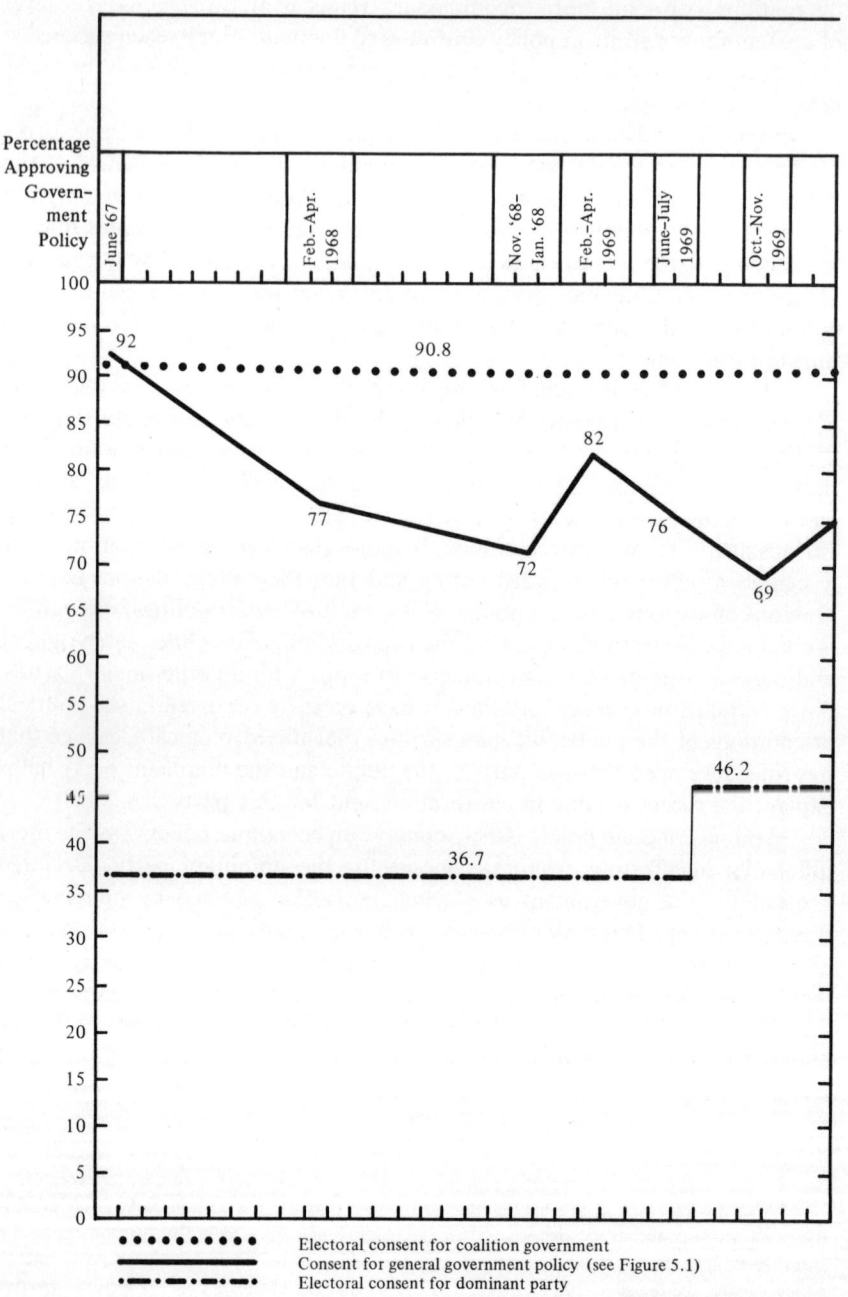

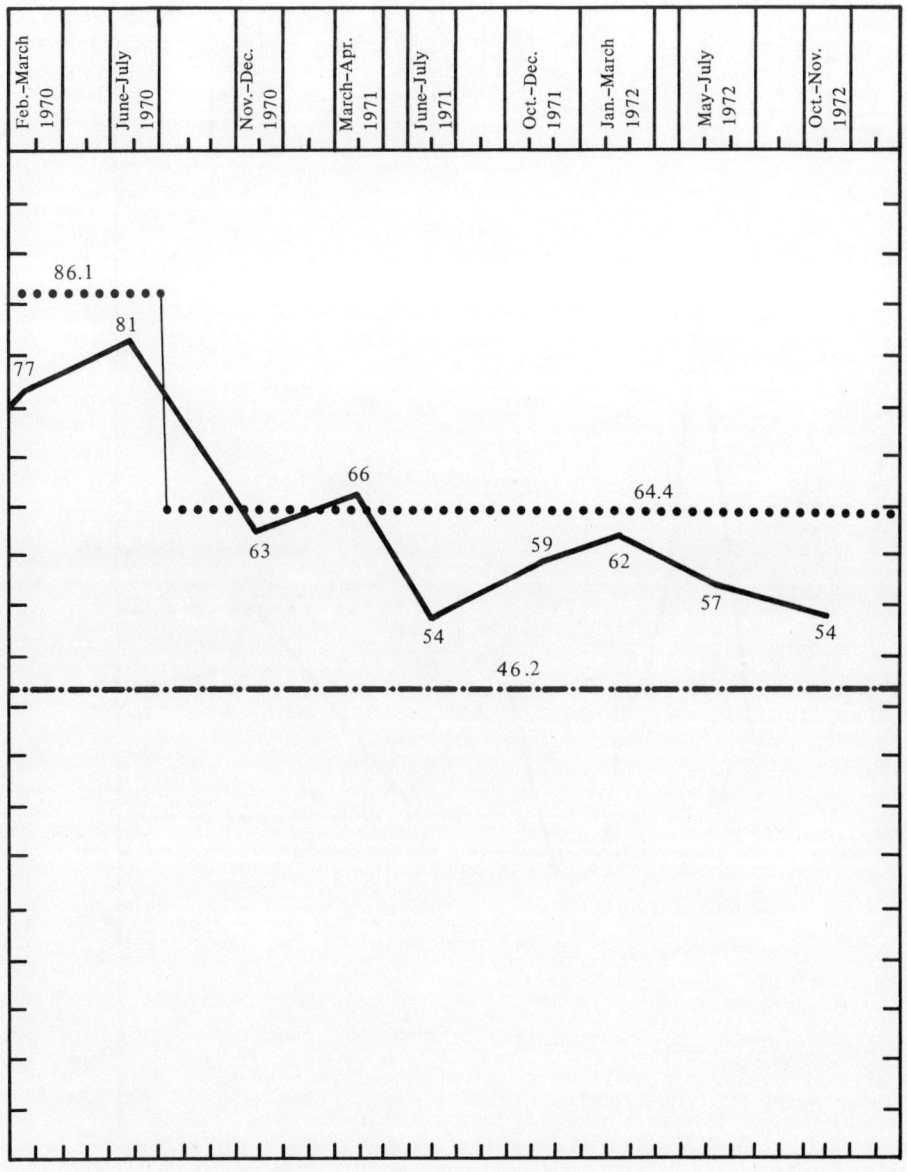

Note: Each 5mm symbolize one month. Spaces left blank are months in which no surveys were carried out, or in which the item of consent was not included.

(continued)

Figure 5.2 (continued)

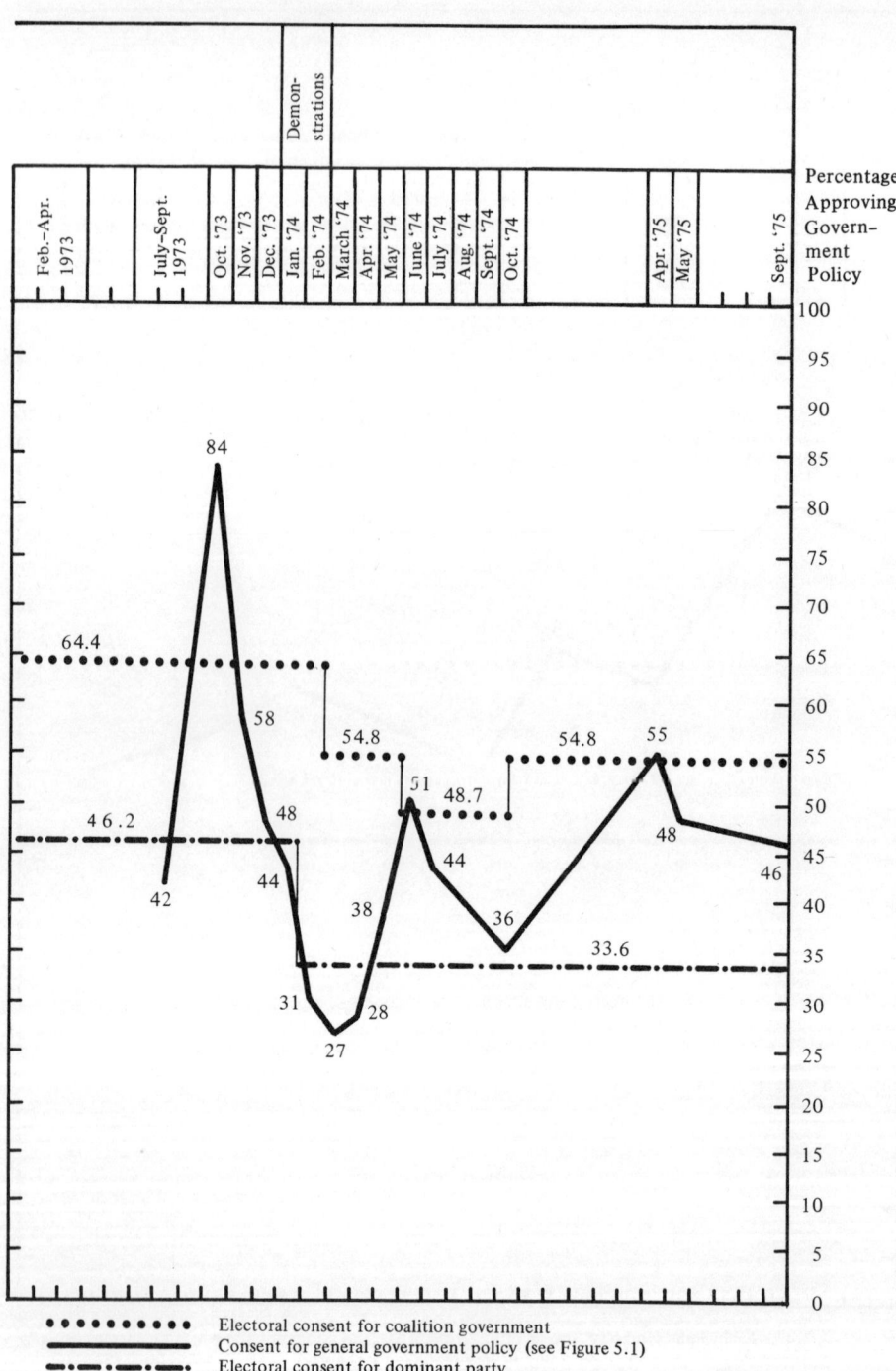

●●●●●●● Electoral consent for coalition government
———— Consent for general government policy (see Figure 5.1)
—··—··— Electoral consent for dominant party

handling of education and on its aid to the disadvantaged),* while consent for government policy in general served as the independent variable. Table 5.1 gives the net effect (standardized regression coefficients) of each item on support for the government's overall policy.

It is surprising that opinions on domestic policy have a greater effect on consent than do opinions on the handling of the Israeli-Arab conflict, in view of the overwhelming importance of this conflict in Israel's general situation.† Perhaps this has to do with the time at which this particular survey was conducted: during the Israeli-Egyptian ceasefire, a latent period of the conflict in which domestic affairs apparently became more salient. Alternatively, this is related to the particular wording of the question; possibly opinion on whether the policy towards the Arabs should be more or less adamant than it actually is does not carry significant weight for consent, while satisfaction (or dissatisfaction) with the government's general success in handling this conflict does. Thus, Matrix 5.1 shows that support for the government's secu-

TABLE 5.1

Net Effect (Standardized Regression Coefficients) of Opinions on Domestic and Foreign Affairs on Support for the Government, in 1971

Policy Item	Beta
Domestic policy	
Handling of education	.25*
Aid to the disadvantaged	.17*
Foreign policy	
Handling of terrorism	.08*
Policy toward Arab countries	.07*

N = 1,620

*Significant – p < 0.01

Source: Supplied by the IIASR on the basis of data from the survey of March-April 1971 (Levy and Guttman June 1971A).

---

*For wording of the questions, see Appendix A. For some questions, the precoded answers placed those satisfied with government policy between those dissatisfied for one reason and those dissatisfied for the opposite reason. These answers were recoded to place the satisfied at one end of the continuum and the dissatisfied at the other end.

Unfortunately, the item of opinion on economic policy was not included in this survey.

†Since we are dealing with ordinal (not with interval) scales we emphasize the *relative* weight of the various items in affecting consent, rather than the absolute magnitude of that effect.

rity policy, for its economic policy, and for its overall policy are all closely interrelated.

The close association between consent for the government and the exigencies of the Israeli-Arab conflict is further evident when developments over time are traced. Figure 5.1 shows that some of the fluctuations in oral consent were clearly related to the advent and cessation of the conflicts:* approval of government policy was highest in the Six-Day War and the Yom Kippur War, as if the public felt obligated to extend its allegiance to the government in times of major crisis. At the end of these wars, and at the end of the War of Attrition as well (August 1970), a notable erosion in support is evident.

Long-range trends, too, seem partially to reflect the Israeli-Arab conflict and the government's method of handling it. Thus, the first period, in which consent was highest, was the period of the Six-Day War and the War of Attrition; the second period, in which consent was intermediate, was that of the Israeli-Egyptian ceasefire; and the third period, in which it was lowest, began with the Yom Kippur War.

It is significant, however, that while the decline in consent was especially pronounced after the Yom Kippur War, it clearly did not begin at that time. Therefore, this decline cannot be attributed entirely to the government's alleged deficiencies in handling this war.

Another factor, related at least to confidence in the government, if not to consent, is the divergence between high political involvement and low political efficacy (see Chapter 4). It therefore seems plausible (although there is no hard evidence to prove it) that this recently widespread divergence, as revealed among the public, has also been conducive to the decline in consent.

MATRIX 5.1

Correlations (Monotonous Coefficients)* among Support for Various Aspects of Government Policy, in 1974

	1	2	3
1. Support for government defense policy		.76	.69
2. Support for government general policy			.84
3. Support for government economic policy			

*Similar correlations are reported in other IIASR surveys.
Source: IIASR Survey; Levy et. al. (May 1974B).

---

*For milestones in the Israeli-Arab conflict, see Appendix B.

All in all, the available evidence does not enable us to supply a full, empirically grounded explanation for the recent decline in support for the establishment. Apparently this decline may be traced to some of the incongruencies between the public and the government (discussed in previous chapters), and to the public's dissatisfaction with some of the government's policies—including its manner of handling domestic affairs and the Israeli-Arab confrontation. However, fuller evidence would be required to reach more definite conclusions.

What can we learn from the recent trends in consent on the effectiveness of the various devices of manipulating such consent? There is no evidence to show to what extent such devices may have impinged on consent,* attenuating what might have been an even steeper decline. However, comparing trends in various forms of consent, one point stands out as particularly significant. Assuming that the samples interviewed represent the voting public,† it can be seen (Figure 5.2) that, during a certain time span, consent for government policy as expressed orally declined to a much greater extent than did electoral support for the party that heads this government and is chiefly responsible for these policies.‡ Thus, comparing both types of consent at the time of the October 1969 election and at the time of the December 1973 election, we see that the decline in orally expressed consent for the government's policy was 21 percent as against only a 6 percent decline in electoral support for the ruling party.**

It has been argued (Lukes n.d.) that the supreme power is that of controlling other people's attitudes. However great its recent power in other respects (see Chapter 1), then, the Israeli establishment has not been very successful in wielding this particular kind of power. To put it differently, the control that the establishment has had over electoral consent, is greater than the control

---

*Except for mergers and alignments, whose effect is rather obvious.

†This assumption, of course, is not entirely accurate, since only about 80 percent of the public usually vote and the surveys cover only the urban population. But since the urban population is the great majority in Israel (see Introduction), the voting public and the population from which samples are drawn seem to be sufficiently overlapping to justify this assumption as a rough approximation.

‡It is also of interest in this context that, with the exception of June 1967 and October 1973 (the height of the war crises), the percentage approving of government policy was mostly lower than electoral support for the government coalition parties. It may thus be presumed that some who voted for the parties constituting a certain government were not satisfied with the government that their vote helped put into office.

**Since orally expressed consent for government policy tends to fluctuate, it might be claimed that the comparison of two specific dates does not reflect the overall decline of this form of consent. But if so, it is clear (see Figure 5.2) that it *underrates* this decline. All in all, we can see that from 1969 until the end of 1973 oral consent declined considerably more than did electoral consent.

it has been able to exercise on the public's opinions or attitudes. This may be interpreted in a number of ways, for example, by some voters' customary allegiance to the ruling party or by their reluctance to endorse an alternative that might not be more promising.

We suggest, however, that a complementary interpretation could be supplied in terms of the above mechanisms for eliciting consent. It may be reasoned that electoral consent for the ruling party and oral consent for the government are both equally influenced by the government's national policy. Beyond this, it is apparent that electoral consent for the ruling party may be influenced by both symbolic and nonsymbolic mechanisms for eliciting consent, including the votes-for-benefits exchange, cooptation, organizational penetration, as well as mergers and alignments. On the other hand, support for the government, as orally expressed, is likely to be less susceptible to nonsymbolic devices of eliciting consent, and lies more in the domain of symbolic persuasion. If this argument is to the point, then the fact that electoral support for the ruling party declined to a lesser extent than did oral approval of government policy may be attributed, in part, to the contribution that nonsymbolic devices have made, as over the contribution of symbolic measures of eliciting consent.

We have cited some conceptions that stressed the importance of symbolic mechanisms in molding dispositions towards the establishment. In view of the foregoing, however, it seems that in Israel such devices, though abundantly employed, have been of relatively limited efficacy, while nonsymbolic devices for eliciting consent have played a relatively prominent role in this domain.

Even the nonsymbolic mechanisms of fostering consent could not prevent a certain decline in electoral support of the ruling party. Might this be due to the fact that the establishment has lately been less proficient in their administration? It is well known that the economic dependence on state bureaucracies has been especially great for new immigrants in relatively new settlements, (Hendelman and Deshen 1975). Therefore it stands to reason that, as the multitude of new immigrants who had reached the country shortly after the establishment of the state were absorbed, they came to be somewhat less susceptible to the votes-for-benefits exchange.* But, as noted, this, as well as certain other mechanisms of eliciting consent, is inherent in some deeply ingrained features of the Israeli sociopolitical system, especially the tight political control over the economy and the pervasiveness of political organizations. These patterns have their roots in a period that long preceded the mass immigration of the late 1940s and early 1950s, and there are no indications of basic changes in these patterns in recent years. Hence it is not likely that there

---

*Subsequent immigration was on a much smaller scale.

has been any substantial decline in the application of nonsymbolic devices of eliciting consent. Rather, it appears that the inherent limitations of such devices become evident from the very fact that electoral consent for the dominant party declined to some extent *despite their continuous application.*

Israel, of course, is not the only country in which nonsymbolic devices of eliciting consent, and especially exchanges of benefits for votes, have been employed.* In Israel, however, the economic dependence of large parts of the population on the political establishment is significantly greater than it usually is in Western countries. Accordingly, the Israeli public is more susceptible to this device. In many non-Western societies (and especially in communist states) the dependence of the population on the establishment is similarly great, or even greater, than it is in Israel. But in most of these countries, if there are elections, they usually have a somewhat different significance in the respective political systems compared to Western democracies.† Thus the Israeli combination of a stable, Western-style multiparty system with excessive economic dependence of the populace on the establishment is not a common one. Hence, the control that the Israeli establishment has been able to exert on the public by means of the various nonsymbolic devices, and especially the exchange of votes for benefits, is formidable compared to other countries of the relevant universe. *If, in spite of all this, the electoral consent for the dominant party declined significantly in recent years, the cleavages between the public and the establishment, and the resulting dissatisfaction on the part of the public, must have been formidable as well.*

Devices for eliciting consent may be seen as part of the overall interaction between the public and the establishment. Therefore, one may speculate, their success depends on a more diffuse rapport between the two. It seems that in recent years the Israeli establishment has been decreasingly effective in establishing this kind of rapport with the public.

It is possible that the trend of declining consent has now exhausted itself, reaching certain limits. For instance, there may be a hard-core nucleus within the public that is especially susceptible to the various devices for eliciting support and that, therefore, is unlikely to change its voting patterns. Or, there may be a hard-core nucleus within the public, that is apt to maintain its traditional allegiance to the dominant party under any circumstances. But as far as the past is concerned, the trend of declining consent and the various tensions and dissatisfactions that brought it about should be evident.

---

*On similar phenomena in various other countries, including the United States, see, for instance, Gosnell (1968 and 1969); Heidenheimer (1970); Key (1970); and Scott (1970).

†See Scott (1970, pp. 552, 560). Note also the recent developments in two of the few non-Western countries that have been considered to be relatively stable democracies: India and Lebanon.

The Impact of Consent on the Israeli Establishment

Since patterns of consent in Israel apparently have a certain degree of independence *from* the establishment, the question is whether these dispositions in turn have had any impact *on* the establishment.

Reviewing the Israeli situation, we came to the conclusion that in a certain limited and indirect way the decline in consent did have such an impact. After the Yom Kippur War, when electoral support for the ruling party diminished and support for its adversary increased, and when consent for government policy reached its lowest point, government instability ensued: within nine months, three governments came into existence; the first took three months to set up and maintained its seat for only one month (see Appendix D).

Furthermore, as the Alignment earned less electoral support and as the margin between the Alignment and its major adversary (the Likud) was reduced, the Alignment's dependence on its traditional coalition partners was thought to increase. Consequently, so did the price that the National Religious Party demanded for its support.* Since the Alignment was unable or unwilling to pay this price, even the third government it eventually formed had to be based on the most narrowly feasible electoral support. At that time, too, various Knesset members of the Alignment were constantly thought to be on the verge of defecting, which would have toppled the government. In fact, observers were repeatedly predicting the downfall of this government and the advent of new elections.†

However, this instability was temporary and, on the whole, rather mild; after a somewhat turbulent period, the new government (formed in June 1974) was able to consolidate itself. Although at first it was based on a very narrow electoral margin, the coalition basis was broadened after a short while (see Appendix D). Thus the government was able to consolidate itself despite the fact that electoral consent and oral consent (per survey research) remained relatively low.

Furthermore, the replacement of the government that decline in consent helped to bring about resulted in nothing more than some personal substitutions (see next chapter). The party that headed the government was not replaced, and the major power centers and the basic political processes also remained intact.

In conclusion, it seems that the Israeli establishment has had only a limited impact on the public's consent, but, on the other hand, the public's declining consent has had only a limited impact on the establishment.

---

*This had to do with the legal definition of who is a Jew, which is not our concern here.
†The growing disapproval of the government's policy at the time also culminated in large-scale demonstrations in which thousands participated. These are discussed in the next chapter.

THE DECLINE OF CONSENT?

It has been claimed that "A democratic political system cannot survive for long without the support of a majority of its citizens. When such support wanes, underlying discontent is the necessary result and the potential for revolutionary alteration of the political and social system is enhanced" (Miller 1974A, p. 951). How is it that in Israel declining support has not had any far-reaching effect on the stability of the system? In the following chapters it shall be argued that this has to do with the mildness of Israeli protest, with the skillful manner in which it has been handled, and especially with some extra political processes that have impinged on the political scene and have mitigated the potential or actual tensions between the public and the political establishment.

CHAPTER 6

THE POLITICS OF ISRAELI PROTEST

INTRODUCTION

Although not one of the established constitutional procedures, protest has been regarded by some observers as an integral part of democracy, since it may channel various political tensions and the grievances of various groups of citizens into concrete claims confronting the establishment. It thus may serve as an effective means for the public to make an impact on the decision-making process, and may effect essential (and sometimes long-overdue) transformations when other channels of influence are partially or totally blocked (Carter 1973). On the other hand, it is feared that such direct action may jeopardize democracy—because, in Kornhauser's words "it abrogates constitutional procedures intended to guarantee both majority choice and minority rights," and thus may lead to extremism (Kornhauser 1959, p. 46). In this chapter it is argued that neither of these conceptions is fully corroborated on the Israeli scene: although there have been severe political tensions and grievances, these have not been fully translated into protest, which has remained on a low key. On the other hand (and perhaps for this very reason) protest has not jeopardized established democratic procedures.

The democratic role of protest as a means of channeling citizens' claims for changes is still under dispute. But the responsiveness of a political elite to citizens' claims, as measured by its willingness to introduce such changes into existing policies and power structures, is widely considered as an important

---

This chapter is a revised version of an article that appeared in the *Political Science Quarterly*, Vol. 90 (Winter 1975–76).

criterion of democracy.* This holds especially for a system such as the Israeli one, in which (unlike the Anglo-American case) the probability of periodic replacement of the party in office is limited, and where, therefore, the public's ability to influence policy through the electoral process is markedly decreased. The majority of the Israeli public has repeatedly expressed the feeling that there is little it can do to influence policy, especially in interelectoral periods (Chapter 4). Do these subjective feelings correspond to objective reality and is the Israeli political establishment indeed impervious to the claims of various groups of citizens?

There has been no unanimity on this topic. The diversity of opinion is somewhat reminiscent of the controversy among observers of the contemporary political scene in general—some of whom maintain that wider social groups and strata are being drawn into political participation and are pressing their mark on the political center; while others hold the opposite to be the case —stressing that power is increasingly concentrated at the top and that the masses, merely an object of manipulation, are impotent politically (see Chapter 4).

Observers of the Israeli scene are similarly divided. Some view the Israeli regime as highly oligarchic because the ruling party holds tight control over the political system, and, through it, the economic system as well (Arian 1973, pp. 3–9), and because the ruling party is itself a highly centralized hierarchical body (Brichta 1972; Aronoff 1972). According to this view, the governing elite frequently forestalls or neutralizes public opposition by incorporating the needs of various groups into its policy or by avoiding controversial decisions altogether; nevertheless, the voice of the public rarely plays an effective role in shaping policy (Arian 1973, passim).

In contrast, other observers perceive the Israeli regime as much less of an oligarchy. They view the ruling party itself as far from monolithic; rather they see it as a federation of (or even a framework for the confrontation of) various factions, interests, and pressure groups that, in turn, are representative of the party's membership. These observers also impute to the leadership a much greater willingness to modify policy in response to shifts in public opinion (Etzioni 1966A; Fein 1967, esp. p. 197).

In this chapter we examine these contradictory conceptions in the specific area of protest. We examine the manner and the extent to which the Israeli establishment has in fact been responsive to the claims of various groups of citizens as expressed through social protest. They also analyze the manner in which such responsiveness has helped to prevent protest from jeopardizing the long-standing stability of Israel's political system.

---

*For an analysis of this topic as conceived in various theories of democracy, see Pateman (1970).

THREE CASES OF PROTEST

Three instances of protest have been in the public eye in the past few years: first, ethnic protest, instigated by the Black Panthers and their offshoots; second, protest against the housing situation, initiated by the "Young Couples"; and third, the Yom Kippur War protest, initiated by a conglomeration of groups that came to be known as "Our Israel."* These, in fact, are practically the only instances of viable, overt protest on the Israeli social scene.† In many ways they differ a great deal from each other; however all of the protestors confronted the Israeli political center. Hence their joint analysis may tell us something on the patterns of action evolved by the establishment to deal with the claims of various groups of citizens.

The Grievances

Ethnic protest had its source in the socioeconomic gap between Oriental and Western Israelis. The situation was aggravated by the fact that, contrary to what the official ideology had led Israelis to expect, the disparities did not narrow perceptibly as time went on but were perpetuated for second-generation Orientals as well (see Chapter 1). In view of these persistent inequalities, and in view of the gap between the ideological precepts and actual reality, some Israeli sociologists have long been prophesying the advent of active, overt ethnic conflict.‡ Yet surprisingly little such conflict appeared in Israel during the first 20 years of its existence.**

At the beginning of 1971, however, a group of Oriental youngsters established a protest movement that, following a Negro-American example, called

---

*The analysis of these instances of social protest is based on previous research, on systematic content analysis of newspaper reports (of Israel's most prominent newspaper, *Ha'aretz*, and of the two most popular newspapers, *Ma'ariv* and *Yedioth Achronot*) from the beginning of 1971 until the end of 1974, and on participant observation of "Our Israel" by Moshe Livne.

†Demonstrations as such have taken place in Israel from time to time, but they did not crystallize into prolonged, viable protest. In contrast to many Western countries, Israel has not experienced student protest and the Women's Liberation movement has not made much headway in this country.

‡Not all Israeli sociologists have shared this view; for a different view see for instance Deshen (1972).

**In fact, through all this period, only one wave of public manifestations of ethnic conflict has been recorded—known as the Vadi Salib incident. In 1953 a group of North African immigrants, inhabitants of Vadi Salib, a slum area in Haifa, staged violent demonstrations against alleged discrimination. Although this was followed by a few similar incidents in other places, the outcry soon subsided and has had no sequel.

itself the Black Panthers. It was active for several years and is still in existence, although at present it is only rarely engaged in active protest. When this ethnic protest finally broke out, it was one of the rare instances in which some sociologists could triumphantly demonstrate that their predictions had come true. Yet what strikes one with regard to this protest is not the fact that it occurred, but that it took such a long time to materialize and that, when it finally did, it remained basically limited in scope.

The second instance of protest is that of the Young Couples. While young married couples exist all over the world, the existence of a protest group composed exclusively of such couples is probably a uniquely Israeli phenomenon. The issue that sent the Young Couples onto the barricades was that of the soaring prices of housing.

This problem dates back to the mass immigration after the establishment of the state, when the new nation had to provide housing for hundreds of thousands of its swelling population within a short time. Not surprisingly, housing prices began to soar; a gap developed and widened between these prices and the population's ability to pay. Concomitantly, rental of apartments became unprofitable and rental housing almost disappeared.* Faced with a situation in which a large proportion of the population was incapable of acquiring its own housing on the free market, the government and various public agencies assumed increasing responsibility for financing, constructing, supervising, allocating, and extending credit for what was meant to be low-price housing. Since 1948, public construction has accounted for two-thirds of all dwelling units put up in Israel (Krivine 1965, p. 7; Eisenstadt 1967, p. 68). As a result, an increasingly large sector of the population looked to the government to provide its housing needs.

But although government action was a major factor in making the housing situation bearable for the less-well-off sectors of the population, it did not provide a solution to the problem; housing prices continued to rise steeply. From 1950 to 1961 the index of housing expenses went up almost six times, while the average cost of living went up only 3.5 times (Darin-Drabkin n.d.) In the 1960s, with the gradual decline in immigration and the onset of an economic recession, the increase in housing prices was temporarily slowed down. At the end of the 1960s and the beginning of the 1970s, however, the soaring prices reached new heights.

While such a situation affects the entire population, it has its greatest impact on newly married couples who must acquire their first dwellings. In recent years, young couples (most of whom have just been released from the army) who want to live in an urban area have been forced to depend on

---

*For an analysis of these developments, see Darin-Drabkin (n.d.) and Darin-Drabkin (1957).

financial aid from their parents; couples without such aid face the gravest difficulties. To acquire even a modest apartment on the strength of their own salaries, even if both husband and wife hold jobs, has presented a problem that many claim is almost insurmountable. To gather the initial sum required for a down payment would necessitate years of strenuous saving, while prices in all probability would continue to soar, making the accumulated sum inadequate. Even if successful in gathering such a sum, the couple would then have to repay various loans and mortgages, which would weigh heavily on their budget precisely at the time they were starting a family.

It is difficult to tell the exact number of young couples affected by this situation; in 1971, however, there were 70,000 Jewish couples in Israel who had been married within the previous three years. Of these, 10 percent were still living with their parents, and 48 percent were unsatisfied with their housing conditions.*

At the beginning of 1971 the Young Couples began organizing for social protest. Like the Black Panthers, they too have remained active for several years; recently they have acted only intermittently, which is rather surprising in view of the situation.

Both ethnic and housing protest focused not only on absolute hardships but also on alleged relative disadvantages. The major grievance that finally triggered the ethnic protest movement was that the Orientals were less favored than were the latest newcomers from Europe and America (Cohen 1972, p. 99). One of the major recurring demands of the Young Couples is to have housing privileges equal to those of the new immigrants.† Thus, although the specific grievances of the protest groups differ, they both revolve around the problem of relative deprivation vis-à-vis new immigrants.

In this respect, the Yom Kippur War protest was of an entirely different order; it was not triggered by a specific group's sense of relative deprivation or by demands for benefits for that group. Rather, it focused on grievances that the protestors felt concerned Israeli society as a whole. Although the active participants were all reserve soldiers and officers who had served in the Yom Kippur War, practically the entire male population up to a certain age had been in the war—so this can hardly be regarded as a specific group. Furthermore, the activists were, if anything, members of overprivileged rather than of deprived groups. Most of them had Ashkenazi background, possessing

---

*On this, see Central Bureau of Statistics (1972, pp. 13, 16, 33).

†This point is also exemplified by the following: Shortly after they came into being, the Black Panthers put up posters in the streets of Jerusalem that read: "New Immigrants get housing—We get nothing." Similarly, the Young Couples carried posters worded as follows: "New Immigrants Have a Right to Housing—We don't." (See *Ha'aretz* May 25, 1971.) It should be pointed out that new immigrants do, in fact, obtain special assistance in solving their housing problems.

higher education and relatively high socioeconomic status. They did not clamor for improvements in their own socioeconomic situation; if they demanded the closing of socioeconomic gaps, it was the upgrading of *other* groups that they had in mind. They did voice some complaints about treatment of Yom Kippur War veterans, especially the dismissal of some of them from their civilian jobs and the paucity of financial assistance extended to them. But complaints such as these were marginal. They were not the grievances that had triggered the protest and, although they were voiced at the beginning, they were soon abandoned.

The Yom Kippur War protest, which began as soon as large numbers of soldiers had been released from active service, was precipitated by the alleged failures of the government in handling the war. These failures, generally referred to as the "mechdal,"* were held to be responsible for the less-than-successful outcome of the war and for Israel's relatively high casualty list. What was especially resented was the fact that no cabinet members or senior officials were willing to assume responsibility for the failures and to resign their posts.

This, the protestors felt, had its source not merely in errors of judgment by specific people, but in deep-seated patterns of Israel's political system. They complained of the leadership's imperviousness to public opinion—a barrier between the government, the Knesset members, and party officials on one hand, and the multitudes of citizen-soldiers on the other. In effect the protestors gave vent to precisely those feelings of low political efficacy that have been found to be so widespread among the public at large (see above). The imperviousness of the elite, in turn, was attributed to what were claimed to be the nondemocratic procedures of Israel's political system.

Thus, although the specific grievances that triggered the protest had to do with the government's handling of security, the source of these failures was sought in the domestic sphere; it is on this sphere that the protestors' claims were focused.

The Moderation of Protest

Both ethnic protest and housing protest presented well-demarcated, rather mild demands. These centered on the redistribution of some well-defined rewards, rather than on any major restructuring of Israeli society or of its political regime. When the Black Panther movement was launched, it asked the government to stop alleged discrimination; to provide adequate

---

*There is no precise English translation for this term. The closest would be "omission."

housing, schooling, and employment for Orientals; and to admit into the armed forces those of their numbers who had been rejected as unfit (Cohen 1972, p. 93).

The striking fact about these demands is that they indicate the Panthers' *acceptance* of some of the basic premises of the Israeli system. For instance, they acknowledge the legitimacy of Israel's government, which makes it appropriate to address demands to it; they accept the tenet that the government is responsible for allocating certain economic rewards, such as housing and employment; and, finally, they acknowledge that the supreme test of full acceptance into (and participation in) Israeli society is admittance to the Israel Defense Forces. As time went on, the Black Panthers did not radicalize their demands; in fact, they have reiterated precisely the same rather moderate demands on every occasion, right up to the present.

Analysis of the Young Couples' demands leads to similar conclusions. They focus exclusively on housing and do not clamor for radical, revolutionary transformations. Like the Black Panthers, they accept the basic fact that the government is (and should be) in charge of housing—and, hence, the government is to be presented with claims. Thus the Young Couples implicitly accept the basic premise of the Israeli regime: that it is the government that is (and should be) in charge of allocating major economic resources and rewards. Their goal is simply to pressure the government into devising a solution to the housing problems of young couples in Israel. What the Black Panthers' and the Young Couples' demands amount to is an upgrading of their own positions in the present form of Israeli society, rather than an upheaval of Israel's ideological, economic, or political systems.

In contrast to the Panthers and Young Couples, Our Israel aimed for significant alterations in Israel's sociopolitical structure. It began with demands for the resignation of senior Cabinet members, but soon broadened its claims to include structural changes as well. Specifically it clamored for the repatterning of major political procedures: transforming the electoral system, so that the elected would be responsible to the electors rather than to the party; holding intraparty elections for candidates to the Knesset and other senior posts; abolishing nominating committees; and limiting the terms of office of cabinet and Knesset members. In addition, it demanded the depoliticization of the military, a similar depoliticization of the economy, and effective public control over the various government bureaucracies. In short, its major aim was democratizing Israel's political life and limiting the power of the political establishment. In addition, it aimed at greater equality and a general upgrading of morals and human relations.

The changes envisaged by the Yom Kippur War protest were thus more fundamental than those that the other two movements aimed at. Nonetheless, the war protestors were not intent upon a radical transformation of the sociopolitical system and its ideological premises. On the contrary, they considered themselves to be the true champions of Israel's basic values and ideologies, such as Zionism and democracy. They repeatedly proclaimed their loyalty to Israel, which they symbolized by the movement's name (Our Israel), by using citations from the Bible as slogans, by singing the national anthem, and by reciting poems by Bialik (Israel's national poet). Their claim was that Israel's basic values, to which they pledged their allegiance, had been increasingly disregarded, and that social practices increasingly diverged from their precepts.

Thus, the Yom Kippur War protest clamored for far-reaching reforms but not for revolutionary changes. It clamored for the restructuring of social patterns, but this restructuring was to be in line with the society's existing, accepted values. Like the other two instances of protest, Our Israel may thus be perceived as a basically moderate, nonradical protest movement.

The three protest movements also held some resemblance to each other with regard to scope. The ethnic- and housing-protest groups have been active for several years, but have been rather limited in their number of participants. None of the Black Panthers' activities, from the beginning of 1971 to the middle of 1974, had more than a few hundred participants; the greatest number was about 500. Usually only about 100 attended any particular gathering; in fact, only 11 gatherings with more than 100 participants have been recorded. It must also be taken into account that many of those present at meetings or demonstrations were merely bystanders or sympathizers, rather than actual participants. Thus, while it is not possible to estimate the exact number of participants in ethnic-protest activities, it seems to be relatively small.

The number of participants in housing protest is similarly small. In most activities reported from the beginning of 1971 through the end of 1973, less than 100 couples participated. Only nine instances were reported in which the number of participant couples was estimated at 100 or more, and in none of these activities was the number of couples estimated as exceeding 300.

It may be claimed that with movements of this type, what counts is not so much the number of active participants but rather the pervasiveness of the support that they can muster. Even considered in this light, the Black Panther movement has not had very impressive results. The fact that it did not gain widespread support even among the most disadvantaged Orientals in Israel is well exemplified by an incident that occurred on June 16, 1971. When the Black Panthers attempted to stage a demonstration in a lower-class Oriental neighborhood in Tel Aviv (Shechunat Hatikva), they were beaten and driven off by the inhabitants. Furthermore, although Orientals comprise more than 50 percent of the Jewish population in Israel, the Black Panthers were able to secure only 1.63 percent of the vote in the (September) 1973 election of the Histadrut (Israel's major federation of labor unions), and only 0.7 percent in the general election (December 1973).

Support for the Young Couples is more difficult to assess. In 1971, at the founding of their organization, 1,500 couples were reported to have become members. While this in itself is not a very impressive number, it was also reported that 12,000 citizens had signed their petition. Thus the Young Couples did have a larger number of sympathizers, many of them presumably from among their compeers, who favored their campaign and probably expected to benefit from it themselves. It is significant, however, that these sympathizers did not become sufficiently involved in the issue to take an active part in the struggle; they left the acts of actual protest to a small (albeit conspicuous) minority.

Ostensibly, the Yom Kippur War protest followed a different pattern. From February through April 1974 it burst upon the scene with several large-scale demonstrations, each involving 4,000 to 5,000 participants. There were also several smaller demonstrations, as well as a great variety of assemblies and meetings of various groups all over the country; these mustered from several score up to several hundred participants. In addition, the movement issued a petition that was signed by 10,500 citizens. Thus, it seemed for a while that large-scale social agitation was evident and that the country was being swept by a massive protest movement. However this movement was rather short-lived; by May 1974 it was evidently on the decline. Several demonstrations and meetings scheduled at that time were poorly attended. Many activists had dropped out; the press, which had previously given sympathetic coverage to the movement, now began to publish its obituaries. Little activity took place in the summer of 1974. The movement's formal founding convention in the fall of 1974 was attended by only 40 or 50 persons, and in effect constituted its funeral service.

Thus the ethnic and housing protests were relatively prolonged over time, but were limited in numbers of participants. The Yom Kippur War protest mustered relatively large numbers of participants, but was relatively limited in time. None of the protests succeeded in mobilizing large numbers of participants for lengthy time spans. In a sense, then, they were all limited in scope.

The protest groups also resembled each other in the mildness of their modes of expression. Little violence was employed; when it was, it was aimed at property rather than at persons. Our Israel refrained from violence altogether; it acted strictly within the confines of the law, limiting itself to peaceful demonstrations, assemblies, and the like. The Black Panthers and the Young Couples also utilized these peaceful means; but, in addition, they engaged in some sit-ins and rioting. The Black Panthers also engaged in occasional acts of violence, including the throwing of stones and (in one case) the throwing of a Molotov cocktail. However these acts of violence were rare; although some property was damaged, no one was injured.

All this, of course, is in marked contrast to the protest scene in some Western countries, notably the United States, France, and Germany. In those countries, at least the absolute (if not the relative) numbers of participants in the various protest activities were far beyond those in Israel* and, particularly in the United States and France far more violence was involved.†

Furthermore, although the various protest groups of the New Left were not unanimous in their approach, they had a common nucleus of radicality in the sense that they did not merely claim for reforms, but negated the basic assumptions and core values of the existent system, and aimed for a complete transformation.‡

In comparison, then, protest in Israel has been moderate in its aims, modest in its scope, and mild in its modes of expression. This, in turn, seems to be related inter alia to the manner in which protest has been handled by the authorities.

THE RESPONSE TO PROTEST

The authorities have not worked out consistent patterns of handling the protest activities as such.** Sometimes they have attempted to discourage such activities, and at other times they have not. For instance, when the Black Panthers first applied for a license to demonstrate, the application was denied and some preventive arrests were made. However, when the demonstration took place anyway, the government did not impose additional restrictive measures (except for the now-famous caution by Jerusalem's mayor to the demonstrators to "get off the lawn"), and those who had been arrested were set free.

---

*It has been estimated, for instance, that in racial outbursts occurring in the United States in 1964–68 some 150,000–200,000 blacks participated, and these constituted up to 15 percent of the black population in the outburst areas (Downes 1969). While only a small proportion of the American student population has been continuously active in radical student movements (Lipset 1972), a significantly greater proportion has supported these movements and, in some demonstrations instigated by these movements, more than 200,000 students and other citizens participated (Teodori 1970). In Germany some demonstrations mustered between 10,000 and 50,000 participants; in France the numbers ranged between 50,000 and 70,000 and one demonstration allegedly mustered no less than a million participants (Ben Raphael 1973).

†In racial outbursts in America throughout the years 1964–68, millions of dollars were lost through arson and looting, 8,000 persons were wounded, and 191 persons were killed (Downes 1969). In student protest in 1968 alone, there were 9 incidents in which one or more persons were killed and at least 45 incidents where some persons were injured. (Campus Tensions 1970). In France, too, valuable property was destroyed, two persons were killed, and more than 2,000 were injured in street battles (Ben Raphael 1973).

‡"Following this analysis of the total nature of the technocratic system . . . the new opposition changes from being essentially reformist to being essentially *radical*. The demands for specific changes . . . give way to a struggle for redistribution of power at all levels and to a different conception of the way in which society should be organized." (Teodori 1970, pp. 36–37, et passim.)

**As distinct from the protestors and their demands.

The police handling of the Black Panthers was also inconsistent: sometimes licenses for demonstrations were granted on request, sometimes they were granted only after the voicing of threats, and sometimes they were not granted at all. However, when demonstrations took place nevertheless, they usually were not forcefully disbanded.

A similar situation exists in regard to the Young Couples: sometimes the police were willing to be patient and forebearing, and even to mediate between the protestors and the authorities; at other times the protestors were forcibly removed from the scene of action and legal procedures were initiated against them. Some protestors were arrested for transgressing the law; mostly, however, these arrests did not result in imprisonment and the protestors were soon released. As for the Yom Kippur War demonstrators, no attempts have been made to hamper them.

Despite inconsistencies, then, one guiding principle seems evident: in all cases, although the authorities have discouraged some of the protest activities, they have carefully refrained from suppressing these activities. Even more coherent patterns have evolved in response to the protestors' demands.

Response to Ethnic Protest

The establishment's response to the Black Panthers' demands include the following steps: first, public announcements are made expressing recognition of the problem and presenting various plans for rehabilitating marginal youth, for clearing slums, for constructing low-priced housing developments, and for other improvements in the conditions of the low socioeconomic strata. The allocation of additional funds for these purposes is made public. Second, various committees are set up to look into the problems of underprivileged groups; it is understood that any large-scale action will have to await their conclusions. Third, various types of personal assistance and benefits are offered to the Panthers' leaders and active participants, including admission to vocational-training programs and the solution of personal employment or housing problems. Eventually activists come to occupy posts in various government-affiliated agencies. Also the representation of Orientals in high-ranking posts of authority is somewhat increased: Orientals have been appointed to the posts of Speaker of the Knesset (Parliament) and chairman of the Foreign Affairs and Security Committee. The number of Oriental government ministers has been increased from a token one (Minister of Police) to two (Minister of Agriculture); however, this is not a real change, since some previous cabinets also contained two Oriental ministers. Furthermore, the major key positions of authority are retained by Westerners: the other 21 ministers, including the Prime Minister, are Ashkenazim, and the major ministries, such as the Ministry of Defense, the Ministry of Foreign Affairs, the Treasury, and the Ministry of Education and Culture, are retained in Ashkenazi hands.

Finally, the government sees to it that the situation of Orientals in Israel actually improves; for instance, in education or in their general standard of living. However, the situation of Westerners improves as well, so that the disparity between them is maintained. This is illustrated by Table 6.1, which presents the salary increases of urban employees' families of various backgrounds between 1970 (shortly before the advent of the Black Panthers) and 1973 (two years after their appearance).

The salaries of all families increased within this time span,* but the percentage increases for Western and for Oriental families were practically identical. In other words, the Orientals' relative situation remains more or less as it has been.

TABLE 6.1

Average Gross Annual Income of Urban Employees' Families by Continent of Birth*, in 1970 and 1973

	1970	1973	Percent Increase
Asia-Africa	9,700	14,300	47
Europe-America	13,200	19,300	46
Israel	13,600	21,700	60

*Of family head
Note: Western families are on the average much smaller than Oriental families so that the disparities between the groups are actually much greater than appears from the table.
Source: Central Bureau of Statistics (1974D, p. 272)

Response to Housing Protest

The government's response to the Young Couples' demands includes the following elements: first, various reassuring public statements are being made, various promises for assistance with their housing problems are extended to the Young Couples' representatives, and various programs for the solution of

---

*Of course part of this increase was offset by inflation.

these problems are made public;* the allocation of funds for this purpose is also made public;† second, committees are set up to study the problem and suggest solutions; third, some of the most active and militant protestors are provided with housing. Finally, the Ministry of Housing actually implements various measures designed to alleviate the hardship of young couples' housing problems, including: provision of rental apartments, extension of long-term loans on relatively easy terms to cover part of the expenses of purchasing an apartment, and construction of apartments whose prices are lower than those available on the open market.‡

Through a combination of these three devices, the Ministry of Housing has actually increased very significantly the number of "housing solutions" for young couples. In the years 1965–71, prior to the protest, the Ministry of Housing had provided only some 2,000–3,000 "housing solutions" a year for young couples. In 1971–72, however, the number was 4,430; in 1972–73 it was 6,500; and in 1973–74 the number reached 9,200.** Since the increase occurred precisely in the years in which the Young Couples' protest was at its peak, it seems safe to conclude that it was in response to the protest.

The question, however, is whether the government's response actually made a significant improvement in young couples' housing conditions; on further examination, it appears that this was not the case. Table 6.2 traces the rises in salaries and prices, especially the prices of housing in recent years.

The prices of housing practically tripled between 1969 and 1974, while salaries only doubled. This means that housing problems were vastly aggravated and the number of young couples in need of government aid increased significantly; consequently, the increase in government aid merely served to keep pace with the growing needs of the young populace, instead of leading to any basic improvement. Furthermore, people do not finance the purchase of an apartment from their current salaries; they finance at least the substantial down payment from what they have saved during previous years—when their salaries were lower. As housing prices soar, savings become increasingly inade-

---

*See *Ha'aretz,* June 2 and June 24, 1971. See also the Ministry of Housing (1971, 1972).
†Ibid.
‡It was not possible to ascertain in overall figures how much these price reductions actually amounted to; it is known, however, that different types of reductions are being offered to couples in different socioeconomic situations.
**See the Ministry of Housing (1971, pp. 7, 10; 1972, p. 1); see also the Ministry of Housing (1973, pp. 3, 12). The housing solutions listed include only those that form part of the Ministry of Housing's own budget. Other solutions in which the government was instrumental but that were not financed by the Ministry of Housing itself have not been listed, since the full, relevant figures for each year could not be ascertained. However, the number of these solutions grew approximately in the same proportions as those included in the budget—which have been listed.

Table 6.2
Index of Salaries and Prices in Israel, 1968–74

Year	Index of Average Monthly Salary per Employee (Baseline 1968)*	General Consumer Price Index (Baseline 1969)†	Housing Price Index (Baseline 1969)‡
1968	100		
1969		100	100
1970	114.2	106.1	
1971	131.7	118.8	130.3
1972	150.5	134.1	159.1
1973 (October)	204.7	168.9	231
1974 (March)		207	292.9

Sources: *Central Bureau of Statistics (April 1974B, p. 52).
†Central Bureau of Statistics (March 1974A, p. 15).
‡Central Bureau of Statistics (March 1974A, p. 10).

quate, and the number of those in need of government aid in housing increases. Savings can be linked to the general consumer price index, ostensibly in order to preserve the money's value. However, this is not a solution to the problem, since it can be seen (column 2) that the increase in the housing price index is vastly greater than the rise in the general consumer price index; while the latter increased by a little over 100 percent, the former increased by almost 200 percent within the same time span.

Not only have the prices of housing been soaring, but increases in prices have been much higher in recent years than they had been for several years before. This can be seen in Table 6.3.

Following the steep mounting of prices in the first years of Israel's existence, there was a certain easing of the situation in the 1960s (especially in the mid-1960s). Towards the 1970s, however, the situation became markedly aggravated and price increases became higher each year. Furthermore, while in the mid-1960s, the rises of housing prices did not as a whole exceed the rises in the general consumer price index, this definitely began to happen toward the 1970s.

It seems clear that despite a general improvement in the standard of living, the housing situation has become increasingly aggravated from year to year. Hence, increased government aid merely serves to keep abreast of the problem rather than to provide a substantial restructuring of the situation.

TABLE 6.3

Relative Yearly Increases in Prices, 1960–72
(in percentages)

Year	In Housing Price Index	In the General Consumer Price Index
1960	+ 8.1	
1961	+15.2	
1962	+21.7	
1963	+23.9	
1964	+15.7	
1965	+10.9	+ 7.7
1966	− 2.1	+ 8.0
1967	+ 0.4	+ 1.6
1968	+ 6.2	+ 2.1
1969	+13.9	+ 2.5
1970	+17.5	+ 6.1
1971	+25.8	+12.0
1972	+29.3	+12.9

Source: Central Bureau of Statistics (1973, pp. 245, 250).

Response to the Yom Kippur War Protest

In November 1973 the greater part of the Israeli male population was still mobilized and stationed at the fronts, and the actual protest movement had not yet come into being. But it was already evident that public furor over the mechdal was mounting. The government made its first response by setting up a high-ranking investigation committee to fix the blame for the mechdal and to suggest ways to preclude its reoccurrence. The act of forming the committee temporarily alleviated the public's agitation to some extent. It was understood that any action to be taken must be postponed, to await the results of the committee's investigation.

Once the protest movement appeared, the response of the establishment was not monolithic. Some parts of the establishment were quick to express solidarity with the protestors and support for their demands. Thus, several Knesset members (including MKs from the Alignment) and other senior officials met with the demonstrators and encouraged them. The representatives of some Labor Party factions collected a large number of signatures for the protestors' petition, and released a statement in support of their claims. Not surprisingly, those who supported the protest movement were the ones who had little affinity with the cabinet members whose resignations were demanded; the protest fitted their own aims, and was therefore favorably received.

The cabinet members under attack (and their associates and supporters) reacted differently. Some of them severely criticized the protestors at first, but this line of action was soon abandoned; instead, two other approaches were adopted. Some of those who felt themselves (or their associates) to be threatened expressed criticism, not of the movement itself, but of their colleagues who had associated themselves with the protestors; they accused them of encouraging nondemocratic procedures. Others expressed ambivalent attitudes: they praised the protestors for caring enough to become involved, but took exception to their methods and urged them to express their claims through traditional democratic channels.

The secretary-general of the Labor Party declared that, in line with the protestors' demands, arrangements were being made for secret, democratic, intraparty elections; he invited the protestors to send observers to the elections. Some attempts were made to convince the activists to join the Labor Party (and other parties) in order to work for changes from within the system; however, after much internal discussion, the activists rejected these invitations, preferring not to confer legitimation on existing frameworks by their own presence.

Finally the establishment took a number of steps to meet the protestors' demands. A law was passed to provide special benefits for Yom Kippur War veterans.* However, this issue had always been marginal with the protestors. The main sphere in which the demands of the demonstrators were ostensibly met was the resignation of the government, and the constitution of a new government without those ministers who were held to be chiefly responsible for the mechdal. It seems that the resignation was not a direct result of the protest movement; rather, by lending impetus to those within the ruling party who had similar aims, the protest movement had a significant but indirect influence in bringing about this result (Etzioni-Halevy and Livne 1976).

As time went on, it became increasingly clear that the replacement of the government had been nothing more than some personal substitutions. The major loci of power, the basic political procedures (for instance, those for nominating Knesset candidates), and the government's fundamental policies remained unaffected. However the resignation of the government took the wind out of the protestors' sails. After this event (April 1974), the movement could no longer mobilize large numbers of participants, even though their more important demands had not been met.

---

*Actually, this legislation had been introduced before the protest movement became highly active; (perhaps in anticipation of such agitation) but later, some small additional benefits were provided.

Reviewing the establishment's responses to the three types of protest, some general patterns emerge:*

1. The protests are not suppressed, but are allowed to express themselves to a certain degree.
2. Little direct criticism of the protests is voiced. Various symbolic reassurances are given to the protestors about the legitimacy of their aims, the understanding with which they are met, and/or the establishment's positive attitude towards the protestors themselves.
3. Public announcements are made that steps are being taken to ameliorate the situation and to meet the protestors' demands.
4. Devices are employed to attenuate the demands or the involvement of the protestors. These include procrastination, the granting of personal benefits to activists, and cooptation (or attempts at cooptation).
5. In one case, the controversy between the protestors and the establishment is turned into a controversy within the establishment itself—the protest supplying ammunition to the contending parties. The impression is thus created (perhaps inadvertently) that the protest is taken seriously and that it has made a significant impact on the political scene.
6. Some of the protestors' demands are actually fulfilled.
7. The basic allocative patterns and power structures of Israeli society are left unchanged.

Have protest movements in other countries attained better results? It is clear that even in countries where recent protest was much more widespread, violent, and radical, no basic transformations of the existent systems were effected.† Nevertheless, in the United States at any rate, (besides withdrawal from Vietnam) some significant changes in the allocation of rewards were introduced, resulting specifically from civil rights legislation and the consequent increased voting participation of Negroes in the South,‡ from partial school desegregation, and from some changes in the criteria of acceptance and advancement both in higher education and in the occupational structure. Not so in Israel, where the major criteria of allocation remained unaffected.

This is not to say that Israel is necessarily a closed and rigid society and that no social developments take place, but merely that protest has not been

---

*Similar patterns are evident in the establishment's response to labor conflict. See E. Etzioni-Halevy (June 1975).

†It has even been claimed (Lipset 1972) that in France student protest had the inadvertent result of strengthening the right in the 1968 election, and that in the United States student protest inadvertently "contributed" to the Republican victory in 1968.

‡See Converse (1972, p. 304).

allowed to sidetrack these developments in any fundamental way from the course on which they were launched.

THE LIMITATIONS OF PROTEST: AN INTERPRETATION

Protest in Israel has been both modest and moderate. How is it that larger-scale and more radical protests have not emerged in Israel as they have in, for example, the United States?

Obviously the background was rife with prospects for such protest. The ethnic grievances, the soaring prices of housing, the alleged mechdal of the Yom Kippur War, the generally widespread public feeling of political impotence, and the declining consent for the establishment, all these would have led one to expect more extensive protest than actually took place. How is it that these grievances and tensions have not been translated more fully into social protest?

It is possible that the majority of the public perceives the political center to be so impervious that even direct action is futile. Alternatively, it is sometimes claimed that the Israeli public is not sufficiently involved even to try. Most Israelis profess political involvement (Chapter 4); possibly, however, this involvement is not sufficiently intensive to prompt large-scale and long-range commitment to direct action that is time-consuming and inconvenient. But if so, this raises the question why this should be the case; why the various grievances have not been sufficiently salient to bring about this reaction.

It is the contention that there are some integrative mechanisms that have counteracted the various grievances of the Israeli public, and prevented or moderated the public's negative involvement in the polity.

The external conflict, and the continuous threat it poses to Israel's existence, is usually considered to be such an integrative mechanism. Has this, in fact, been the case? In his comparison of 77 countries Tanter (1966) found a limited negative effect of external conflict on internal turmoil and violence. Probably the effect revealed would have been even stronger had Tanter taken into account as well the factor of threat to a country's existence (see Chapter 9). Nevertheless, it seems that when one country only is examined the chronological relationship between external conflict and internal protest is far from clear-cut.

Thus, it is true that in Israel overt, prolonged ethnic and housing protests made their appearance approximately half a year after the 1970 Israeli-Egyptian cease-fire came into effect, that is, at a time of relative relaxation of external tension, but even at that time they did not gain large-scale active participation. On the other hand, the Yom Kippur War protest came into being before the ceasefire with Syria was reached, when external tension had not yet abated; conversely, it disintegrated after this cease-fire, when relative normalization had set in.

But while the effect of external warfare on internal protest does not find direct expression in the chronological order of events, it has apparently had a more diffuse, though indirect, effect on such phenomena: The hostility of Israel's neighbors, to which the state has been exposed since its inception, has probably contributed to a sense of being in siege, and hence to internal solidarity and to widespread commitment to Israel's most basic collective values (see Chapters 8 and 9). These commitments, in turn, have had a restraining effect on protest.

This conception is indirectly supported by the finding (see Chapter 8) that commitment to collective values is extensive among Israelis, that it has been intensified in the wake of the Six-Day War, and that such commitment has positive implications for tolerance and support of the political regime. Thus it is suggested that the specially strong collective commitments of the Israeli public have directly affected protest and have been partly responsible for its attenuation; they have thus served as one major integrative mechanism on the Israeli political scene.

Of special relevance is Israel's widely acclaimed ideology of national unity, which is part of the ideology of Zionism; it holds that Jews all over the world, by virtue of their common past, religious culture, fate, and mutual identification, constitute *one* nation whose dispersion has not impaired its basic unity. Hence it stresses the ingathering of the exiles and the fusion of the various subgroups into a single closely knit community. Since the unity of the Jewish nation is so greatly emphasized, basic differences and inequalities among its various segments are either negated or considered to be temporary; no basic conflicts of interests are recognized (Cohen 1972, p. 95).

While this ideology is relevant for *any* type of conflict or protest in Israel, it has been of special significance on the ethnic scene. It encouraged Orientals to expect full integration and equal opportunity; consequently, it fostered a sense of deprivation when these failed to materialize. Thus, the ideology helped generate ethnic protest—but it also helped to *limit* the protest. For it has caused the protestors to exercise a certain amount of self-restraint, limiting themselves to demands for the alleviation of specific grievances *within* the existing framework, rather than becoming a full-fledged radical movement that, in certain circumstances, might have jeopardized this framework. As Cohen states (1972, pp. 106–07), "They themselves and those they addressed were still too much attached to the fundamental assumption of unity of the Jewish nation and had too strong a stake in the survival of Israel as a Jewish state to create a radically separatist Oriental ideology. It is, moreover, doubtful whether under prevailing conditions such a separatist call could indeed be effective." (See also Peres 1976, p. 79.)

Widespread adherence to this ideology of Zionism and other collective identities (Chapter 8) may also explain why there are practically no completely alienated groups among the Jewish Israeli public;* why the Yom Kippur War protestors put such emphasis on their loyalty to the nation; why the basic legitimacy of the regime has not been questioned; and why the only protest in which the younger generation as such was involved has focused on the limited issue of its own housing problems.

However, it seems that national solidarity and commitment to collective values may help explain only the moderation of protest. It can hardly explain why the mild protest movements that did appear (and which did not present a threat to Israel's basic solidarity) could not mobilize more participants and supporters for longer time spans. We suggest that the latter can be explained by the fact that the potential members and leaders of protest groups have been siphoned off by various processes of social mobility.

This is especially evident on the ethnic scene. In the following chapter it will be seen that various channels of social mobility have been opened to Orientals in Israel: including occupational upgrading; some, albeit limited, advancement into higher education; and interethnic marriage. We shall also see that some of these channels have been open to Orientals in Israel to a greater extent than have parallel channels for blacks in the United States before the advent of the civil rights movement.

While the average social position of Orientals in Israel is and remains lower than that of Westerners, they are not a totally blocked group. Various mobility channels have opened and these have been geared to single out and advance the more talented and ambitious among the Orientals, opening ways for their fuller integration into Israeli society. Thus, they have siphoned off precisely those elements of the Oriental population that could have served as potential leaders for social protest.

We know, for instance, that Orientals who marry Westerners are usually the better educated and the economically better off (Schrift 1975). We also know that Orientals who successfully attend university, an especially mobile segment of the Oriental population, have chosen the path of conformity and individual advancement rather than that of collective ethnic protest (Shapira and Etzioni-Halevy 1973). Since students frequently instigate or supply leadership for protest movements, it is significant that Oriental students are unlikely

---

*There exists a group of Jewish-Israeli youngsters by the name of *Mazpen* which totally rejects the ideological premises, the national identity, and political structure of Israeli society. It is estimated, however, that this group numbers no more, probably less, than a hundred members, and it has not made any noticeable impact on Israeli public life.

to be willing to do so. Thus, the most mobile Orientals seem unlikely to supply the leadership for ethnic protest. (See also Peres 1976, p. 79.)

Social mobility also influences the situation in the housing protest. Young married couples are a major part of Israel's younger generation and a formidable part of Israel's population; if all of them had participated in the housing protest, this would have resulted in a large-scale mass movement.

However, many of these young people are highly mobile, so they eventually solve their housing problems on their own—perhaps with the aid of their parents or the companies in which they are employed. Others move out of urban centers or out of the country, temporarily or permanently. Still others are eventually aided by the authorities. Thus, the potentially large number of young couples who could fill the ranks of the protest movement is depleted by social mobility, whether vertical or geographical or by government aid. Since the most resourceful and ambitious are also likely to be the most mobile, potential leadership for this type of protest too is constantly being skimmed off.

This effect of social mobility also holds for the Yom Kippur War protest. The participants were mostly well established, of high SES; many of the activists held prominent positions in various occupational areas. They were already successfully launched on their careers; they perceived that excessive, prolonged involvement with social protest would sidetrack their occupational efforts.* No doubt this was one major factor in the depletion of the movement's activists and its eventual disintegration.

In sum, we suggest that the external threat and the commitment to collective, unifying ideologies may help explain the moderation of protest in Israel—while existing avenues of individual social mobility may help explain its limitations.

Finally, it is the contention that one of the explanations for the limitation of protest in Israel lies in the way in which the protest movements and their demands have been handled by the Israeli establishment. The establishment's manner of responding was designed to prevent further alienation and additional grievances, and to decrease resentment. It is of interest, however, that it has succeeded in doing so without introducing any perceptible changes into the distribution of rewards among the various groups that compose the Israeli society.

The establishment was aided in this by the fact that protest in Israel was rather limited and tame. Larger scale, more violent, and radical protest would

---

*Many of them stressed the fact that they could not spare the time required for the organization of prolonged protest.

possibly have met with somewhat greater responsiveness, as was the case in the United States. But, we suggest, the integrative mechanisms of collective commitments and individual advancement, as well as the establishment's skillful handling of protest, had the effect of forestalling precisely this development.

CONCLUSION

Israel may be characterized as a society in which, despite potential grievances and tensions, protest has been mild and limited to demands for specific reforms rather than being subversive of the sociopolitical system itself; and contrary to the pronouncement of some theorists, Israeli protest has not effected essential, basic transformations. At the same time, the fears of other theorists that direct action might be conducive to irresponsible extremism, and, hence, to totalitarianism, have not been vindicated in Israel; here, protest has shown no signs of endangering established democratic procedures. On the contrary, it seems that Israeli-style protest has even contributed to the vitality (and, accordingly, to the viability) of these procedures, by making it necessary for members of the political elites to remain at least somewhat open to opinions from below, thus decreasing the likelihood of these elites becoming completely out of touch with social reality and with the public they are supposed to represent. But the fact that protest in Israel did not present a threat to democracy is itself due, in part, to the alertness of the establishment to this phenomenon, and to its resourcefulness in dealing with it.

Various observers have been at odds with each other concerning the responsiveness of the Israeli establishment to the demands of the public. It seems that those who perceive this establishment as being responsive, as well as those who perceive it as being unresponsive, can both establish a solid basis for their contentions—since the Israeli establishment has evolved typical patterns of action that comprise both responsiveness and rigidity in an intricate pattern. Perhaps as the result of a balance of forces and interests within the establishment itself (rather than as the result of a deliberate plan), these patterns include symbolic reassurances, partial responsiveness, and devices for attenuating demands and for depleting the aggrieved party and decreasing its involvement—as well as the maintenance, relatively unchanged, of the establishment itself, its policies, and the basic socioeconomic framework of Israeli society.

This type of response may be termed "absorption of protest"—since it has the effect of forestalling potentially disruptive and subversive forces of social protest without suppressing them, but without allowing them to generate substantial transformations. Protest, like other kinds of conflict, exerts pressures for social change. The absorption of protest represents certain measures by which such pressures are contained within a basically unchanged sociopolitical system.*

The ability and readiness of an elite to incorporate changes (and changes of previous changes) into a sociopolitical system has been considered as an important measure of modern democracy, while rigidity and democracy do not go hand in hand (Eisenstadt 1966). In view of this, Israeli-style absorption of protest may be seen to have two-sided implications for democracy. On one hand, it has entailed some flexibility; hence it helped prevent the radicalization of protest and the eruption of large-scale violence. In this manner it has evidently served to check a potential threat to Israeli democracy. But, on the other hand, it has acted as a buffer between existing conglomerations of economic and political power and the claims of various groups of citizens, and as such can hardly be regarded as a democratic device.

The various devices employed by the establishment for the absorption of protest have helped to prevent the various political grievances and tensions from being fully translated into such protest, and thus have served to protect the stability of Israel's political regime. But these devices, however skillfully employed, could not have been effective had they not been aided by some extraneous integrative mechanisms, opening avenues of individual mobility and strong collective commitments of the Israeli public. These mechanisms have not only attenuated some specific protest movements but have generally counteracted the various cleavages and tensions on the Israeli political scene. Hence they will be explored at greater length in the following chapters.

---

*The term "absorption of protest" has been used by Leeds (1964) in organizational analysis to designate the handling of protest by the conversion of a nonconforming group into a subunit of the organization. This is certainly an intriguing device for the absorption of protest; however it seems that this term may be profitably employed in a somewhat more encompassing sense to designate *any* handling of protest aimed at checking its threat without suppressing it, but without permitting it to engender basic upheavals in the structure. In fact, this concept is of special relevance in the political context, for it is the political establishment that is most frequently confronted by social protest.

PART II
INTEGRATIVE MECHANISMS

CHAPTER

7

SOCIAL POSITION, SOCIAL MOBILITY, AND POLITICAL INTEGRATION

Several sets of factors may impinge on the interaction between the public and the political establishment, factors that, as such, are not part of this interaction. One of these concerns individuals' "life chances" in a given society. By this we mean the chances of various individuals and groups of individuals to share in the major rewards the sociopolitical system has to offer. If people think and act rationally, then it may be expected that persons who enjoy a greater share of these rewards, that is to say, people with higher social positions, should be more supportive than others of the political regime and of its dominant ideology. Since they enjoy more advantages, they have the most to gain from the status quo and the most to lose from its transformation. Conversely, the disadvantaged, those who receive a smaller slice of the national cake, feeling deprived, should be more likely to oppose the status quo as embodied in the political establishment and its political trend. Apparently positing such a rational basis for political attitudes, Tumin (1953) claimed that one of the dysfunctions of social stratification was that those lower on the ladder were apt to be less than supportive of the system. If this should be so, then the accumulation of disgruntled and resentful elements at the bottom of the stratificational ladder may weaken the political establishment and strengthen the opposition; it may also have an adverse effect on political quiescence.

A related factor is that of expectations for the future and the possibility for their realization. The divergence between aspirations for social mobility and the actual opportunity to realize them (sometimes referred to as blocked mobility) has long been perceived as a major source of frustration, resentment of the political regime, adherence to radical ideologies, and political unrest (see Introduction). Conversely, if individuals of lower social positions have reason to expect improvements in the future, their resentment against the regime is likely to be mitigated. This holds even more for socially mobile persons, that is, for persons who have actually improved or are in the process of improving their positions, who might be expected to be especially supportive of the system. We shall argue that in Israel, in fact, disproportionate resentment of the establishment is not clearly evident among the disadvantaged, inter alia because of opening channels of mobility; and that these, in turn, have counteracted recent cleavages between the public and the establishment, thus promoting political integration.

THE RELEVANCE OF SOCIAL POSITION

The relevance of social position for support of the political status quo was examined by various studies that relate SES and country of origin to political orientations and to consent for the government. Such studies show that persons of higher SES more frequently favor the left, while persons of lower positions are disproportionately attracted to the right. Thus, Antonovsky, in his study conducted in 1962* reports that professional and large-scale businessmen tend to the left more frequently than skilled workers,† and that supporters of the right are more numerous among manual workers than they are among nonmanual workers.‡ Further, support for the left is greater among the better educated, while the less educated tend to favor the right.**

Similar results emerge from the General and Panel Study in 1973: only 15 percent of those with elementary education or less adhered to the left, as opposed to 28 percent of those with partial or full higher education; only 19 percent of persons in the lowest income bracket adhered to the left, as against 31 percent in the highest income bracket.

Somewhat less clear-cut, are the results of various studies for adherence to socialism versus capitalism: thus Antonovsky reports that the rate of prosocialists was lowest at the lowest educational level, increased at the intermediary level, and once more decreased at the highest level. Unskilled workers were less prosocialist but also less procapitalist than all other occupational categories.††

---

*On 1,170 respondents—a cross section of the Jewish population outside of kibbutzim (Antonovsky 1963A).

†36 percent of the former against 28 percent of the latter.

‡8–11 percent among the former against 4–5 percent among the latter.

**41 percent of persons with higher education adhered to the left as against 23 percent of those with less than full elementary education. Conversely, the percentages of rightist supporters were 6 and 12 respectively. See Antonovsky (1963A)

††The rate of nonresponse was highest for this group.

At the same time, Zloczower (1972) reports that people who were more satisfied with their positions more frequently adhered to socialism, whereas persons unsatisfied with their status showed more of a tendency to favor "free enterprise" (see Table 7.2 below).

These findings, at any rate, complement the results of the Antonovsky study and of the General and Panel Study, which showed that persons of higher SES more frequently opt for the left. Together they indicate that people with a favorable status-balance show a disproportionate tendency to favor leftism-socialism.* In general, then, most studies show that in Israel the less satisfied, the less established, groups are the least supportive of the left, and vice versa. This is at variance with the general pattern prevailing in Western democracies. In practically all Western countries persons with lower-ranking occupations, persons with relatively low income and with low education—in short, people of lower SES—are disproportionately supportive of left-of-center parties. In various countries, disadvantaged ethnic groups similarly opt for the left.†

Israel's uncommon pattern is evidently related to the fact that the Israel Labor Party (Mapai) has been in power for almost half a century, so that the left has apparently come to be associated with the establishment (Zloczower 1968). Hence the tendency of the less established, the less favored, to be less

---

*In his study on a representative sample of male Jewish residents of Haifa, Zloczower also reports that, at least among some categories of people, self-identification with the working class is positively related to socialist adherence. Similar results are reported by Antonovsky on the basis of his 1962 study: only 17 percent of those who identify themselves as "working-class," as against 32 percent and 40 percent of those who categorize themselves as middle-class and upper-middle-class respectively, are procapitalist. At the same time Antonovsky reports that no relationship was found between identification with the working class and left-right adherence (Antonovsky 1963A and 1963B). From the results of the General and Panel Study different conclusions emerge (see Chapter 2). Thus it seems that more research is needed before any clear-cut, comprehensive conclusions may be reached on the relationship between *subjective* class identification and political adherence.

In addition, Zloczower reports that persons who are self employed and/or more highly educated, less frequently adhere to socialism compared to employees and/or persons with lower education. Interpreting these results, Zloczower maintains that they point to a greater socialist adherence among people in the lower social strata. This, however, is so only if we assume that employees are necessarily lower in SES than the self-employed. It is highly doubtful whether this assumption is justified in the Israeli context. Since the variables of education and manner of employment were not isolated from each other, there is little that can be concluded on the basis of these results concerning the relationship between SES and socialist adherence.

†See Lipset (1963, pp. 230–40); Smith (1972, pp. 36–42); Rose (1974, passim). For voting patterns of disadvantaged ethnic groups, see also Free and Cantril (1967, pp. 42, 153).

supportive of the left may symbolize a kind of resentment against the establishment.

However, in Sweden and Norway, for instance, where socialist parties have also been traditionally dominant,* lower-class people have nevertheless tended to favor the left. The Israeli pattern therefore seems to be related to the additional fact that the differences between the left and the center-right political blocs on the issue of equality are no longer as unequivocal as they were once thought to be (see Chapter 2). The Israeli left-of-center establishment has never formally abandoned its official egalitarian ideology (Lissak 1970). But on the level of concrete policies there is no clearcut polarization on egalitarianism between the left-of-center ruling party and its center-rightist opposition.

Commenting on the leftist tendencies of lower-class persons in various European countries Lipset (1963, p. 239) says: "The leftist parties represent themselves as instruments of social change in the direction of equality; the lower income groups support them in order to become economically better off." Following this general line of reasoning, and extending it to general leftist orientations as well, it makes sense that in Israel this pattern does not hold, because the left-of-center political bloc (which is also the political establishment) is no longer associated with social change in the direction of equality. Moreover the center-rightist bloc—the Likud (and especially Herut)—has had considerable success in building up its image as champion of the disadvantaged, thus mobilizing their commitment.

If this were the only evidence for us to go on, we would have to conclude that persons of lower social positions have indeed been resentful of the political establishment, whose policies, they have felt, have not been sufficiently egalitarian and thus have not worked in their favor. However a different picture emerges when social position (education and country of origin) is related to consent for the government, as measured by the various IIASR surveys. Following the findings reported so far, it might have been expected that the lesser educated and the Orientals (that is, the less advantaged), feeling themselves to be deprived, would be less supportive of the government. Furthermore, it might have been expected that the lesser educated among the Orientals, an especially disadvantaged group, would be conspicuously dissatisfied with the government.

Surprisingly, however, no consistent differences were found over the years between Orientals and Westerners in their support for government policy; and, whenever differences existed, Orientals tended to be more supportive of the

---

*In both countries Labor parties have been almost continuously in power since the beginning of the 1930s. In Norway, however, the Labor party was out of office from 1966 until 1971 and from 1972 until 1974.

government than were Westerners. It also came as a surprise that, as a rule, the lower the level of education the greater the tendency to support government policy, as Table 7.1 shows.

Additionally, wherever correlations between level of education and approval of the government's policy are reported, they are usually negative. Thus, in March-April 1971, the correlation between level of education and approval of various facets of government policy ranged from −.29 to −.36 (Levy and Guttman June 1971).

Since the average level of education of Orientals is lower than that of Westerners, it is of interest that, when country of origin is held constant, the differences by education still persist for Westerners: lesser-educated Westerners tend to support the government more than do the better-educated of similar origin. For Orientals, the situation is unclear: sometimes the better-educated tend to support the government more than do the poorer-educated; sometimes the opposite is the case; and sometimes there are no differences at all. Thus, even the least privileged group, the poorly-educated Orientals, do not tend to be especially nonsupportive of the government.

We reasoned that if the attitudes of the poorer-educated and the Orientals (and especially the poorer-educated Orientals) had a rational basis, they should have been less supportive of the government that represents a regime from which they obtain fewer rewards than do other groups. Yet it does not seem to work out this way. It seems that the patterns that have been found to exist

TABLE 7.1

Approval of the Government's General Policy, by Education, in 1971 and 1972 (in percentages)

Date	Education	Elementary or Less	Partial High School Education	High School or More
October* December 1971	Approve	68	61	53
	Disapprove	32	39	47
	n =	1,172	944	1,732
May–July† 1972	Approve	64	54	51
	Disapprove	36	46	49
	n =	493	382	731

Sources: *IIASR Survey: Peled and Shimmerling (March 1972A).
†IIASR Survey: Ben Sira (December 1972).

can be explained in part by what Shils (1965) has called the charisma of the political center—to which the less-privileged seem to be exposed no less (and perhaps even more) than are the more highly privileged. For Orientals, and for the lesser-educated, then, two tendencies seem to work at cross purposes to each other: they tend to oppose the political trend of the ruling party more often than do Westerners and the better-educated; but once a government has been elected, they are exposed to its charisma and hence tend to support it no less than do others. In fact, since they oppose the ruling party and its ideology more frequently than do others, and yet support the government no less, it stands to reason that the charisma factor is of more weight for them than it is for Westerners.

All in all, the evidence points to two divergent tendencies. Therefore it must be concluded that there are no clear-cut indications that disproportionately disgruntled elements have gathered at the bottom of the stratification ladder.* Another explanation for the apparent lack of this tendency may be given in terms of social mobility, as will be seen below.

THE RELEVANCE OF SOCIAL MOBILITY

The conception that social mobility is conducive to support of the system, while blocked mobility breeds resentment, is usually supported by empirical research. Students of social mobility in various countries have repeatedly found that upward mobility results in political conservatism, that is, in support of the ideology of the status quo.† At the same time Wilensky (1966) reports that among professional men in the United States, blocked mobility of the ambitious fosters alienation.

Similar results are reported in Israeli studies. Thus Zloczower (1972) found that upwardly mobile persons were more likely than were the downwardly mobile to adhere to socialism (the ideology of the establishment). This can be seen from Table 7.2.

In almost all categories of respondents the upwardly mobile show a greater tendency toward socialism. Also, Shapira and Etzioni-Halevy (1973)

---

*Another factor commonly thought to be of relevance for attitudes toward the political establishment is that of status discrepancy. However, a study of a representative sample of the adult, male, Jewish, urban population in 1974 revealed no consistent differences between persons with or without status inconsistencies with regard to support of government policy (see Blau-Luksemburg 1976).

†See, for instance, Lipset (1963, pp. 267–73); Lipset and Zetterberg (1959, p. 70, and 1964, p. 456); Lopreato (1967).

TABLE 7.2

Percentage of Socialist Adherents among Five Categories of Respondents—According to Status Satisfaction and According to Intergenerational Mobility, in 1964

	Status Satisfaction	N	Percentage of Socialist Adherents	Mobility	N	Percentage of Socialist Adherents
I	Low satisfaction*	(61)	10	Deterioration	(46)	4
	High satisfaction	(78)	13	Improvement	(44)	14
II	Low satisfaction	(36)	17	Deterioration	(25)	16
	High satisfaction	(46)	30	Improvement	(28)	32
III	Low satisfaction	(70)	34	Deterioration	(37)	30
	High satisfaction	(41)	32	Improvement	(37)	30
IV	Low satisfaction	(50)	26	Deterioration	(29)	17
	High satisfaction	(36)	39	Improvement	(29)	48
V	Very low satisfaction	(79)	24	Deterioration	(86)	27
	Low satisfaction	(77)	30	Improvement	(65)	42
	High satisfaction	(66)	48.5			

*Includes low and medium satisfaction.

Explanatory Remarks:

1) The table (second column) does not include non-mobile respondents. These are consistently *in between* the upwardly and the downwardly mobile.

2) The five categories of respondents are as follows:

I Self-employed and/or high school graduates who identify themselves as middle-class.

II Self-employed and/or high school graduates who identify themselves as "working intelligentsia."

III Self-employed and/or high school graduates who identify themselves as working class.

IV Employees, not high school graduates, who identify themselves as middle-class.

V Employees, not high school graduates, who identify themselves as working class.

Source: Zloczower (1972, pp. 352, 359).

in their follow-up study of university students* found that students who expressed concern over blocking of mobility in Israel† and students who were worried that they might not be able to realize their own occupational aspirations were significantly less supportive of the government and less satisfied with the general situation in Israel than were students who expressed no such concern.‡ Shapira and Etzioni-Halevy also found that students who had viewed the chances for realizing their own occupational aspirations as favorable were much more likely than others to have changed their attitudes from negation toward support of the government six years later.** This is all the more remarkable since (as noted) they had been more supportive than others —to begin with.

At the same time, the majority of students in the general student sample (70 percent) were confident of their ability to realize their occupational aspirations in Israel. Since students in other countries frequently instigate, or supply the leadership for, social protest—while in Israel they do not—this finding seems to be of special relevance.

Similar results are reported by Shapira et al. (1975) in their study of high school graduates.*** These authors compared the effect of political orientations on support of the government with that of concern over advancement. For this purpose, a multiple regression analysis was employed in which political orientations††† and concern over blocking of mobility‡‡‡ served as independent variables, while satisfaction with the government's performance served as the dependent variable. The results, as reported in Table 7.3, indicate that concern over advancement has a significant net effect on support of the government, even though this effect is somewhat smaller than that of political orientations.****

---

*A representative sample of a class of Tel Aviv University students (N= 560).
†Respondents were presented with three statements concerning the possibilities of "getting ahead" in Israel—with which they could express various degrees of agreement or disagreement. The statements were combined into a scale of "concern over blocking of mobility in Israel." For wording of all questions see Appendix A.
‡Of the students who expressed concern for blocked mobility, 64 percent supported the government and 54 percent expressed satisfaction with the situation in Israel, against 79 percent and 74 percent respectively of those who expressed no concern.
**47 percent of those who regarded the chances to realize their occupational aspirations as very good changed their attitude from negation to support of the government as against only 12 percent of those who regarded their occupational chances as poor.
***A representative sample of 1,387 graduates.
†††On the left-right continuum and on the socialism-capitalism continuum.
‡‡‡The statements were identical to those employed in the student project.
****Since we are dealing with ordinal (rather than with interval) scales, we emphasize the relative rather than the absolute magnitude of the effect.

Also an IIASR survey among the general public found that persons whose economic situation has recently improved, persons who expect their economic situation to improve, and persons who are satisfied with their present situation, tend to be more approbative of the government's economic policy and general policy. This can be seen from Matrix 7.1.

MATRIX 7.1

Correlations (Monotonous Coefficients) between Past, Present, and Expected Economic Situation and Approval of Government Policy, in 1971

	Approves of Government's Economic Policy	Approves of Government's General Policy
Economic situation has improved	.34	.21
Expects his economic situation to improve	.36	.26
Is satisfied with his situation	.25	.37

N = 1,770
Source: IIASR Survey; Peled (October 1971).

In all, the available evidence indicates that past and expected upward mobility is indeed conducive to support for the political regime. Hence, it is significant that Israel has been characterized as a society with unusually high rates of social mobility. Matras (1965) reported that rates of intergenerational mobility were conspicuously higher in Israel than in most modern Western societies. It is true that, in contrast to the latter, the trend in Israel (as reported by Matras) was predominantly from nonmanual to manual work; ostensibly, this was a trend of downward mobility. But it was not regarded as such in the yishuv era. One of the major precepts of the Zionist ideology called for the reversion of the "occupational pyramid" of the Jews in the diaspora—for a return to the soil and to productive occupations; there was even a time when the many people who personally realized this precept were highly regarded. An anecdote is fondly told about the construction of Naharia (a small town in northern Israel), originally inhabited mainly by Jews from Germany. A traveler passed by when the town was being built, and heard a strange murmur of voices emanating from the construction site. Curious as to its origin, he approached the scene, and saw a multitude of construction workers standing in line, passing bricks hand to hand. As they did so, they said to each other, "Thank you, Doctor" and "You are welcome, Doctor," over and over again.

Since then, of course, times have changed, as have the ideologies of the Israeli public (see Chapter 3). But so, too, have the avenues of social mobility open to Israelis. Israel still has open channels of social mobility, but these are now more frequently in the opposite direction. This can be learned, indirectly, from Table 7.4.

The table presents the number of workers in each occupational branch and their average monthly salaries in 1961 and in 1974. The branches are arranged by level of salary in 1974. There is a certain difficulty in interpreting the table, because the category of "finance" was not included in 1961 (see explanatory remarks). Nevertheless, the table is illuminating from several points of view. It shows that the highest-ranking branches (in terms of salary) are not the primary and secondary "productive" occupations of agriculture, industry, and construction, but rather (as is probably the case in other contemporary societies as well) the "tertiary" occupations. From this it may be deduced that these are also the most highly regarded occupations, in marked contrast to what the Zionist ideology originally called for.* It can further be

TABLE 7.3

Net Effect (Standarized Regression Coefficients) of Political Orientations and of Concern over Advancement on Satisfaction with the Government

	Beta
Political Orientations	
on the left-right continuum	.26*
on the socialism-capitalism continuum	.17*
Concern over Advancement	
anybody can get ahead if he invests efforts	.22*
can get ahead only with personal contacts	-.13*

N = 1,387
Source: Data supplied on the basis of Shapira et al. (1975).

---

*This conclusion is corroborated by research on occupational prestige in Israel, which shows that tertiary occupations (especially those included in "public services") are invariably ranked higher than the primary and secondary "productive" occupations (Lissak 1961; Hartman 1975).

TABLE 7.4

Numbers and Percentages of Workers
in Various Economic Branches, Average Monthly Salary,
and Rank Order of Salary, in 1961 and in 1974

Economic Branch	Average Monthly Salary, Number of Employees (in parentheses), and Percentage of Total Labor Force		Difference in Percentage of Total Labor Force from 1961 to 1974	Rank Order of Average Monthly Salary	
	1961*	1974†		1961	1974
Transport, Storage and Communications	IL. 345 (33,400) 6.3	IL. 2,553 (63,600) 6.7	+0.4	2	1
Electricity and Water	IL. 485 (9,600) 1.8	IL. 2,238 (11,100) 1.2	−0.6	1	2
Finance and Business Services		IL. 2,089 (76,200) 7.8	+7.8		3
Public and Community Services	IL. 298 (152,900) 28.7	IL. 1,799 (336,100) 35.3	+6.6	3	4
Industry and Mining	IL. 278 (146,600) 27.5	IL. 1,712 (249,000) 26.1	−1.4	5	5
Construction	IL. 260 (60,400) 11.3	IL. 1,542 (84,300) 8.8	−2.5	6	6
Commerce (incl. hotels and restaurants)	IL. 295 (53,900) 10.1	IL. 1,531 (71,200) 7.5	−2.6	4	7
Agriculture, Forestry, and Fishing	IL. 143 (52,400) 9.9	IL. 1,175 (27,600) 2.9	−7	8	8
Personal Services	IL. 204 (23,200) 4.4	IL. 1,104 (35,300) 3.7	−0.7	7	9

Explanatory Remarks:

1. In two economic branches, (Public and Community Services and Commerce) the categories of employees included for 1961 are not completely identical with the categories included for 1974. However, the overwhelming majority of employees included in each economic branch in 1961 are also included in the same branch in 1974, so that, for the purpose of gaining an overall picture, the comparison may be regarded as valid. The branch of "finance" appears in 1974 but not in 1961; in 1961, the employees in this category were divided between "commerce" and "public services."

2. For 1974 workers from the Administered Territories are included. These workers (who numbered 68,000 in 1974) are employed mainly in construction, agriculture, and (to some extent) industry. This means that the shift toward higher-ranking occupations among Israelis, at the very least, has not been any smaller than it appears from the table.

Sources: *Central Bureau of Statistics, (1969, pp. 288–89).
†Central Bureau of Statistics, (May 1975, pp. 50–51).

seen that, except for "electricity and water" (which is a well-demarcated branch with objectively limited possibilities), the higher-ranking categories have grown in numbers to a significantly greater extent than have the lower-ranking ones, and the low-ranking category of agriculture is the only one that was conspicuously depleted in numbers.* In fact, the higher-ranking occupations (except for "electricity and water") are the only ones that have grown both in absolute numbers and in relative terms.† Thus, when taken together, the four higher-ranking occupations have increased by 14.2 percent, while the five lower-ranking occupations have decreased by the same percentage.‡

A similar picture emerges from Table 7.5, which deals with the Jewish population only. It compares the proportion of various occupational groups in 1954 and in 1974.

Even in the 1950s, the proportion of white-collar workers was rather high; it grew even further toward the 1970s, with close to 50 percent of the working force being engaged in such occupations. Although interpretation of such shifts in terms of precise rates of mobility is far from simple (Duncan 1966, p. 96), they indisputably imply the opening of mobility channels and the upgrading of significant proportions of the population.

Of special interest is the category of "public and community services" in Table 7.4, which includes (besides education and other professional branches) the various government and government-affiliated bureaucracies. In Table 7.5 this category appears even more distinctly under the heading of "administrators, etc." Complaints are frequently voiced in the Israeli press about the unnecessary swelling of government bureaucracies. The tables indicate that these have indeed gained disproportionately in recent years, but whether this growth has been "necessary" or "unnecessary" is an entirely different matter. Considered from the viewpoint of productivity and efficiency, it was probably not warranted; however, different conclusions are indicated when the problem is considered from the viewpoint of social mobility and political quiescence.

---

*Only salaried workers in agriculture are included in this category. Members of collective settlements and independent farmers are not included.

†Even though the category of "finance" was previously divided between "commerce" and "public services" this does not alter the fact that it is now a high-ranking occupational category. The fact that "commerce" declined percentagewise and dropped in salary rank is undoubtedly because the category of "finance" was separated from it. But it should be remembered that "commerce," too, is a tertiary occupation; consequently, even if "commerce" had not been depleted, this would not have invalidated our thesis.

‡Even if the category of "commerce" were included in the higher-ranking occupations, this would not basically change the picture: the higher-ranking occupations would still have grown by 11.6 percent. In other words, this growth is not an artifact of the difference in the arrangement of the categories between 1961 and 1974 but is quite a real phenomenon.

TABLE 7.5

Jewish Employed Persons by Occupation and Continent of Orgin, 1954 and in 1974
(in percentages)

	1954*				1974†		
	Total‡	Israel	Asia & Africa	Europe & America	Total‡	Israel	Asia & Africa	Europe & America
Total (in thousands)	474.4	56.6	119.5	292.3	989.1	46.4	398.6	544.1
Scientists, Professionals, Technicians, etc.	10.4	14.6	3.4	12.4	19.6	22.4	9.6	26.8
Administrators, Managers, Officials, Clerical, etc.	16.3	23.1	7.3	18.7	21.8	30.1	17.3	24.4
Merchants and Salespeople	10.4	6.0	9.1	11.7	8.0	8.4	6.7	9.0
Service workers	8.5	6.2	12.0	7.5	11.9	9.2	17.3	8.2
Farmers & Agricultural workers	13.5	11.3	22.6	10.2	5.5	5.0	5.8	5.3
Skilled workers in Industry, Construction, Crafts & Transport	28.2	33.4	23.1	29.3	27.9	22.7	35.5	22.8
Unskilled workers	12.7	5.4	22.5	10.2	5.3	2.2	7.8	3.5

‡The grand total for each year is more than the sum of all categories because the country of origin was not known for all employed persons.
Sources: *Central Bureau of Statistics (1957, pp. 45–46).
†Central Bureau of Statistics (1975, pp. 316–17).

Since bureaucracies usually assume the form of a pyramid, most of the new openings in the bureaucracies are necessarily of the lower-ranking type. Even so, they are now more highly regarded than, say, construction work,* and many of them are stepping stones for further advancement. Moreover, the higher-ranking bureaucratic posts overlap into administrative (and, in some cases, political) elite positions. Hence, the growth of the bureaucracies indicates that some sectors of the political establishment itself, in the widest sense of the term, have been relatively open, constantly absorbing additional elements of the population. While it is well known that the highest-ranking political posts are still mainly in the hands of a clique of old-timers of East European origin, and only in exceptional cases have others gained a foothold in these positions, it seems that second- or third-rank elite posts are open to much wider segments of the population.

This fact seems to have special significance for support of the political regime. Like the blocking of social mobility, the blocking of political mobility has been considered to be a major source of political unrest. Thus, Pareto (1935, pp. 1422–32) has viewed the closing of the ranks of a ruling elite, and the consequent accumulation of potential leadership on the outside, as a major precipitator of revolt. Similarly Brinton (1959, pp. 64–67), accepting Pareto's point of view, considers the stoppage of this "circulation of elites" as one of the distinguishing traits of prerevolutionary societies. He points out, for instance, that in both prerevolutionary France and prerevolutionary Russia, avenues of economic mobility were open to the bourgeoisie while avenues of political mobility were blocked. He also considers the stoppage of mobility into bureaucracies as characteristic of prerevolutionary regimes (including, for instance, the Weimar Republic). In the same vein, Seligman (1966, p. 361) maintains that when the routes to political mobility are blocked this may lead to provocative acts culminating in violence (see also Apter 1955, p. 117).

If this point of view is accepted, the evident growth of Israeli bureaucracies (and their consequent ability to absorb additional elements of the population) takes on new significance: while not promotive of economic efficiency, it has probably been conducive to political quiescence; while it did nothing to improve Israel's balance of payments, it probably did a lot to stabilize its political regime.

The relative growth in the higher-ranking occupations is not unique to Israel. In fact, the partial shift from manual to nonmanual occupations usually accompanies economic development (Moore 1966, p. 206), and high rates of social mobility have been common in practically all "advanced" societies (Lipset and Zetterberg 1959; Germani 1966, p. 379). In the United States for

---

*As is evident from the salary scale, and from Lissak (1961) and Hartman (1975).

instance, the proportion of white-collar workers has grown perceptibly in recent years; within 20 years (from 1950 until 1970) the growth (in percentages) was approximately equal to that in Israel.*

In Israel, however, this growth is beyond what is warranted by economic development. Ofer (1967, Chapter 2) compared the employment share of services† in Israel to that of other countries. He calculated the regression of the share of employment in services on per capita income for all countries;‡ the Israeli figure was then compared with that predicted by the regression line. He reports that in Israel in the early 1960s some 50 percent of the working force was employed in services, compared with 37.9 percent predicted by the regression line for other countries with the same level of economic development as Israel, and 36.2 percent ($\pm$ 1.4) predicted for all countries regardless of economic development. Since most services involve white collar occupations, it may be concluded that Israel has an overconcentration in such occupations.** This, reports Ofer, is evident mainly in the public services, especially in the government and other public administrations. In the United States and the United Kingdom for instance, about 15 percent of the working force were employed in public services at the beginning of the 1960s, contrasted with Israel's 29 percent. Since the large and growing proportion of white-collar workers (especially public officials) in Israel has not been fully warranted economically, their political relevance is especially evident.

From this point of view it is also significant that the occupational upgrading, and the opening up of avenues of sociopolitical mobility, have not been restricted to Ashkenazim; they have been available to Israelis of Oriental origin as well. Thus, the percentage of Orientals in higher-ranking white-collar occupations has more than doubled since the 1950s.*** Orientals have been making considerable headway into secondary power positions, especially in party hierarchies and on the municipal level, and, although a relatively small minority of Orientals attain higher education, their attendance at the universities has tripled since the 1950s (Smocha and Peres 1974).

Following the thesis on the political significance of social mobility, it is interesting to compare the situation of Orientals in Israel to that of blacks in the United States in the periods preceding the two countries' protest move-

---

*See Bureau of the Census (1972, p. 230). Compare to Table 7.5 above.
†"Services" are almost identical to "white-collar occupations," except that they also include the minor categories of personal services, transport, and electricity and water (see Table 7.4).
‡Per capita national income was used as indicator of economic development.
**See also Halevi and Klinov-Malul (1968, Chapter 5); Moore (1966, p. 207).
***See Table 7.5.

ments. Data for 1940–60 in the United States and 1954–74 in Israel* show that the upgrading of Orientals in Israel has been significantly greater than that of blacks in the United States: the percentage of black Americans in white-collar occupations grew by 7 percent,† while the percentage of Israeli Orientals in such occupations increased almost twice as much (see Table 7.5).

Another potential avenue of social advancement for Orientals in Israel is that of interethnic marriage. The rate of marriages between Orientals and Westerners has been relatively high, and has been growing from year to year: 2.6 percent of all marriages in 1944, 9 percent in 1952, and 18.5 percent in 1971. This growth was larger than what could have been expected on the basis of the increase in the percentage of Orientals in the population. Moreover, the rate of actual interethnic marriages (out of what could have been expected if all marriages had disregarded ethnic preferences) is higher in Israel than the similar rate of interracial marriages in the United States. These conclusions emerge from a cross-cultural comparison of intermarriages by Schrift (1975), summarized in Table 7.6.

Some scholars would regard this cross-cultural comparison as problematic, since being a black in the United States is not entirely equivalent to being an Oriental Jew in Israel. However, this is precisely what Table 7.6 demonstrates: rejection of Orientals in Israel is far weaker than rejection of blacks in the United States,‡ so the chances for Orientals to improve their social standing by marrying into the "dominant" group are far better than they are for blacks in the United States.

---

*Actually, the years 1950–70 were the two decades preceding the appearance of Israel's ethnic protest movement in 1971. In 1950, however, the mass immigration to Israel was not yet completed (see Chapter 1), so data for that year would not have been meaningful. Later on there were some further waves of immigration but they were on a much smaller scale.

†See U.S. Bureau of Labor Statistics, (December 1962, pp. 1963–64). Apparently the recent educational attainments of blacks have been somewhat better. But the fact that educational attainments have not been fully translated into occupational ones is in itself a source of stress.

‡The United States data are for only two states, but there is no reason to assume that rejection of blacks is stronger in these states than it is in others. As Schrift notes (p. 106), data on the United States in general are difficult to obtain because some states do not register the racial backgrounds of marrying couples. These two states have been selected by the author because they seem most representative of the United States in general (excepting the South, where intermarriages are even less widespread).

The United States data go only up to 1963. However, this is sufficient for our purpose, since we are interested chiefly in the period immediately preceding the peak activity of the civil rights movement.

TABLE 7.6

Rates of Interethnic Marriages in Israel and Interracial Marriages in the United States
(Expected, Actual, and Index of Rejection)

	Israel				United States		
Year	Expected Rate (e)	Observed Rate (o)	Index of Rejection $\frac{(o-e)}{e}$	State	Expected Rate (e)	Observed Rate (o)	Index of Rejection $\frac{(o-e)}{e}$
1944	33.10	2.60	−0.92				
1947	34.60	6.40	−0.82				
1949				California (Los Angeles)	15.00	0.14	−0.99
1952	48.60	9.00	−0.82	California	11.15	0.26	−0.98
1955	49.70	11.80	−0.76	Michigan	15.73	0.12	−0.99
1963	49.80	15.40	−0.69	Michigan	16.10	0.27	−0.98
1971	50.00	18.50	−0.63				

Note: The rate of expected intermarriages was computed on the basis of all persons married each year, as follows: N = number of marriages in a particular year; Md = number of grooms from the "dominant" group (Westerners in Israel, whites in the U.S.); Fd = number of brides from the "dominant" group; Mm = number of grooms from the "minority" group (Orientals in Israel, blacks in the U.S.); Fm = number of brides from the "minority" group; E = expected number of intermarriages; e = expected rate of intermarriage.

There are two patterns of intermarriage: "dominant" male with "minority" female (DM), and minority male with dominant female (MD). The expected number of intermarriages of the first type (DM) was computed by multiplying the number of Md's by the number of Fm's and dividing the result by the number of marriages in that year: $EDM = \frac{Md \cdot Fm}{N}$

The expected number of intermarriages of the second type (MD) was computed by multiplying the number of Mm's by the number of Fd's and dividing the result by the number of marriages: $EDM = \frac{Mm \cdot Fd}{N}$

To obtain the expected percentages for each type, each of the above results was divided once more by the number of marriages:

$$eDM = \frac{EDM \cdot 100}{N} \quad ; \quad eMD = \frac{EMD \cdot 100}{N}$$

The index of expected intermarriages is the sum of the expected rates for the two patterns of intermarriages.
In addition, an index of rejection was computed, taking into account the relationship between expected mixed marriages (e) and actual observed mixed marriages (o), for each year as follows: $Re = \frac{oDM, MD - eDM \cdot MD}{eDM, MD}$

Source: Schrift (1975, pp. 69-70, 99).

As Smocha and Peres (1974) point out, there is a striking similarity between the two countries: in both, the overall intergroup discrepancies have not declined significantly before the advent of protest (see Chapters 1 and 6). At the same time, various avenues of mobility for especially talented and ambitious Orientals in Israel have opened to a significantly greater extent than did avenues for blacks in the United States. This, we argue, may partly explain why Orientals in general have not been disproportionately critical of the regime and why protest in Israel has been more limited, milder, and more moderate than black protest in America (see previous chapter).

Related to the apparent openness of some avenues of social mobility in Israel is the fact that until the Yom Kippur War, the general standard of living had been rising.* From 1970 to October 1973 the index of average monthly salaries went up 90.5 percent, while the general consumer price index rose only 62.8 percent (see Table 6.2). Theoreticians have emphasized that such improvements are not necessarily conducive to satisfaction unless they keep pace with, or surpass, rising expectations. This, in fact, seems to have been the case in Israel. Perhaps the well-known difficulties in Israel's situation in general, and in its economic situation in particular, have had a restraining effect on expectations, so that improvements were accepted as a bonus. At any rate, it seems that until recently most Israelis have been satisfied with their occupational situation. In two surveys done by the IIASR (in August-September 1973, and March-April 1974), 81 percent and 82 percent of the respondents respectively declared themselves to be satisfied with their jobs† (Levy et al. May 1974B). This too, seems to have benefited not only the job holders, but also those who rule them.

CONCLUSION

We asked whether persons with better life chances, that is, persons of higher social positions, persons whose positions had improved in the past, and persons who expected their positions to improve in the future, would be more supportive than others of the political establishment and its ideology and of

---

*It has been rising for Westerners and Orientals in approximately equal proportions (see Table 6.1).

†Some observers would not consider findings such as these significant. Their claim is that a "social desirability effect" is at work, so that respondents are inclined to overstate their work satisfaction. It is not clear, however, why satisfaction should be more socially desirable than dissatisfaction.

the government as its representative. The evidence indicated that persons of higher social positions were indeed more supportive of the ideology of the establishment and of the ruling party, but they were no more supportive than were persons of lower positions (and, at times, even less so) of the government and its policy. All in all, then, the disadvantaged groups do not display disproportionate overall resentment of the political regime. This, in turn, may be related among other things to Israeli patterns of mobility.

Upwardly mobile persons, or persons who had confidence in further upward mobility, were more supportive than others of both the establishment's ideology and the establishment itself, as is the case in other countries as well. In light of this, it is significant that in Israel the percentages of the population engaged in higher-ranking occupations have been growing; that some avenues of social mobility have consequently been opened; that these have opened for Orientals as well as for Westerners; that until recently the standard of living has been rising steadily; and that no widespread resentment with blocked mobility and with the occupational situation has so far been evident.

While the upgrading of the occupational structure is rather widespread in contemporary societies and is an integral part of economic development, in Israel it has not been fully warranted by such development. Hence, it is most likely to be the result of pressures on various organizations such as universities and government bureaucracies to absorb growing numbers of applicants, pressures that coincided with the expansionist tendencies of these organizations themselves. Regardless of whether the elite has been conscious of the political significance of this expansion, the process clearly had a politically stabilizing effect.

Ostensibly, this conclusion is at odds with the decline in consent for the political establishment that has been evident in Israel in recent years (see Chapter 5). However, as has been argued, this decline had its source in factors other than social mobility, such as dissatisfaction with the government's handling of the Israeli-Arab conflict, and these could not be fully counteracted by mobility. Moreover, it seems safe to presume that the opening of avenues for social mobility has had a restraining effect on the decline in electoral consent, and has also been partly responsible for the fact that orally expressed consent (which, during a certain period, declined more steeply) has frequently bounced up again as if the public was ever willing to give the government another chance. The main effect of opening mobility channels, however, is probably that the decline in consent has not had any more visible effects on the Israeli political scene, which on the whole has been rather quiescent (see Chapter 6); they have thus had an integrative effect on the Israeli political system.

In conclusion, the Israeli political establishment may draw confidence from the fact that the less favored groups in Israel have not shown disproportionate overall resentment of the regime and from the fact that opening channels of social mobility have apparently been counteracting potential resentment both on the part of the disadvantaged groups and on the part of the Israeli population in general.

It is thus evidently in the interest of the ruling elite to have improvements in the standard of living continue and to keep avenues of social mobility open. However, in the final analysis neither element is independent of Israel's general economic situation. For although occupational upgrading in Israel is beyond what is justifiable economically, there is obviously a limit to the possible discrepancy between developments in the occupational structure and developments in the country's economic situation, and the latter must necessarily have a restraining effect on the former. The economic situation, in turn, may be manipulated by the establishment, but only partly so—being related, inter alia, to rates of immigration, to amounts of foreign aid (especially from the United States), and especially to external conflicts.

In fact, there are some indications that, following the Yom Kippur War, the trend of a rising standard of living has been halted and that a reverse trend is now setting in. Apparently this process is about to find expression, among other things, in reductions in higher-ranking, tertiary occupations, and therefore in a certain tightening of mobility channels. It is not possible to foretell, however, how far this process may go.

Thus, despite the pervasiveness of political control of the Israeli economy, Israel's general economic situation, the resultant standard of living, and the related rates of mobility are partly outside the control of the political establishment; consequently, so is the impact that these factors may have on the public's support for the establishment, and on political quiescence in the future.

CHAPTER 8

NATIONAL IDENTIFICATION AND POLITICAL INTEGRATION

NATIONAL IDENTIFICATION AND THE POLITICAL ESTABLISHMENT

In most contemporary societies, political systems represent certain national entities;* hence, it may be argued, the national identifications of the citizens are highly relevant for the cohesiveness of political systems. Probably not all scholars would share this view. Some recently fashionable schools of thought have belittled the importance of value orientations; they probably would not regard national identifications as an exception. However we follow another school of thought in arguing that basic, diffuse national commitments have significant implications for the manner in which individuals confront political reality (and, indirectly, for the political system). (See Introduction and Chapter 2.) In Verba's words:

> The importance of this belief cannot be overstressed.... The question of national identity is the political version of the basic personal problem of self-identity. Erik Erikson has argued that "the crisis of identity" must be resolved if a mature and stable personality is to develop. Similarly one can argue that the first and most crucial problem that must be solved in the formation of a political culture if it is to be capable of supporting a stable yet adaptable political system, is that of national identity ...

It is the sense of identity with the nation that makes it possible for the political elites to mobilize the commitment and support of their followers:

---

*As defined historically, culturally, linguistically, and by common acceptance.

> The most potent kind of commitment ... is to the political system *per se* ... over and above its actual performance. It is only such a rain-or-shine commitment that will allow a system to survive the many kinds of crises that are likely to arise during processes of rapid social change. And unless most members of a system identify themselves as members of that system, such generalized loyalty will be hard to generate. Verba 1965, pp. 529–30; see also Introduction.)

While the problem of national identity is significant for all political systems, it becomes crucial under conditions of external or internal stress: where the boundaries of national identity are unclear, especially where various types of boundaries (religious, national, political, and the like) are not coextensive; where the system is challenged from without; and where internal discrepancies or other internal difficulties are evident (Verba 1965, p. 531). In cases such as these, strong, unambiguous national identifications are essential for sociopolitical integration, while weak, ambiguous, or conflicting identifications may be a source of tension and may detract from the viability of the political system.

Israel doubtlessly fits all three criteria of stress. The national boundaries of the Jewish community in Israel are unclear: do these include only Israelis, or do they include Jews in the diaspora as well? In the Jewish religious tradition, Jews have been regarded not merely as a religious community, but as a people. The Zionist ideology, translating this assumption into modern terms, has maintained that Jews all over the world form what is basically a single nation with a common history, a common culture, a common identity, and therefore a common future in a renewed common state. With the establishment of the Jewish state, however, the majority of Jews preferred to remain in the diaspora. While many of them have given evidence of unfailing allegiance to Israel, they have also maintained their basic loyalty to the political entities in which they have found themselves. In view of this, Jewish Israelis face the dilemma of defining the boundaries of their own national identity, and of coping with the potential of dual national identifications: Jewish identification and Israeli identification.*

Also, Israel is constantly challenged from without. Not only do Israel's Arab neighbors present a constant physical threat to the Jewish community in Israel; but, in addition, they challenge the Jewish-Israeli nationhood, dis-

---

*This raises the problem of the Arab minority in Israel. Does the Israeli national identification include or exclude this minority? What are the national identities of the Israeli Arabs themselves? These problems, though fascinating, are of an entirely different order and will not be dealt with here.

claiming the right of the Jewish state over the territory in which it exists, and defining it as a usurper of another people's land. It may be argued that especially strong, collective national identifications would be necessary to meet this dual challenge.

While Israel must cope with external threats, some claim that domestic social problems present no less of a challenge and are no less difficult to cope with. These include cleavages between the public and the political establishment (Chapters 1, 3, 4, and 5), as well as ethnic cleavages and controversies between the religious and the nonreligious.* It seems that staunch, collective national commitments are required to enable the political system to overcome crises of this nature. We shall argue that the generally strong and widespread commitments of Israelis have indeed fulfilled such politically integrative functions.

NATIONAL IDENTIFICATIONS: THE INTEGRATIVE COMMITMENTS OF ISRAELIS

It has been argued that in a society where the potential for multiple national identities exists the relationship among them assumes primary importance from the point of view of the political system. Only mutually supportive national identities are likely to make a positive contribution toward political integration, and toward basic support for the political regime; conflicting identities are likely to detract from this support and integration (Verba 1965, p. 534). What is the case in Israel? As noted, there is a potential for dual national identifications in Israel. Are Jewish and Israeli identifications at odds with each other (as has sometimes been claimed), or are they mutually reinforcing?

The national commitments of Israelis are also expressed in adherence to the basic ideology of Zionism, in attachment to the Land of Israel and (if the Jewish people is regarded as a national entity) in affinity with Jews all over the world. How are these various commitments related to each other?

The empirical evidence indicates that they are all positively interrelated and mutually supportive. Thus Herman (1970), in his study of high school students and their parents,† reports that the great majority of both students and parents stated that when they felt more Jewish, they also felt more Israeli.‡

---

*These have precipitated numerous crises (which are not our concern here).
†The project was on a nationwide sample of 3,679 high school students aged 16 and 17 and their parents.
‡70 percent of the students and 83 percent of the parents felt that way.

Also Etzioni-Halevy and Shapira (1975), in their project on Israeli university students,* report a positive correlation of .35 between Jewish identification and Israeli identification,† and Levy and Guttman, in their IIASR surveys, report strong positive correlations among sense of belonging to the Jewish people in the world, and sense of affinity with Jews abroad on one hand and commitment to Zionism on the other hand.‡

Finally, Levy and Guttman (1974C) report a correlation of .46 between sense of belonging to the Jewish people in the world and attachment to the Land of Israel (as measured by the desire to live in Israel), and Etzioni-Halevy (1971) reports positive relationships between Jewish identification, Israeli identification, and solidarity with Jews abroad on one hand, and attachment to Israel on the other, as documented by Table 8.1:**

This study also reported that the relationship between Israeli identification and attachment to Israel was maintained when Jewish identification was held constant and vice versa, which means that Israeli identification and Jewish identification are each independently related to attachment to Israel.

Some of the relationships between national affinities and attachment to Israel require an interpretation. While it is obvious that Israeli identification should have positive implications for Israel, it is not self-evident that *Jewish* identification should have such implications. Since many Jews residing in other countries similarly profess strong Jewish identification, this means that residence in Israel is not a sine qua non of Jewishness. How, then, are Jewish identity and attachment to Israel related? Could not attachment to Israel be based exclusively on *Israeli* identification?

---

*This was a follow-up study on a representative sample of a class of Tel Aviv University students (N=560) who had enrolled in 1966/67 (and a comparison group of 174 students who had enrolled in 1970). This project is reported on in Etzioni-Halevy (1971), Shapira and Etzioni-Halevy (1973), and Etzioni-Halevy and Shapira (1975).

† Israeli and Jewish identifications were established by questions in the form of six-space continua on which the respondents were requested to place themselves according to the degree of their identification. For wording of all questions see Appendix A. The questions were combined to form scales of Jewish and of Israeli identification. For details see Etzioni-Halevy and Shapira (1975).

‡Correlations ranged between .31 and .76 (see Levy and Guttman, August 1971B, June 1974C and 1974D). All correlations reported in IIASR surveys are monotonous coefficients.

**In this study, attachment to the Land of Israel was measured by a question divided into six subquestions. Each subquestion was a statement concerning the circumstances under which it would be justifiable for an Israeli university graduate to settle in another country. The subquestions were combined into a scale; those who opposed emigration under most eventualities were classified as disapproving of emigration, that is, as displaying strong attachment to Israel.

TABLE 8.1

Students with Strong Attachment to Israel
(Disapproving of Emigration) by Jewish Identification,
Israeli Identification, and Sense of Affinity
with Jews in the Diaspora, in 1969
(in percentages)

Strength of Identification	Sphere of Identification		
	Israeli Identification	Jewish Identification	Affinity with Jews Abroad
Weak	52 (N = 23)	67 (N = 190)	67 (N = 89)
Strong	79 (N = 528)	84 (N = 359)	81 (N = 461)
	$p < 0.001$	$p < 0.001$	$p < 0.01$

Source: Etzioni-Halevy (1971, p. 99).

While such a possibility cannot be excluded, we suggest that Jewish identification has an additional contribution to make, in that it lends deeper significance and sense of mission to life in Israel. Without Jewish identification, life in Israel would derive its significance merely from the residence of Israelis here during a few decades—a somewhat meager significance. From the point of view of Jewish identification, on the other hand, Israel is the country in which the Jewish people has come into independent being, which has served as the focus of Jewish yearning throughout many generations, and which may serve as the potential spot for the ingathering of the whole Jewish people in the future. In other words, it is only on the basis of Jewish identification that the ideology of Zionism makes sense, and it is this ideology that supplies a major raison d'être to life in Israel.

The positive relationship found between attachment to Israel and affinity with Jews abroad lends further support to this interpretation. Logically, the two affinities might well have been entirely independent of each other, or even negatively interrelated. The apparent paradox that attachment to *one* country is positively related with attachment to people living in *other* countries, makes sense only in terms of the above interpretation: affinity with Jews abroad (as part of Jewish commitment) lends a deeper significance to life in Israel by imbuing it with a sense of mission.

In summation, the various national commitments of Israelis, far from being in conflict with each other, are mutually supportive. And they are mutually supportive, although not coextensive, because they are in some way consistent with each other; some national commitments make more sense in terms of other national commitments, which thus enhance their significance.

We have cited Verba's conception that consonant national identities are likely to lend "rain or shine" support to the political regime. It may also be argued, however, that national identities that are not coterminous with the political system promote loyalties that are incongruent with the regime, hence are likely to be a source of political tension. The national identities of Israelis are indeed consonant with each other, but only part of them are coextensive with the political system: Jewish identification and a sense of belonging to the Jewish people in the world extend beyond it. Hence the question arises: to what extent are such identifications supportive of the regime?

Shapira and Etzioni-Halevy's study of university students indicates that people who are attached to the Land of Israel are more likely to approve of the government.* The effect of national identification on support of the government was also explored in Shapira et al.'s study of high school graduates (1975).† A multiple regression analysis was employed in which various national identifications‡ served as independent variables and support for the government served as dependent variable. On the basis of this analysis, the authors report a multiple correlation of .32 between the various national commitments and support for the government. In concurrence with this, Levy and Guttman's study (June 1974C) indicates that persons who profess strong national identifications are less likely than others to consider the Israeli political regime and various (presumably unpleasant) features of that regime as grounds for leaving the country. This is illustrated by Matrix 8.1.

When people are strongly committed, even when their commitment is with the Jewish people of the world (most of whose members are part of other political systems), they show more willingness to put up with alleged deficiencies of the Israeli regime. We conclude that national identities may promote support (or tolerance) of a political system even when they are not coextensive with it, so long as they are congruent with other national identities that are; this, in fact, seems to be the case in Israel.

---

*Of students with high attachment to Israel, 59 percent expressed support for the government; of students with low attachment to Israel, only 42 percent expressed such support (Shapira and Etzioni-Halevy 1973).

†A representative sample of 1,387 high school graduates.

‡Jewish identification, Israeli identification, and attachment to Israel.

MATRIX 8.1

Correlations (Monotonous Coefficients) between National Commitments and Tolerance of the Regime, in 1974

	National Commitments	
Tolerance of the Regime	Regards Self as Zionist	Feels Part of the Jewish People of the World
Does not consider the political regime as a ground for leaving Israel	.46	.44
Does not consider the manner in which authorities treat citizens as a ground for leaving Israel	.38	.33
Does not consider tax policy as a ground for leaving Israel	.45	.35

N = 2,270

Source: Levy and Guttman (June 1974C).

Hence, the next question would be: How strong and widespread are national commitments among the Israeli public and, therefore, how much of a mellowing force may such commitments present on the Israeli political scene?

NATIONAL IDENTIFICATIONS: THE COLLECTIVE COMMITMENTS OF ISRAELIS

All studies on these topics have invariably reported that the great majority of Israelis profess strong national identifications. Herman's study on high school students, for example, produced the results shown in Table 8.2.

The overwhelming majority of both students and their parents expressed strong Israeli identification. Strong Jewish identification, though less wide-

TABLE 8.2

Centrality of Jewishness and Israeliness for High School Students, in 1964-65 (in percentages)

	Does the fact that You Are Jewish Play an Important Part in Your Life?		Does the fact that You Are Israeli Play an Important Part in Your Life?	
	Parents	Students	Parents	Students
Plays a very important or an important part	91	68	92	90
Is of little importance or plays no part	9	32	8	10
N	434*	2,980	434	2,980

*Only a subsample of parents was interviewed.
Source: Herman (1970, pp. 49 and 51).

spread among the students, was still professed by two-thirds of them. Similar results were reached in their project on university students by Etzioni-Halevy and Shapira (1975). The pertinent results of that study are presented in Table 8.3.

The data attest to an almost total professed commitment of Israeli youngsters to their Israeliness, and to a lesser, but still widespread, commitment to Jewishness. Similar results emerge from studies of the public at large. The Katz-Gurevitz study (1973)* presented a list of 35 personal, social, and political needs, to be rated as "very important," "important," or "not too important." The need to feel pride in the state of Israel was felt to be "very important" by a greater proportion (90 percent) of respondents than any other need (p. 15).

---

*On a national cross section of 3,697 Jewish respondents.

TABLE 8.3
Israeli Identification and Jewish Identification of Tel Aviv University Students
(in percentages)

Strength of Identification	The Sample Group at the Beginning of Studies (1966-67)		The Sample Group at the End of Studies (1969)		The Comparison Group at the Beginning of Studies (1970)	
	Israeli Identification	Jewish Identification	Israeli Identification	Jewish Identification	Israeli Identification	Jewish Identification
Strong	90	56	96	66	97	67
Weak	10	44	4	34	3	33
N	560	560	560	560	174	174

Explanatory Remarks:
A. As will be recalled, the questions on Israeli and Jewish identification were combined into scales. On each scale scores ranged from one to six. Respondents whose scores were one to three were classified as "weak"; the rest were classified as "strong."
B. The first questionnaire was administered to the sample group shortly before the Six-Day War.
Source: Etzioni-Halevy and Shapira (1975).

The overwhelming majority of Israelis sense themselves to be part of the Jewish people in the world, as can be seen from Table 8.4 below.

A sense of belonging to the Jewish people implies a certain affinity with Jews abroad. Not surprisingly, then, a majority of Israelis expressed such an affinity as well. Katz and Gurevitz (1973) report that two-thirds of their respondents thought that the Jewish people in the diaspora could not survive without Israel, and three-quarters thought that Israel could not exist without strong spiritual ties with the diaspora; similar results are reported by other studies.*

Since the ideology of Zionism establishes a link between Jews all over the world and Israeliness, the above findings lead one to expect a widespread

---

*See for instance Levy and Guttman (1971); Shapira and Etzioni-Halevy (1973, Ch. 2).

TABLE 8.4

Israelis' Sense of Belonging to the Jewish People in the World, Commitment to Zionism and to the Land of Israel, 1970-75
(in percentages)

	June-July 1970	June-July 1971	August-September 1973	October 1973	November 1973	March 1974	April 1974	November 1974	April 1975
N	1,945	1,770	1,825	400	Not reported	Not reported	2,270	Not reported	1,111
Feels self to be part of the Jewish people of the world									
Definitely Yes or Yes				96			90		
No or Definitely No				4			10		
Views self as a Zionist									
Definitely Yes or Yes	77	84	82	90			79	80	
No or Definitely No	23	16	18	10			21	20	
Would like to live in another country if possible									
Very much, or to some extent					5	16	13	14	9
Not so much, or not at all					95	89	87	86	91

Sources: Various surveys by the IIASR: Levy and Guttman (August 1971B, November 1973B, and June 1974C); Adi and Froelich (September 1970B); Peled (October 1971); and Institute Staff (1975C).

commitment to that ideology. Yet it is sometimes argued that Zionism is no longer relevant in Israel today. At one time, so the argument goes, Zionism was a charismatic national movement; its ideology, which called for the return to Zion and for the reconstruction of the Jewish state, exacted intense commitments. But this ideology is no longer relevant for present-day Israelis; for them, the former ideals have become routine facts.

It is therefore significant that the overwhelming majority of Israelis do express allegiance to Zionism. This was attested by Antonovsky's 1962 study;* 83 percent of the respondents said they "identified" or "tended to support" the Zionist idea (Antonovsky 1963A). The extensive adherence to Zionism among the Israeli public is also shown by several other studies, as seen in Table 8.4. While the ideology of Zionism probably no longer has the intensive grip that it once had over the public, it is evidently still relevant to the great majority of Israeli citizens, since they identify themselves as Zionists.

The table also shows that the great majority of Israelis profess a strong affinity with the Land of Israel, as measured by their desire to live in it; similar results are reported by Shapira and Etzioni-Halevy (1973).

It is estimated that since the establishment of the state, more than 250,000 Israelis have emigrated from Israel. The data on attachment to Israel are significant not because they may help predict rates of emigration, but because they indicate that most Israelis who stay seem to be committed to the country. This is not to say that all who stay do so out of such commitment—but merely that for most Israelis, the decision to stay is backed up by (or consonant with) such a commitment.

National commitments were found to be strong among both Orientals and Westerners. Orientals were found to evince somewhat stronger identifications than did Westerners; but the differences were not large (Levy and Guttman 1974B; Shapira and Etzioni-Halevy 1973), and when religiousness was controlled for the differences between Westerners and Orientals in Jewish identification, they almost disappeared (Herman 1970).†

All in all, then, most Israelis, of whatever origin, profess a staunch commitment to Israel and to Israeliness, to Zionism and, to a somewhat lesser extent, to Jewishness and to Jews abroad.‡ Since the research projects on these

---

*On a representative sample of the Jewish population outside of kibbutzim (1,170 respondents).

†"Westerners" and "Orientals" are broad categories embracing a variety of subgroups that may well differ in their national identifications. However, the available data do not enable us to deal with the subgroups separately.

‡Some observers would probably claim that a social desirability effect is at work here, biasing the results. But, if so, how can one explain the fact that Jewish identification is less widespread than Israeli identification, whereas both are official aims of the Israeli educational system. On this, see also Chapter 4.

topics have all been carried out in recent years, long-term trends cannot be traced. However, the data indicate that throughout the last decade or so these tendencies have either been steady or have strengthened in the wake of the Six-Day War and Yom Kippur War. Thus, Shapira and Etzioni-Halevy (1973) report that the Israeli identification and the Jewish identification of Israeli university students was strengthened following the Six-Day War* (see Table 8.3), and so was affinity with Jews abroad: before the Six-Day War, 75 percent of the respondents expressed a strong sense of affinity with Jews abroad, while 84 percent expressed such affinity in 1969. Also, strong national commitments were especially widespread during the Yom Kippur War (Table 8.4). It thus seems that the traumatic experiences of the wars had an intensifying effect on the national commitment of Israelis. Since the wartime crises were also the times when worldwide Jewish solidarity was widely reaffirmed, it is not surprising that the sense of affinity with Jews abroad was also strengthened.

It is difficult to estimate, however, whether these crises had a lasting effect on national identities or merely a temporary one. On one hand, it can be seen that the national identities of university students were still stronger in 1969 than they had been shortly before the advent of the Six-Day War (Table 8.3); on the other hand, it is evident (see Table 8.4) that the sense of belonging to the Jewish people, which had been especially widespread during the Yom Kippur War, declined slightly a year and a half later.[†]

Also, it is clear that the effect of the war on Zionist commitment was temporary. A year and a half after the Yom Kippur War, Zionist commitment had reverted to its prewar level (Table 8.4), which, however, had been very high to begin with.

In all, the data indicate that the strong collective national commitments expressed by most Israelis in recent years have been intensified by the last two wars; that in some cases these have proved to be short-run rather than long-run effects; but that, in any case, no perceptible weakening of national identifications has occurred. Findings such as these may lead one to express a fair degree of confidence in the reservoir of national commitments as a source of strength for the Israeli political regime. And yet it seems that these commitments are beset by a certain vulnerability.

---

*Attempting to isolate the effect of university attendance from the effect of national events, the authors conclude that changes in identification cannot be attributed to the former. Nevertheless, it cannot be proved that the changes occurred *because* of the war.

†Naturally, this sense of belonging may still have been stronger in 1974 than it had been before the war; however, since this item had not been included in adult surveys before the Yom Kippur War, the possibility cannot be checked. But it seems that at least some of the intensifying effect that the Yom Kippur War had on Jewish belongingness was eventually neutralized.

THE VULNERABILITY OF NATIONAL COMMITMENTS: SOME INDICATIONS FOR THE FUTURE

The vulnerability of national commitments becomes evident when such commitments are broken down by age and by religiousness. The data indicate that in some respects youngsters are just as committed to national identities as are their elders, but on other counts their commitment is less widespread. Both Herman's study of high school youth and Shapira and Etzioni-Halevy's study of university students indicate that more than 90 percent of Israeli youngsters evince strong Israeli identification; in this respect, youngsters are hardly less committed than their elders. However, Herman's study also shows (Table 8.2) that the students' Jewish identification is clearly less widespread than that of their parents. Similarly, Katz and Gurevitz (1973) report that the sense of affinity with Jews abroad falls off as one moves from the older to the younger ages.*

Other national commitments of Israeli youngsters, as established by a survey of a countrywide representative sample of Jewish high school students, are presented in Table 8.5.

Comparing Table 8.5 to Table 8.4, it can be seen that the youngsters' sense of belonging to the Jewish people is as widespread as that of their elders, while their adherence to Zionism is not. The fact that Zionist commitment tends to fall off with age is also illustrated by Table 8.6 (below) which gives the Percentage Difference Index (PDI) of Zionist commitment for different age groups. It can be seen that school youngsters are more committed than are young adults, but all young people are clearly less committed than are their elders.

Some observers are quick to point out that members of the younger generation profess less allegiance to Zionism not because they are generally less committed, but because they, more than their elders, regard Israel as a self-evident fact rather than as an ideal. But is this the whole story? To answer this, it would be necessary to know whether youngsters are, in fact, as widely attached to Israel as are their elders.

Shapira and Etzioni-Halevy (1973, p. 193) report that university students evince more widespread attachment than do the faculty. However, university professors are a special type of population: clearly, their professional-academic ties are international rather than intranational, and thus cross-cut their national affinities. Therefore, it is not surprising that entirely different results are obtained when the general population is considered. This can be seen once more from Table 8.6.

---

*74 percent of those aged 65+ thought that Israel needs the spiritual ties with the diaspora, compared with only 53 percent of those aged 18–24.

TABLE 8.5
Israeli High School Students' Sense of Belonging to the Jewish People and Zionist Commitment, in 1973 (in percentages)

	Feels Self to be Part of the Jewish People of the World	Views Self as a Zionist
Definitely Yes or Yes	93	66
No or Definitely No	7	34

N = 5,000

Note: The questions in the youth survey were identical to those in the adult surveys. The adult surveys were on the Jewish urban population only, while the youth survey was on a cross section of the entire Jewish population; yet, since the overwhelming majority of the Jewish population in Israel is urban, this is not a decisive difference. It should be noted, however, that this is a sample of high school youth and not of youth in general.

Source: Levy and Guttman (1974D).

It may be seen that not only commitment to Zionism but the desire to live in Israel declines conspicuously with age.* In conjunction with the lesser tendency of Israeli youngsters to define themselves as Zionists, these differences indicate that the youngsters are less widely committed to the Land of Israel than are their elders.

As noted (Chapter 3), age differences do not invariably indicate trends of change over time, since youngsters may adopt the outlooks of their elders as they mature. But in this particular case the age factor assumes special significance, because it comes on top of another factor whose implications seem to be similar: religiousness.

Practically all studies on these topics point to a positive relationship between religiousness and various national commitments, especially Jewish identification, as illustrated in Table 8.7 from Herman's study.†

---

*Also, in the survey done by the IIASR in April 1975 a negative correlation of -.44 is reported between age and desire to live in Israel (Institute Staff 1975C).

†Similar differences between the religious and the nonreligious are reported by Farago (1968) and Hofman (1970). No relationship was found between Israeli identification and religiousness.

TABLE 8.6

Zionist Commitment and Desire to Live in Israel—Percentage Difference Indices (PDI) by Age, in 1973 and 1974

Age	Commitment to Zionism PDI*	Desire to Live in Israel PDI†
High School Youth	19	
Adults		
18–24	11	32
25–29	16	28
30–34	26	48
35–39	34	57
40–44	35	59
45–49	42	70
50–54	52	72
55–64	52	84
65+	58	89

Note: The PDI indicates the preponderance of positive over negative responses for each variable. In each case the most negative responses are subtracted from the most positive ones. For details, see Chapter 2, Table 2.1.

The desire to live in Israel was measured by answers to three questions: 1) "Do you wish your children to live in Israel?" 2) "If you had the opportunity, would you wish to live outside of Israel?" 3) "Are you sure that you will remain in Israel?" The three questions were combined into a seven-point scale. Scores of 1–3 were classified as a strong desire, 4 as a medium desire, and 5–7 as a weak (or nonexistent) desire to live in Israel.

Sources: *Computed from Levy and Guttman 1974D (N for youth survey: 5,000; N for adult survey: 1,825).

† Computed from Levy and Guttman June 1974C (N = 2,270).

Etzioni-Halevy and Shapira (1975), on the basis of their study of Israeli students, also report a positive relationship between religious commitment and Jewish identification: 100 percent of the religious, 94 percent of the traditionalists, but only 54 percent of the nonreligious and 39 percent of the antireligious were classified as "strong" on Jewish identification.*

---

*In addition, Etzioni (1969) in her study on a group of university students reports positive correlations between religiousness and Jewish identification (ranging from .38 to .42).

TABLE 8.7

Centrality of Jewishness for Religious, Traditionalist, and Nonreligious
High School Students and Their Parents, in 1964-65
(in percentages)

"Does the fact that you are Jewish play an important part in your life?"

	Religious		Traditionalists		Nonreligious		Total Population	
	Parents	Students	Parents	Students	Parents	Students	Parents	Students
Plays a very important or an important part	94	98	91	78	85	46	91	68
Is of little importance or plays no part	6	2	9	22	15	54	9	32
N	147	680	165	942	122	1,358	434	2,980

Source: Herman (1970, p. 49).

On one side of the continuum these findings are almost tautological, for Jewish religiousness is hardly conceivable without strong Jewish identification. However, their interest lies in the opposite pole of the continuum—that is, in the insight they give into the Jewish identification of the nonreligious. The data indicate that strong Jewish identification is not completely absent even among the nonreligious, which shows that such identification is not exclusively a religious phenomenon. But while strong Jewish identification is self-evident and hence practically universal among the religious, this is no longer so among the nonreligious (of whom only half express such identification).*

Jewish identification, in turn, has positive implications for other national commitments, including ties to the Land of Israel (see above). Moreover, religiousness itself was found to be positively related to other national affinities. For instance, Levy and Guttman (August 1971B) report positive correlations (ranging from .23 to .27) between religiousness and various items of affinity

---

*Religiousness was also positively related to a sense of belonging to the Jewish people in the world. While almost all Israelis express such a sense of belonging, the religious more frequently than the nonreligious sense that they *definitely* belong (Levy and Guttman 1974E; Cohen 1975).

with Jews abroad.* Cohen (1975) in his project on high school students[†] reports a positive association between religiousness and Zionist commitment[‡] and Etzioni-Halevy (1971) reports a positive relationship between religiousness and attachment to Israel: only 15 percent of the religious students (as against 36 percent of the nonreligious) approved of emigration from Israel; furthermore, this relationship was maintained even when Jewish identification was held constant.**

The Jewish religion has always been a national religion with great emphasis on the uniqueness and the unity of the Jewish people. It has also put major stress on affinity with the Land of Israel. Consequently, findings such as these were to be expected. Their special significance in the present context lies in the possibility that religious adherence may be gradually diminishing in Israel. Contrary to what some observers (notably Herberg 1960) claim to be the case in the United States, no religious revival has been discerned in Israel; the trend seems rather to be in the opposite direction. It is true that surveys in Israel over the last 15 years or so do not point to any clear decline in religious observance.*** But then, 15 years is a relatively short time span where religious change is concerned.

Quite a different picture emerges when the trend of intergenerational development is observed. This can be done on the basis of Herman's study of high school students, by comparing the extent of the students' religiousness with that of their parents. Such a comparison indicated that 29 percent of the high school pupils whose parents were traditionalists were themselves nonreligious—while only 3 percent of the pupils whose parents were nonreligious were themselves traditionalists.[†††] In addition, Herman reports that 42 percent of the high school students regarded themselves as less religious than their parents, while only 7 percent regarded themselves as more religious. Theoretically, the possibility exists that as students grow older, they return to the fold of religious tradition. But significantly, Herman also reports that 63 percent of the students' parents declared themselves to be less religious than their own

---

*Similar results are reported by Herman (1970).

[†]A sample of 841 students.

[‡]59 percent of the religious, 52 percent of the traditionalist, but only 44 percent of the nonreligious said that the Zionist ideology influenced their desire to belong to Israeli society. 41 percent of the religious against 31 percent of the traditionalists and 29 percent of the nonreligious said it was very important for them to understand Zionism.

**Similar results are reported by Levy and Guttman (1974A).

***For instance, Antonovsky (1963A) reports that 30 percent of his respondents declared that they observed the religious tradition; Arian (1969) reports that 24–26 percent of his respondents identified themselves as observant; and in the General and Panel Study of 1973 once more 30 percent of the respondents identified themselves as observant. All studies were on cross sections of the urban population and an identical question was employed in all of them.

[†††]Similar results are reported by Etzioni-Halevy and Shapira (1975).

parents, while only 5 percent of the parents regarded themselves as more religious than their own progenitors. Since we have here a fully adult population (rather than one of youngsters), this finding, when combined with the previous ones, indicates that an intergenerational decline in religiosity is indeed in progress.

This contention is further corroborated by Matras (1965). Examining a representative sample of 582 maternity cases in Tel Aviv and Jerusalem in 1959–60, he reports that while almost 40 percent of the respondents were less observant than their mothers, almost none were more observant. Matras concludes that a secularization trend of considerable proportions is occurring in Israel.

Comparing intergenerational decline in religious observance by ethnicity, Herman shows that in the previous generation the decline was more pronounced among Ashkenazim—but both Herman and Matras demonstrate that recently it has been more pronounced among Orientals.* Even so, Oriental youngsters are still more religious than their Ashkenazi peers,† but the trend of diminishing observance is found in both groups, and is thus a general Israeli phenomenon.

Now, if nonreligious youngsters are less likely than religious ones to harbor strong Jewish and other national identifications, and if religiousness declines from one generation to the next, the prospects seem to be for a gradual decline of Jewish identification from generation to generation. It is true that even among the nonreligious, more than half express strong Jewish identification. Hence, it may seem, on the face of it, that such a decline will not be pervasive. It should be borne in mind, however, that many of the nonreligious youngsters who harbor a strong Jewish identification have grown up in religious or traditionalist homes. Assuming that the home serves as a major formative influence on Jewish identification, the question arises as to the Jewish identification of nonreligious persons who have grown up in nonreligious homes, and are thus second-generation nonreligious.

This question is of more than academic interest; for, should the present trend continue, not only will there be more and more nonreligious persons in

---

*Herman reports that 48 percent of the Oriental parents (against 71 percent of the Western parents) are less religious than their own parents. But 48 percent of the Oriental students (compared to 37 percent of their Ashkenazi peers) are less religious than their parents (p. 265). Also, Matras reports that of Oriental-born maternity cases, 46.2 percent in Jerusalem and 46 percent in Tel Aviv were less religious than their mothers; while for Western-born maternity cases, the percentages were 22.3 percent and 12.8 percent respectively (p. 100).

†Herman reports that only 22 percent of Oriental pupils (against 51 percent of Westerners) classified themselves as nonreligious. On differences in stand vis-à-vis the religious tradition between Orientals and Westerners and their historical roots, see Deshen (1975).

Israel, but there will also be a growing percentage of second- (or third-) generation nonreligious. Therefore, it is of interest to compare the extent of Jewish identification of first-generation and second-generation secularists. Such a comparison, made by Etzioni-Halevy and Shapira (1975), indicates that the percentage of second-generation nonreligious students displaying strong Jewish identification is somewhat smaller than that of the first-generation nonreligious.* It may be concluded that the Jewish identification of the non-religious does not perish, but diminishes somewhat where no religious home background exists. It is quite possible (although this could not be ascertained) that Jewish identification shrinks even further with third-generation secularists.

Additional (albeit indirect) support for this conclusion may be gained from Herman's study. Herman reports that while the Jewish identification of religious students is close to that of the religious parents, nonreligious students exhibit significantly *less* Jewish identification than do nonreligious parents (see Table 8.7). One plausible interpretation for these findings[†] would be that nonreligious parents are more frequently first-generation nonreligious, while nonreligious students are more often second-generation nonreligious; since more of the latter grew up in a nonreligious home atmosphere, fewer of them feel positive involvement in their Jewishness.

A similar conclusion emerges from Levy and Guttman's study of high school youth. It may be assumed that in Israel, school background varies with home background: religious parents tend to send their children to religious schools and vice versa. Hence the special significance of the results shown in Table 8.8.

Nonreligious or slightly religious youngsters in nonreligious schools profess a less widespread sense of belonging to the Jewish people and less commitment to Zionism compared to similar youngsters in religious schools. Hence, as fewer nonreligious Israelis are likely to be raised in religious homes, and, therefore, as fewer are likely to be educated in religious schools, even the present moderate extent of Jewish identification found among the nonreligious is likely to diminish to some extent from one generation to the next.

Table 8.8 shows that Zionist commitment, too, is likely to be affected by the gradual decline in religiousness. This is also evident from Levy and Guttman's study (1971), which found that a Jewish atmosphere in the home was positively related to the respondents' self-conception as Zionists (.29), to the views that youth should be educated toward Zionism (.27), and that Jews in

---

*56 percent of the first-generation nonreligious students, but only 46 percent of the second-generation nonreligious students expressed strong Jewish identification.

†In view of the intergenerational decline in religiousness.

TABLE 8.8

High School Students' Sense of Belonging to the Jewish People and Zionist Commitment PDI by Religiousness and Type of School, in 1973

	Sense of Belonging	Zionist Commitment
Religious respondents		
Raised in religious school	83	33
Raised in nonreligious school	68	23
Non-(or slightly) religious respondents		
Raised in religious school	76	24
Raised in nonreligious school	48	12

N = 5,000

Source: Computed by Levy and Guttman 1974D.

Israel and Jews in the diaspora have a common fate (.32), and that Jews abroad have an obligation to support Israel (.37). As more and more Israelis become second- and third-generation nonreligious, and as fewer attend religious schools, Zionist commitments and affinity with Jews abroad are also likely to become attenuated.

CONCLUSION

Although various collective identities of Jewish Israelis (or Israeli Jews) are not coextensive, the evidence strongly suggests that they form a system of interrelated and mutually supportive commitments to which most Israelis adhere. In fact, the evidence points to an almost total professed consensus on most of these commitments, and to an intensification of some of them in the recent past.

Despite the difficulty in making cross cultural comparisons, there are several indications that collective national commitments in Israel today are stronger than are similar commitments in Western countries, especially the United States. For one thing, Zionism, which at one time was a charismatic national movement, is still in the process of being institutionalized. Evidently the extensive commitments of Israelis to its ideology are not as *intensive* as they used to be in the yishuv era, when routinization was still in its initial stages. Nevertheless, such commitments are not as routinized as they are in the West, where national entities have been in existence for centuries.

Moreover, the basic assumptions and core values of Western societies (especially the United States) have been of a more individualist bent from the very beginning, putting greater stress on individual liberty and individual achievement; the core ideology of Zionism, on the other hand, has put more emphasis on collective aims and national unity.

This is especially true of the collectivist ideology of socialist Zionism, but not exclusively so. The general ideology of Zionism is also a basically collectivist ideology in which national aims take precedence over individual comfort and safety. While shifts have recently occurred toward greater individualism (see Chapters 1 and 3), the collectivist bent in Israel today is apparently still stronger than it is in countries such as the United States, where the individualist tradition has been paramount since the country's inception.

Also, Israel's continuous external conflict and the resulting sense of being under siege have probably helped to intensify the collective commitments of Israelis. Even though the effects of each war may eventually wear off, the basic effect of the ongoing conflict as a whole is probably toward a greater cohesiveness of Israeli society.

At the same time, we contend that the indications for the future are somewhat different. The routinization of Zionism is apt to continue, and the external conflict may (hopefully) become less intensive (thereby reducing its cohesive effect). In addition, there are some concrete indications of a depletion of national commitments.

Since religiousness diminishes from one generation to the next, and since Jewish identification is lower among the nonreligious (and even somewhat lower among the second-generation nonreligious), the Jewish identification of Israeli youth appears to be in a precarious state, and there are clear prospects of its weakening in the future. How far this trend may proceed, and whether it may eventually be reversed, cannot be foretold.

Jewish identification was found to be related to other national commitments, such as Zionist adherence, Israeli identification, and attachment to the Land of Israel. Although no one directional, causal relationship was assumed to exist, it was presumed that Jewish identification contributes to the strengthening of these affinities by adding a historical dimension and a sense of mission to life in Israel. Consequently, the possibility of a gradually diminishing Jewish identification is of concern not only in its own right but also because it may point to a weakening of other national commitments.

The possibility of alternative bases of Israeliness and of attachment to Israel is, of course, not excluded. Such foci of national commitment seem to have been pronounced in the prestate era, and even today Israeli identification does not depend exclusively on Jewish identification. Nevertheless, it is a fact that people who express less Jewish identification are also less likely to express other national commitments; hence the precariousness of the former is likely to be reflected to some extent in the vulnerability of the latter.

This vulnerability is further evident from the differences in commitment among various age groups. The elder generation is overwhelmingly committed in all spheres, but a certain imbalance seems to have developed in the younger age groups: in some respect their commitments equal those of their elders, and in some respects they clearly do not. Education toward national commitments has always been one of the major, official aims of the Israeli educational system. Consequently the situation should certainly be a source of concern to educators and to others involved with the problem. Even among the younger generation, national commitments are extensive, so no drastic decline is to be expected. But, on the other hand, complacency is not in order, either; the national commitments of the young can no longer be regarded as given.

On a more general level, the data point to the possibility that the submersion of national identifications, including Jewish identification, exists not only where Jews are a minority, but also where they constitute a majority. In this case the problem is not one of assimilation in the usual sense of the term (that is, of national identifications being eradicated by identification with another national group), but of a partial erosion of a national identification for which no clear substitute is in sight.

We contended that national identification, as one type of value orientation, would have significant implications for the manner in which citizens confront political reality. We saw that the Jewish and Zionist commitments of Israelis are indeed associated with tolerance for the political regime, and that Jewish and Israeli identifications and attachment to the land of Israel have positive implications for support of the political establishment. This seems to corroborate the conception that national identifications do have political significance, and that they are conducive to what Verba termed diffuse "rain or shine" support of the political system. By furnishing such support, the extensive national commitments of Israelis seem to have mitigated various potential strains, thus acting as politically integrative mechanisms.

The present widespread national commitments of the Israeli public may thus serve as a source of confidence to the Israeli political leadership. At the same time, since the indications are toward diminishing commitments in the future, the supportive effect that overwhelming national commitments now seem to furnish the sociopolitical system cannot be regarded as assured in the long run.

CHAPTER

9

SOLIDARITY, MORALE, AND POLITICAL INTEGRATION

SOLIDARITY, MORALE, AND THE POLITICAL ESTABLISHMENT

Like the citizens' national identifications and their commitments to common collective values, so too are citizens' commitments toward each other highly significant for political integration. In fact it has been argued that the sense of identification with other political actors is directly relevant for the viability of the political regime (Verba 1965; see also Introduction).

This feature is especially crucial where there are various subgroups with potential cleavages among them. Where members of a political system do not identify with their fellow citizens in general, but only with various subgroups; and where no or little basic solidarity binds the subgroups to each other; then, Verba holds, it is impossible to develop the sense of community on which much of the trust for the political establishment rests. However, as Eckstein (1966, p. 76) points out, political cohesion is, under certain conditions, compatible with any kind of division, and a feeling of solidarity may overcome any number of cleavages and divergencies. Where cleavages are indeed bridged by intergroup solidarity, this may serve as a source of strength for the political regime, and it may act as a politically stabilizing force even in times of major crisis. This, we argue, is what actually happened in Israel, although the stabilizing effects of intergroup cohesion were rather short-lived.

Support of the political establishment should also be dependent on the public's morale, since both morale and support are likely to fluctuate with changes in the country's objective situation. When adverse developments take place (or are perceived to take place), morale is likely to decline; concurrently, the public may be expected to blame the government for these developments (at least in part) and to withdraw some of its support. Conversely, when things are going well and morale is picking up, the government should be getting credit for the situation. Hence, morale and approval of the government should be rising and falling simultaneously. Also, those whose morale is higher (presumably because they take a more favorable view of the situation) should be more favorably oriented toward the establishment than are those whose morale is low. We thus expected solidarity and morale to have something in common: both would be positively related to support for the establishment.

SOLIDARITY AND MORALE: FACING EXTERNAL CONFLICT

Another common feature of solidarity and morale is that both are measures of how a certain public bears up under stress, such as an external conflict. Morale may be viewed as a measure of how people cope with such conditions of stress, while solidarity may be viewed as a measure of how people cope with each other under such conditions. Presumably, then, the higher the morale and the stronger the solidarity, the less frustration will be caused by internal friction, the greater will be the combined strength of the public, and the greater will be its tenacity in their face of external threat.

The problem of how the tenacity of a society is affected by external conflict, especially active warfare, can appropriately be studied in Israel, where different types of active warfare have alternated with periods of relative quiet. Even during the "quiet" periods, small-scale incidents continued, war threats by Israel's neighbors abounded, and both sides prepared for war at full speed. Nevertheless, they differed from full-fledged warfare in that the threat to physical existence was somewhat less tangible, and thus offered Israelis some respite from the acute stress of actual war. Hence, it is against these stretches of relative relaxation of external tension that the effects of active warfare on Israelis' intergroup solidarity and morale may be traced and analyzed.

Solidarity

Israel's popular satirist, Ephraim Kishon, wrote about being involved in a traffic jam. The driver of another car characterized him in a few well-chosen unprintable words, accused him of obstructing traffic, and demanded to be given the right of way. "Didn't you hear?" asked Kishon, "Nasser has just advanced his missiles to the Canal!" Replied the other driver: "In that case, sir, go right ahead!" This satirical tale illustrates (with slight exaggeration) the widely held belief that external conflict subdues internal discord and fosters solidarity. Does sociological analysis uphold popular wisdom, or do the two diverge in this respect?

Following Simmel, Coser (1956) regards the fostering of internal solidarity as one of the major positive functions of external conflict. But he qualifies this generalization by pointing out that such a unifying effect depends on the previous level of solidarity in the social unit, on whether the conflict poses a threat to the unit as a whole, and on the public's satisfaction with the manner in which the conflict is being handled.

Kriesberg (1973), in his comprehensive analysis of social conflict, is even less determinate. He, too, maintains that under certain circumstances an external conflict may have a cohesive effect on a social unit. But he also points out that the manner in which such a conflict affects internal cohesion differs with the structure of the unit, the extent of preexisting discord in it, the degree of threat and danger involved in the conflict, its justification, the manner of waging the struggle, the equity with which its costs are borne, the length of the conflict, the success of its outcome, and any number of other variables (pp. 246–52).

This conception, though doubtlessly correct, is not very helpful as a guideline for empirical research. It is impossible to isolate and control the many variables mentioned (let alone any number of other variables) in order to determine how various types of conflict affect solidarity. We therefore limit our analysis to two that seem to be specially pertinent for the Israeli case.

Both Coser and Kriesberg mention the threat or danger posed by the conflict as one of the major factors in determining its effect on solidarity: a conflict that involves danger to the society as a whole is likely to be more conducive to solidarity than one that does not. Although some scholars maintain that external conflict in general has only a limited effect on internal unity (Tanter 1966), most would probably agree that conflict that involves a threat to the unit does have a significant effect on such unity.* Thus, Smith (1971) reports that in the United States World War II was perceived as more threatening than the Korean and Vietnam Wars, and internal dissent and solidarity responded accordingly. In Israel, all major conflicts posed a threat to physical existence; hence, one would expect that internal solidarity would have been heightened by each of them.

Kamen (1975) notes that most observers attribute a cohesive effect to disasters, and he gives limited support to this claim—although he criticizes the evidence on which it is based. While Israel's wars cannot be characterized as outright disasters, they share with such phenomena a threat to existence and a general sense of crisis. Hence, additional support for the expectation that Israel's wars would have fostered solidarity.

Another variable that seems to be especially crucial to the Israeli case is the manner in which the conflict was waged. If the public is unsatisfied with

---

*Provided that, despite the danger, the social unit continues to exist. Total collapse would probably have different ramifications for solidarity.

the handling of the conflict and blames those who are in charge (as was the case in the Yom Kippur War), some discord between the public and the elite is likely to ensue. Following Verba's conception on the implications of intergroup solidarity for support of the political elite, one would expect vertical discord to have a backlash on horizontal relations as well, dampening, to some extent, the intensifying effect of the external conflict on solidarity.

Since both the Six-Day War and the Yom Kippur War involved the trauma of danger to Israel's physical existence, we expected solidarity to have been heightened in both. But because of dissatisfaction with the waging of the conflict, we expected the Yom Kippur War to have fostered solidarity to a lesser extent than did the Six-Day War.*

Morale

It stands to reason that the morale of a group or a society faced with external conflict would be influenced by the same variables that affect solidarity; but the effect may be of a different order. While the threat posed by the conflict and the danger it entails may have a heightening effect on solidarity, it may have the opposite effect on morale. In their research project on the Wehrmacht in World War II, Shils and Janowitz (1948) concluded that so long as solidarity was strong, morale was maintained on a relatively high level, even in the face of danger and imminent defeat. But this conclusion concerns interpersonal solidarity in small groups; it is not clear whether this would be true for intergroup solidarity as well. It seems more likely that on the macrolevel morale would be affected directly by how, and how successfully, the conflict is handled.

Another factor that is likely to have a major effect on morale is the number of casualties. Even when the war is successful, casualty lists are apt to have a dampening effect on morale; this is even more so when the war is less than successful and casualties are more numerous, as in the Yom Kippur War. We therefore expected that morale would have been heightened to some extent by the victorious Six-Day War, lowered to some extent by the less-successful War of Attrition, and lowered more by the even-less-successful Yom Kippur War.

Considering the effect of external conflict on solidarity and morale simultaneously, we expected that both would have been heightened in the Six-Day

---

*We do not deal with the effect of the War of Attrition (1969–70) on solidarity because the pertinent data for most of this period are lacking.

War. In the Yom Kippur War, we expected solidarity to have been heightened to some (albeit a lesser) extent, while morale was expected to have declined. Working on the assumption that morale and solidarity are both components of the tenacity of a group or society in the face of adverse conditions, we thus expected that the rising solidarity and lowering morale in the Yom Kippur War would have balanced each other out. Thus, the standing power of the Israeli public, though not as staunch as in the Six-Day War, would not have been as negatively affected as is usually thought to have been the case.

MORALE AND SOLIDARITY: HOW ISRAELIS FACE EXTERNAL CONFLICT

Our expectations on solidarity and morale could be examined empirically on the basis of data from surveys carried out at relatively short time intervals since the Six-Day War by the IIASR in conjunction with the Communications Institute of the Hebrew University.

Morale

Reversing the order of presentation, we begin by tracing the effect of external conflict on morale.* As can be seen from Figure 9.1[†] morale is measured by the manner in which Israelis perceive their moods and their worries at various times.[‡]

Within the period studied, the morale of the Israeli public has known several ups and downs—reaching its highest level right after the Six-Day War and sinking to its lowest level after the Yom Kippur War. It can also be seen, however, that all *ongoing* wars were accompanied by low morale. Thus, while the Six-Day War was going on (beginning of June 1967), the public's morale

---

*Strictly speaking, we cannot be absolutely sure that changes in morale or solidarity during or after a war occurred because of that war; but it seems reasonable that this was in fact the case.

†This and the following figures have been plotted on the basis of various surveys conducted by the IIASR and the Communications Institute of the Hebrew University since the Six-Day War and up to the present, on representative samples of the Jewish urban population. For a list of these surveys see the Bibliography at the end of this book. For milestones in the Israeli-Arab conflict see Appendix B.

‡Other measures, such as the individuals' assessment of their ability to adjust to the situation, have been included in the public opinion surveys as well, but only intermittently. The items selected, on the other hand, were included in all surveys from June 1967 onward.

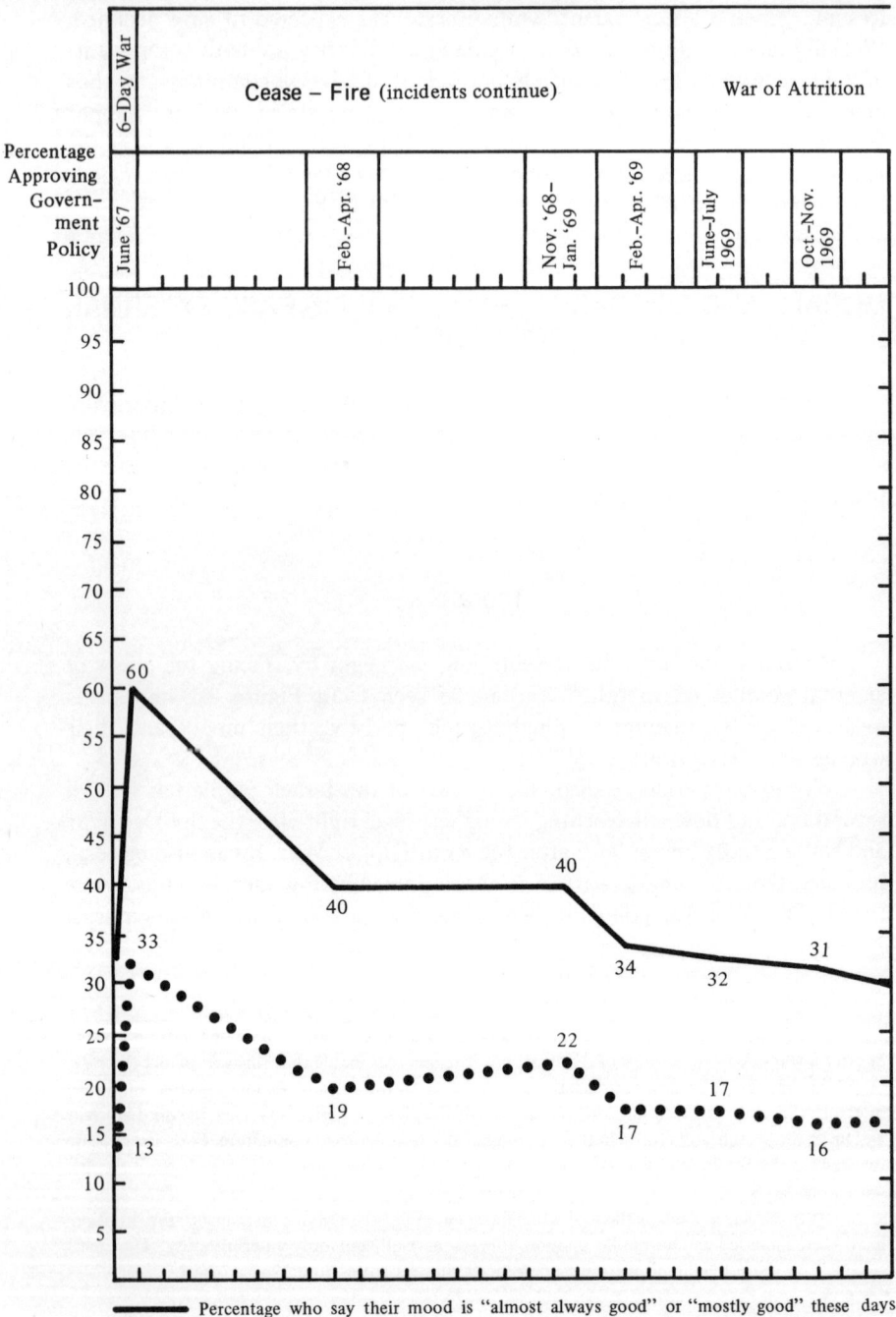

Figure 9.1
Morale, 1967-75
(in percentages)

184

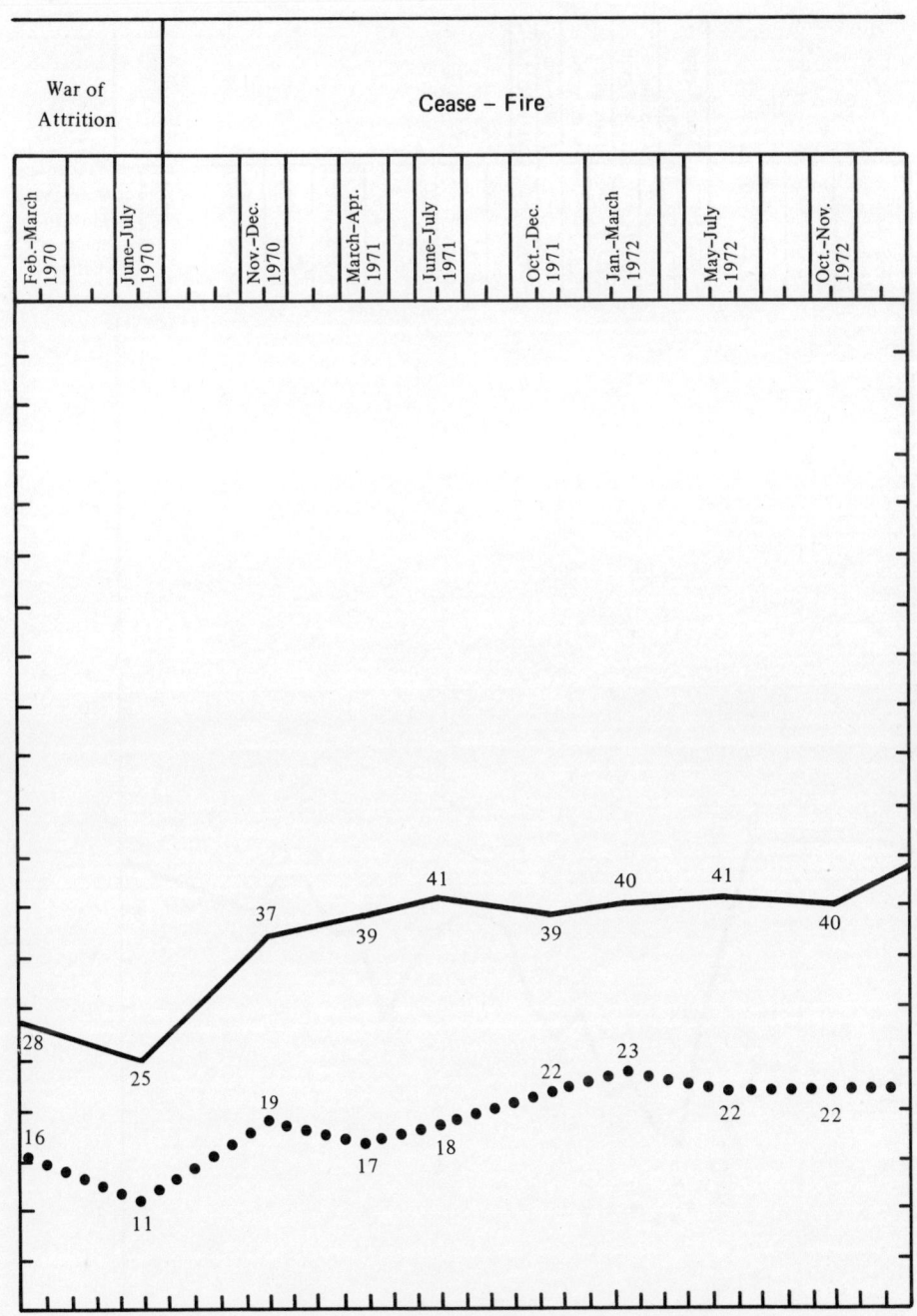

Note: For the period between the Six = Day War and the Yom Kippur War surveys were carried out 2-3 times a year. In June 1967 and from October 1973 onward, surveys were carried out weekly. For June 1967 we report the results at the beginning of the month (during the War itself) and at the end of the month (after the termination of the War). For October 1973 and onward we report the monthly average for weekly results. Since samples of weekly surveys are of similar sizes—this is permissible.

(continued)

Figure 9.1 (continued)

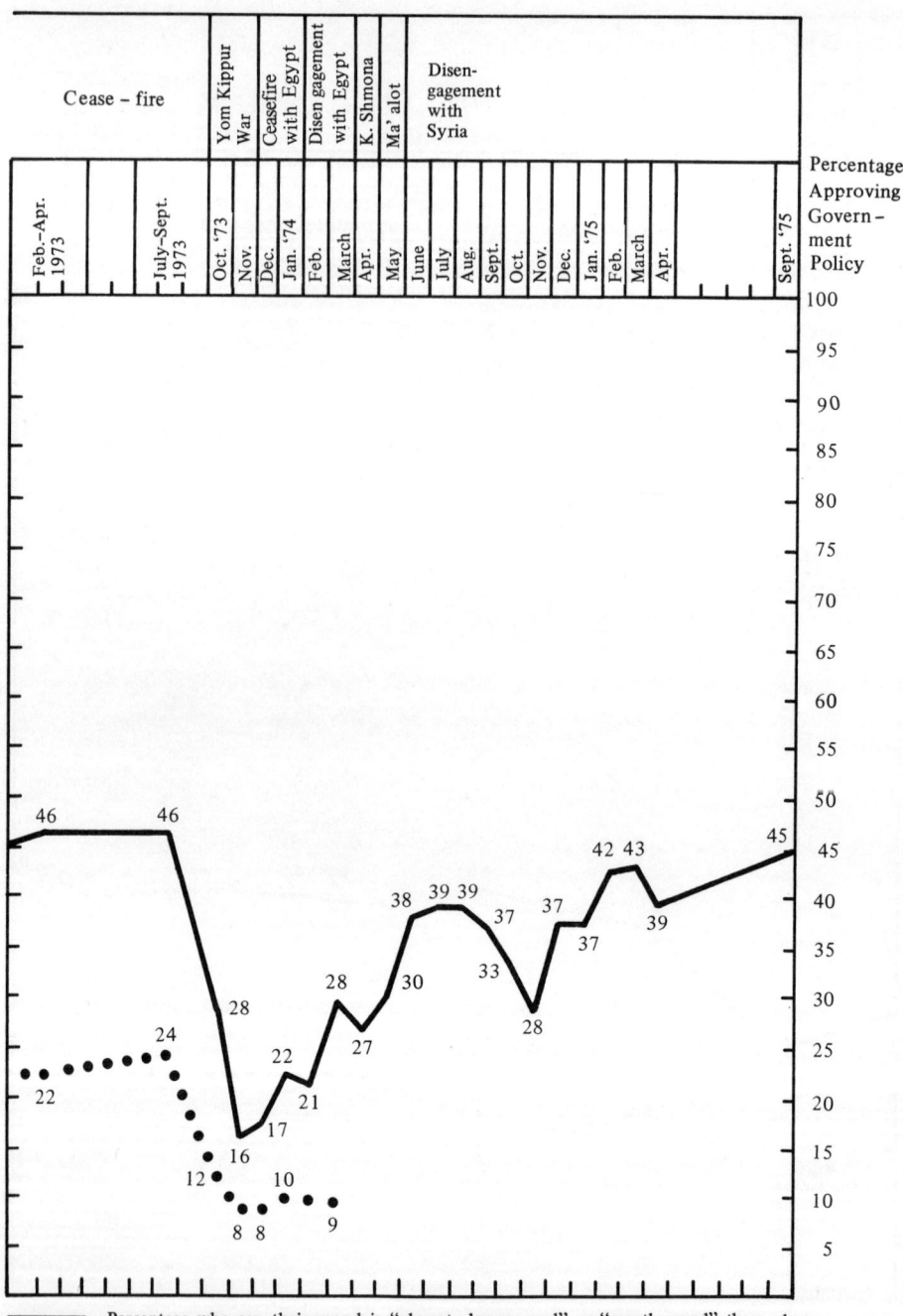

was rather low, in fact, almost exactly as low as it was in October 1973 at the time of the Yom Kippur War. Only as the Six-Day War ended (middle of June), and the public had a chance to become fully aware of the spectacular victory, did morale rise steeply.

Even after the Six-Day War, however, the good mood engulfed less than two-thirds of the public, and less than a third was able to refrain from worry. So, even after Israel's most victorious war, the public did not reach a stage of euphoria. This may be attributed to the casualty list and to the widespread feeling that the victory did not ensure subsequent peace. Once the aftermath of the Six-Day War had receded, morale declined perceptibly; for over a year of relative quiet at the front it maintained a rather steady intermediate level.

Initially, the War of Attrition, which began in the spring of 1969, did not seem to have had any critical effect on the public's morale; rather, its effect seems to have been cumulative. As the war dragged out, morale declined gradually, reaching its lowest point in the summer of 1970 just before the ceasefire; in fact, at that time morale was even lower than it was to be during the Yom Kippur War period. This gradual, rather than abrupt, decline in morale matched the character of the War of Attrition: it was not a major traumatic experience, but casualties were reported almost daily and the pictures of the youngsters killed in action were seen continuously on the front pages of the newspapers.

At the advent of the cease-fire, morale abruptly recuperated, reaching almost exactly the same level as before the War of Attrition. It maintained this level rather steadily for three years (that is, throughout the cease-fire period). Thus, although the Six-Day War was eventually followed by a lowering of morale, and the War of Attrition was followed by a rise in morale, the level during the period of quiet following each of these wars was practically identical. Interestingly, almost the same level of morale was reached in 1975, some time after the Yom Kippur War.

This belies a commonly held view (frequently stated in the press) that before the Yom Kippur War the Israeli public had reached an exaggerated level of collective self-confidence bordering on national megalomania. Actually, when asked what they thought of Israel's situation at that time, some two-thirds of the public pronounced it to be "very good" or "good,"* a percentage that, not surprisingly, declined drastically later on.† While this indicates a certain level of self-complacency, it does not indicate a state of exuberance: less than half of the public was generally in a good mood, and less

---

*While only one-third thought it to be "not so good" or "not good at all."
†This question was not included in the surveys before the middle of 1973.

than a quarter was able to refrain from worry, a level that seems to be "normal" in Israel for nonwar periods.

The Yom Kippur War resulted in an abrupt lowering of morale; it picked up very slowly and gradually some time later. Apparently, this was due not only to the heavy casualties and the less-than-favorable outcome of the war, or to disillusionment in regard to the Israelis' excessively high expectations concerning the capability of their defense forces, but also to the cumulative effect of previous wars. Also, until recently, some hope had usually persisted that no further wars would occur; now it seemed to have struck the public that Israel was inevitably fated to undergo war after war, with no end in sight.

Further, the Yom Kippur War, though formally terminated by a ceasefire agreement, actually gave way to yet another war of attrition terminated only with the disengagement agreement with Syria (June 1974). This period also knew the terrorist onslaughts on Kiryat Shmona (April 1974) and Ma'alot (May 1974) in which civilians (mainly children) were massacred; furthermore, Israel's situation on the international scene suffered a severe setback with the growing power of the oil-producing Arab countries. It is not surprising that morale was so heavily affected and that it took such a long time before it reattained its former level; in fact, the recuperation itself, though hesitant, may be considered as an achievement in its own right.

In sum, the changes in morale since 1967 can be traced to external conflicts, and they faithfully reflect the peculiarity of each. But after each conflict, morale tended to regain the same intermediary level. It may be concluded that external conflicts effected shifts, rather than long-term trends of change, in morale.

It may be claimed, of course, that there were no periods of total relaxation of external tension to which the periods of warfare and semiwarfare could have been compared. But at least we know that the wars did not have any long-range cumulative effect, and that, given Israel's basic situation of perpetual external tension, the even greater stress of active warfare did not leave perceptible long-term traces on morale; even the Yom Kippur War did not have such an effect.

Solidarity

It was suggested that solidarity is an especially crucial aspect of political culture where there are potential intergroup cleavages. Accordingly, we inquired into the kind of solidarity that may bridge over such points of stress. Two of the major potential foci of tension between Jews in Israel are relations between ethnicities (especially between Orientals and Westerners) and between the religiously observant and the nonobservant.* Relations between ethnicities are influenced by the fact that Orientals have tended toward lower socioeconomic strata compared to Westerners (see Chapter 1); this situation has potential interethnic grievances built into it. Relations between the observant and the nonobservant are beset by the controversy on the status of religion; most nonobservant argue for separation of religion and state, while most of the observant demand an even greater convergence of the two. At times this controversy was so intense that some observers envisaged a Kulturkampf.† Thus, the perceptions of Israelis on relations between these subgroups present an especially apt measure of intergroup solidarity, as can be seen from Figure 9.2.

There is a striking similarity in the development of the perceived relations between ethnic groups and the perceived relations between the observant and the nonobservant. Hence, what we have here appear to be two indicators of basically the same phenomenon, namely, a generalized sense of intergroup solidarity within Israeli society.

Solidarity declined perceptibly in the 1970–73 cease-fire period, reaching its lowest recorded points at the end of 1972 and shortly before the Yom Kippur War. Significantly, this was also when ethnic and housing protest appeared on the Israeli scene and the protest groups were most active (see Chapter 6). This seems to corroborate the contention (cf. Peres et al. 1975) that with the relaxation of external tension, internal tensions came to the fore. It can be seen that, like morale, solidarity responded readily to external conflict. Solidarity was at its highest immediately after the Six-Day War‡ (end of June 1967) and during the Yom Kippur War (October 1973), and it was beginning to rise with the advent of the War of Attrition (1969–70).

Although all three wars seem to have fostered intergroup solidarity,** the pattern of influence differed from case to case. The War of Attrition, a prolonged conflict on a relatively low key, led to only a gradual rise in solidarity. Both the Six-Day War and the Yom Kippur War, on the other hand, resulted in a sudden soaring of solidarity to a high peak. Apparently, the traumatic character of these wars, the widespread feeling that Israel had just barely

---

*Another focus of potential tension is that between old-timers and newcomers. This issue is not dealt with here because data on it were not collected continuously over the years.

†See Cohen (1975).

‡Data on the period preceding the Six-Day War and on the Six-Day War itself are not available.

**Although there is no hard-core evidence to prove this, it seems reasonable to presume that before the Six-Day War solidarity had not been as high as it was immediately after the war.

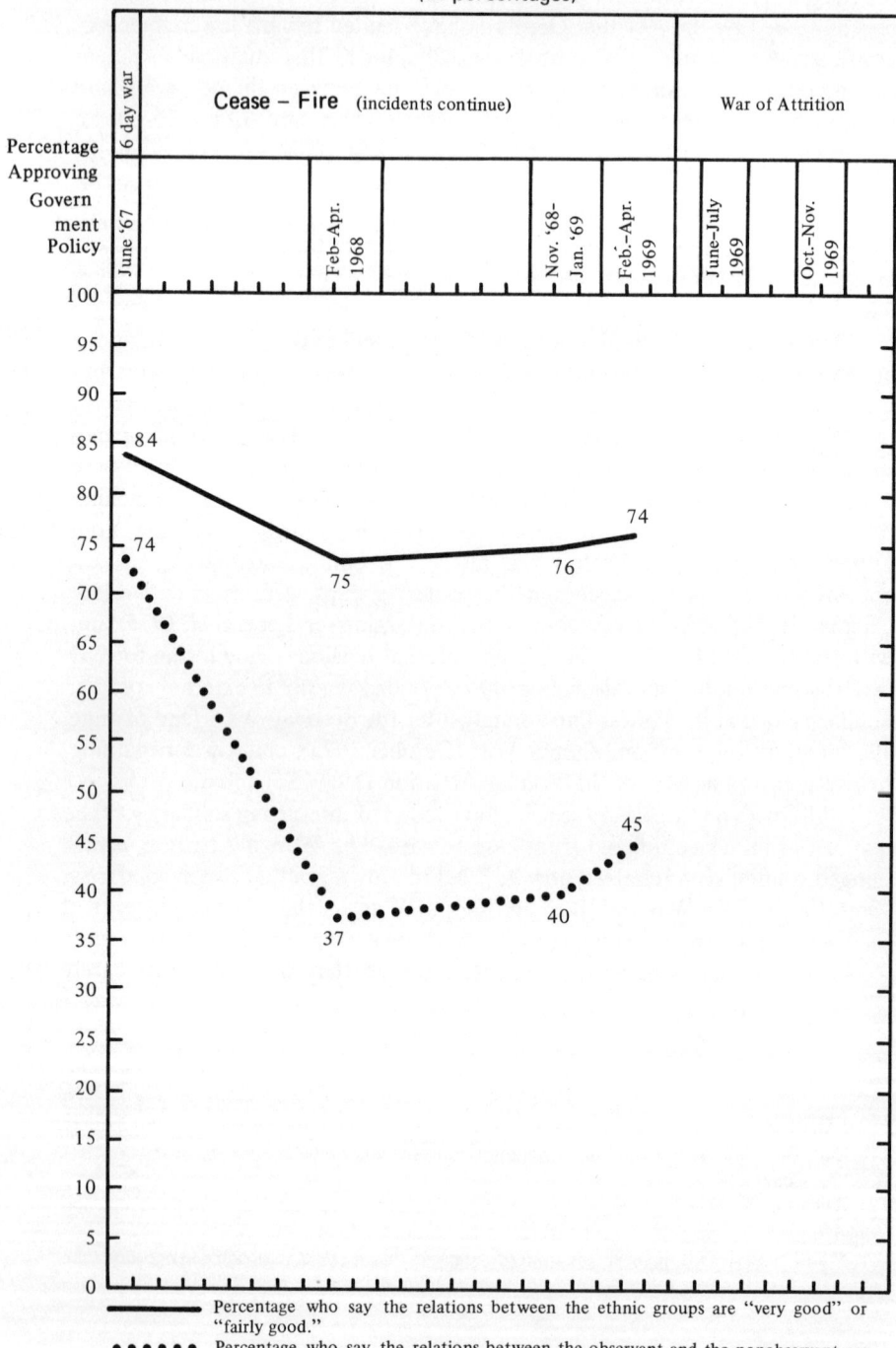

Figure 9.2
Sense of Intergroup Solidarity, 1967-75
(in percentages)

——— Percentage who say the relations between the ethnic groups are "very good" or "fairly good."
• • • • • Percentage who say the relations between the observant and the nonobservant are "very good" or "fairly good."

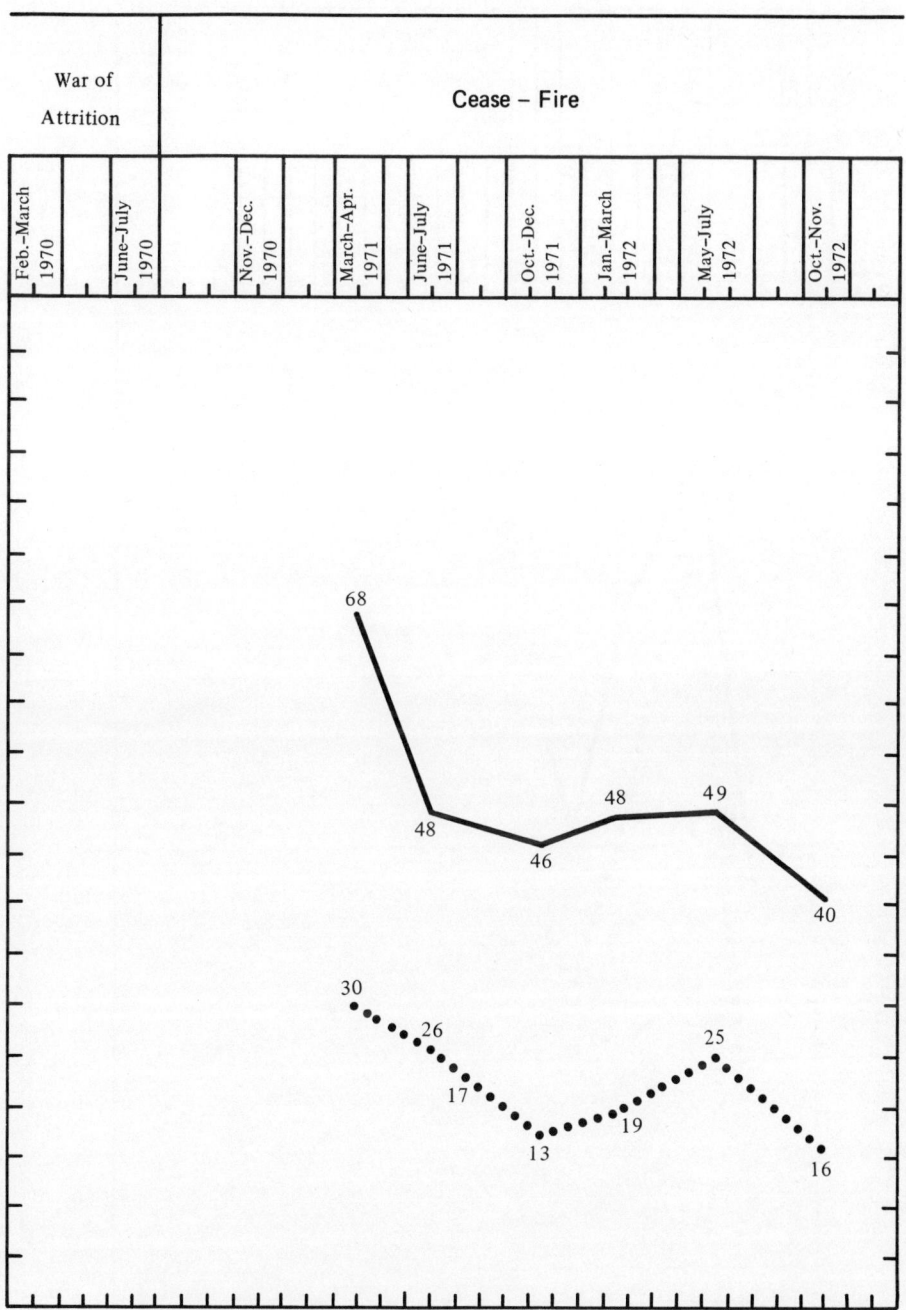

Note: The questions on solidarity were not included in the surveys done at the beginning and the middle of June 1967; they were omitted from several surveys in the interwar period, and from November 1973 onward they were included only bimonthly. After March 1974 they were omitted altogether.

(continued)

Figure 9.2 (continued)

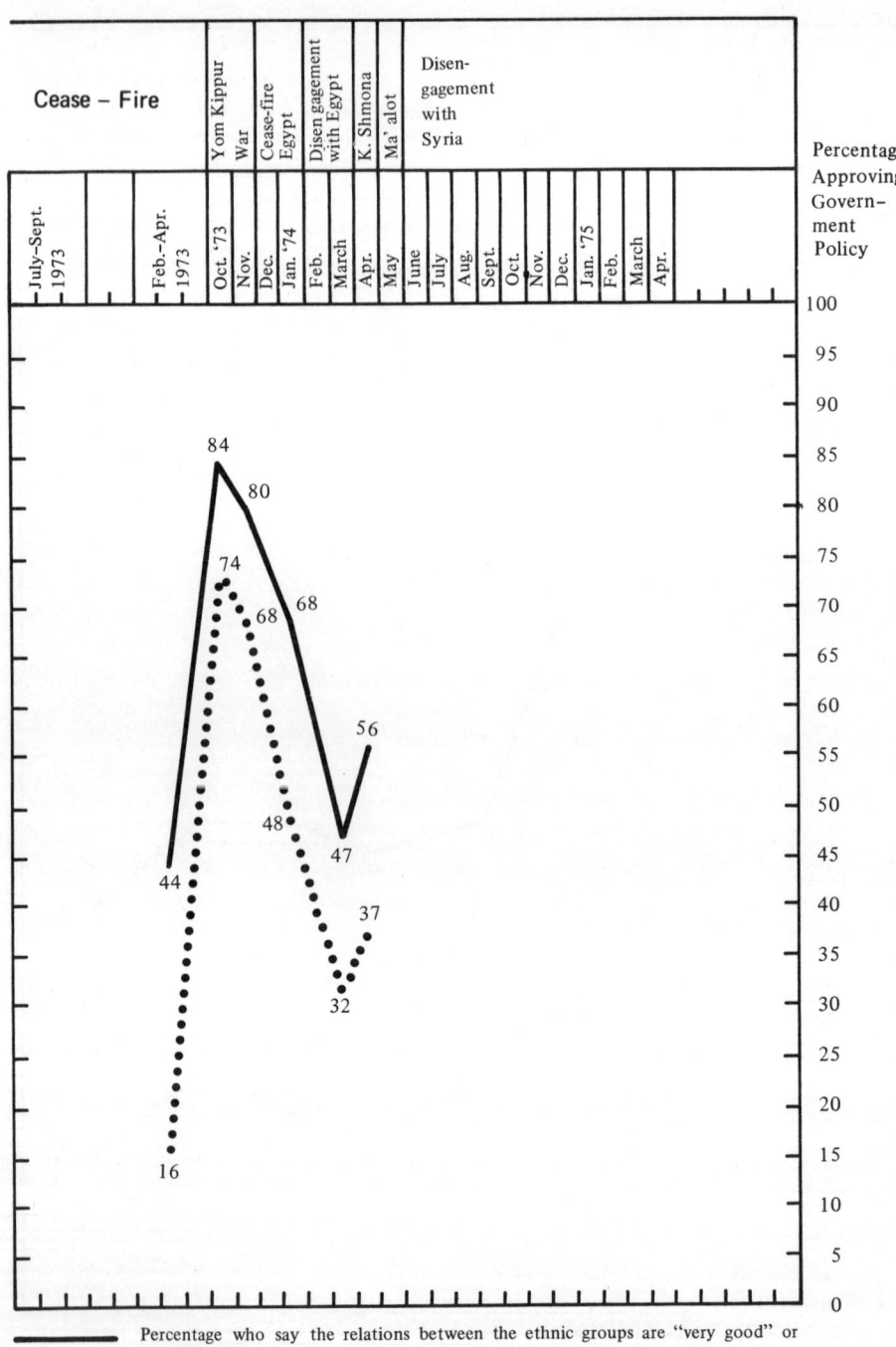

———— Percentage who say the relations between the ethnic groups are "very good" or "fairly good."

• • • • • • • Percentage who say the relations between the observant and the nonobservant are "very good" or "fairly good."

escaped physical destruction, was responsible. In both cases, however, solidarity later declined.

We expected the Six-Day War to have had a more favorable affect on solidarity than did the Yom Kippur War. This expectation was not borne out: both wars resulted in the rise of solidarity to practically the same level. Despite this similarity, the Six-Day War and the Yom Kippur War differed in their effects on solidarity. In the Yom Kippur War, there was a slight decline in solidarity when the war, although no longer full-scale, had not yet been clearly terminated (November 1973). This is in contrast to the Six-Day War: solidarity was at a high peak even when the war had been over for two weeks (June 20-29, 1967). Moreover, shortly after the termination of large-scale warfare in the Yom Kippur War, when battles still continued on a small scale on the northern front (January 1974), interethnic solidarity declined to a much greater extent than it did in the wake of the Six-Day War (February–April 1968). Thus, both wars had a similar intensifying effect on solidarity, but in the Yom Kippur War this effect had exhausted itself before the war was fully terminated.

The peak of solidarity reached in the Yom Kippur War, and its speedy decline before the full termination of the war, may be explained by two factors that worked at cross purposes to each other. On one hand there was the unifying effect of the war and of the threat it posed. On the other hand there was disappointment with the faulty conduct of the war (the "mechdal") and the sense of inadequacy and dissatisfaction fostered by this disappointment. As long as the war was at its height, the first factor prevailed. But as soon as the war had become less intensive, the danger to physical existence had become less pronounced, and more information had filtered through to the public, the sense of dissatisfaction became more salient.

In general, the evidence indicates that external conflict that involves a threat to a society's existence does have a unifying effect on that society—but only in the short run.* Once the peak of the struggle has passed and danger is perceived to have abated, the effect of the external struggle is not uniformly cohesive; it may even provoke intergroup irritability.

Morale and Solidarity: The Convergence of Opposites?

Since both morale and solidarity are related to external conflict, does this mean that they must also be related to each other? Above, we have argued that although morale and solidarity have been found to be interrelated on the

---

*This conclusion has also been reached by Kamen (1975).

microlevel, they are not necessarily related on the macrolevel. And, in fact, the surveys on which this analysis is based report no (or negligible) relationships between morale and solidarity. This being the case, we expected morale and solidarity would respond to external conflict independently of each other.

In line with this, we expected that in the Six-Day War both morale and solidarity would have pointed up; and that in the Yom Kippur War they would have developed in opposite directions, balancing each other out so that the overall tenacity of the Israeli public would have been maintained. To examine this expectation, morale and solidarity are presented here in a joint diagram. To simplify understanding, we selected one indicator for each factor. For morale, the indicator is the one that recurred continuously in all surveys to date.* In the case of solidarity, both indicators were included in an equal number of surveys; hence we selected interethnic relations, which is more pertinent for the present analysis (see Chapter 6). Since the developments in both indicators of morale are largely parallel to each other (Figure 9.1), as are the developments in both indicators of solidarity (Figure 9.2), the selection of one of each for joint presentation should not unduly bias the conclusions. These data are presented in Figure 9.3.†

Both morale and solidarity were high in the wake of the Six-Day War— but in the Yom Kippur War (and at the beginning of the War of Attrition as well) morale and solidarity moved in opposite directions: while morale went down, solidarity went up. After the peak of the Yom Kippur War, as solidarity moved down, morale moved up again. Ostensibly, then, our expectation was borne out. However, in the last war, there was a time lag between the reaction of solidarity and the converse reaction of morale: solidarity reached its peak before morale reached its lowest point. Consequently, there was a time span (toward the late fall and winter of 1973–74 when the war was still going on on a small scale)‡ when solidarity had already started to move down while morale was still declining or was still very low.

Consequently, our expectations were borne out for the Six-Day War, but only partly for the Yom Kippur War: initially, morale and solidarity did indeed balance each other out, so that the general tenacity of the Israeli public was somehow maintained. But this held only for the peak of the war crisis. As soon as the war became less intensive, this mutual balance no longer seemed to be fully at work. The initial drop in solidarity was slight, and the periods

---

*The second item was not included in recent surveys, as can be seen from Figure 9.1.

†In addition, the conclusions may be rechecked by comparing Figure 9.1 and Figure 9.2.

‡The disengagement agreement with Syria had not yet been reached and small-scale battles on the Golan Heights were still going on.

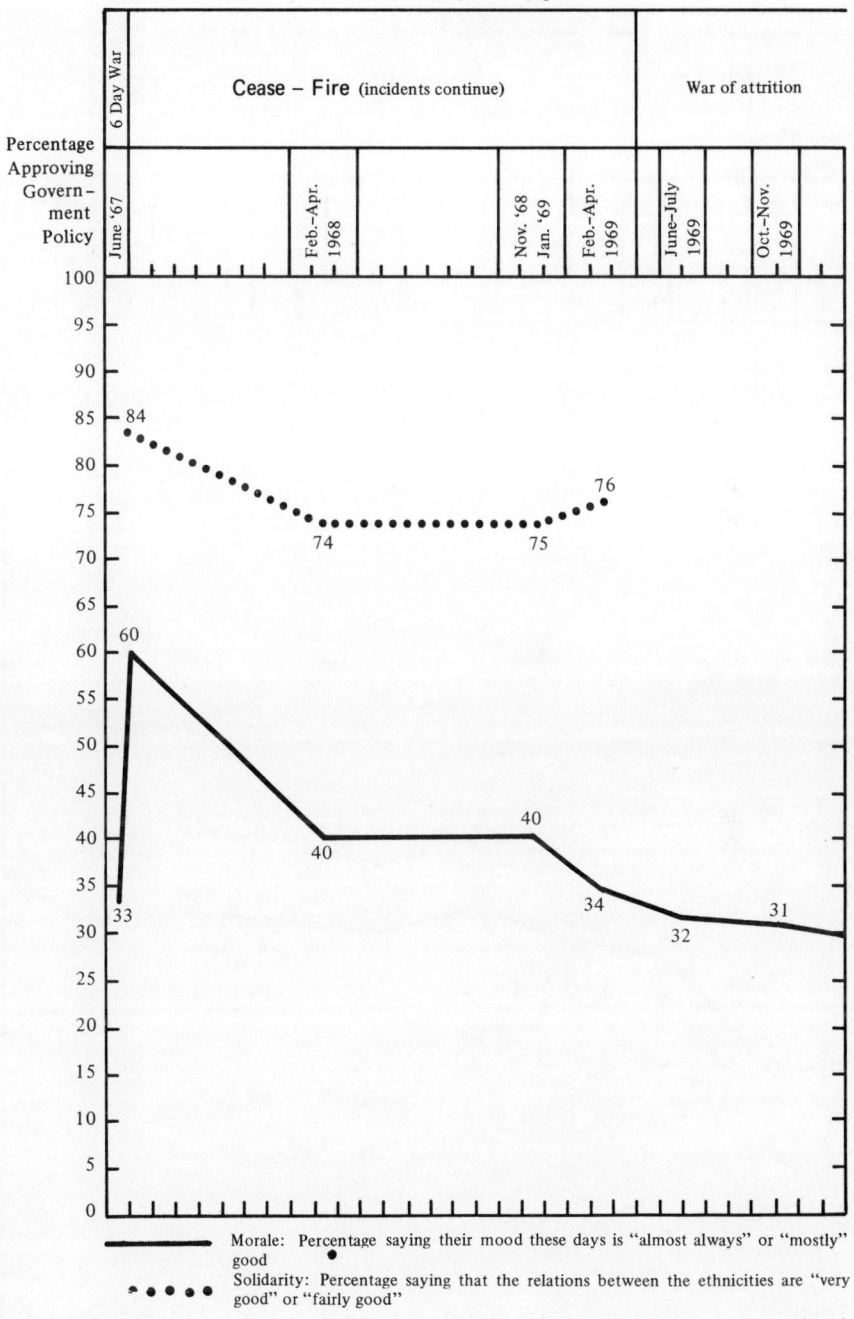

Figure 9.3
Morale and Solidarity, 1967-75
(in percentages)

———— Morale: Percentage saying their mood these days is "almost always" or "mostly" good

••••• Solidarity: Percentage saying that the relations between the ethnicities are "very good" or "fairly good"

(continued)

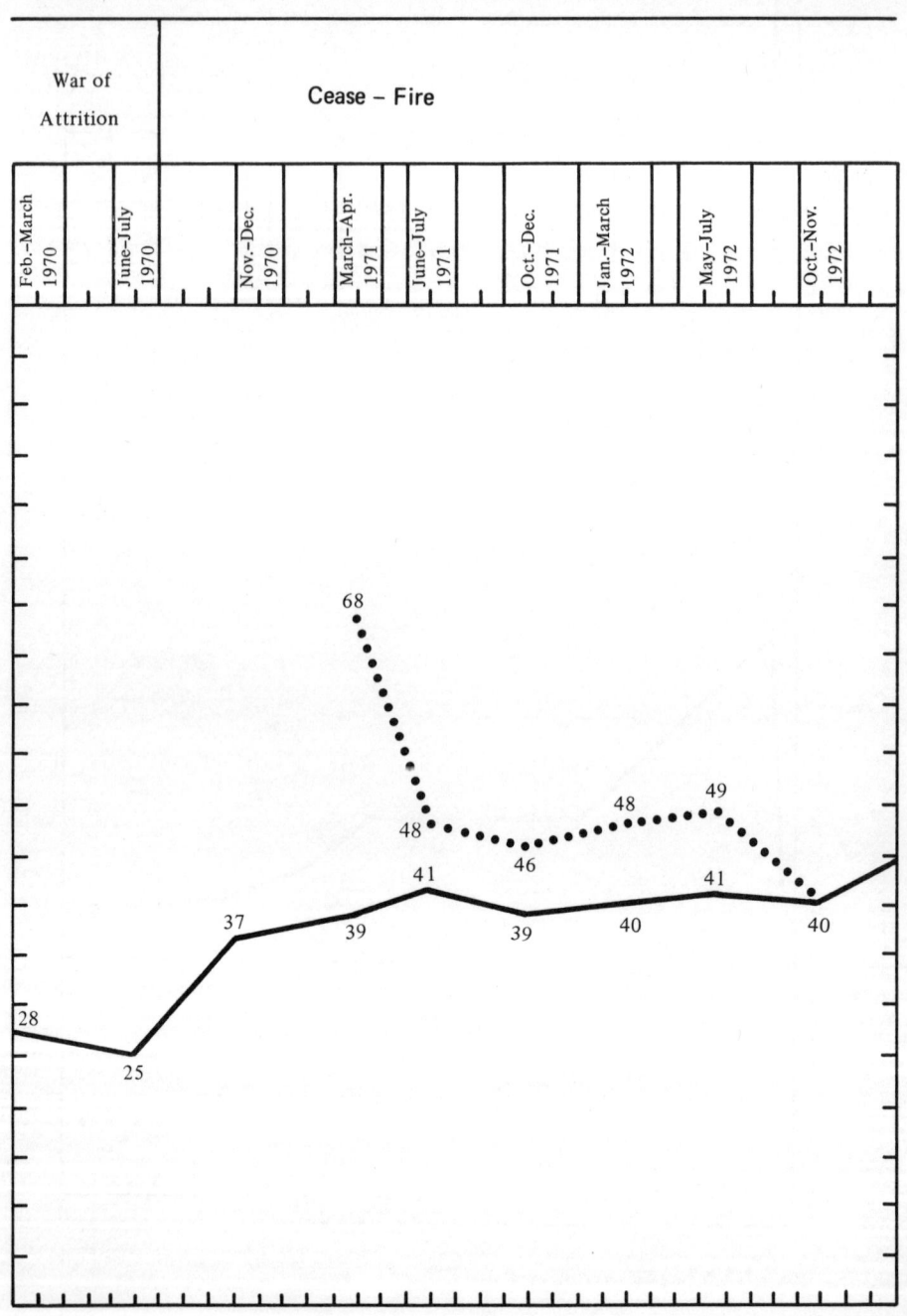

Figure 9.3 (continued)

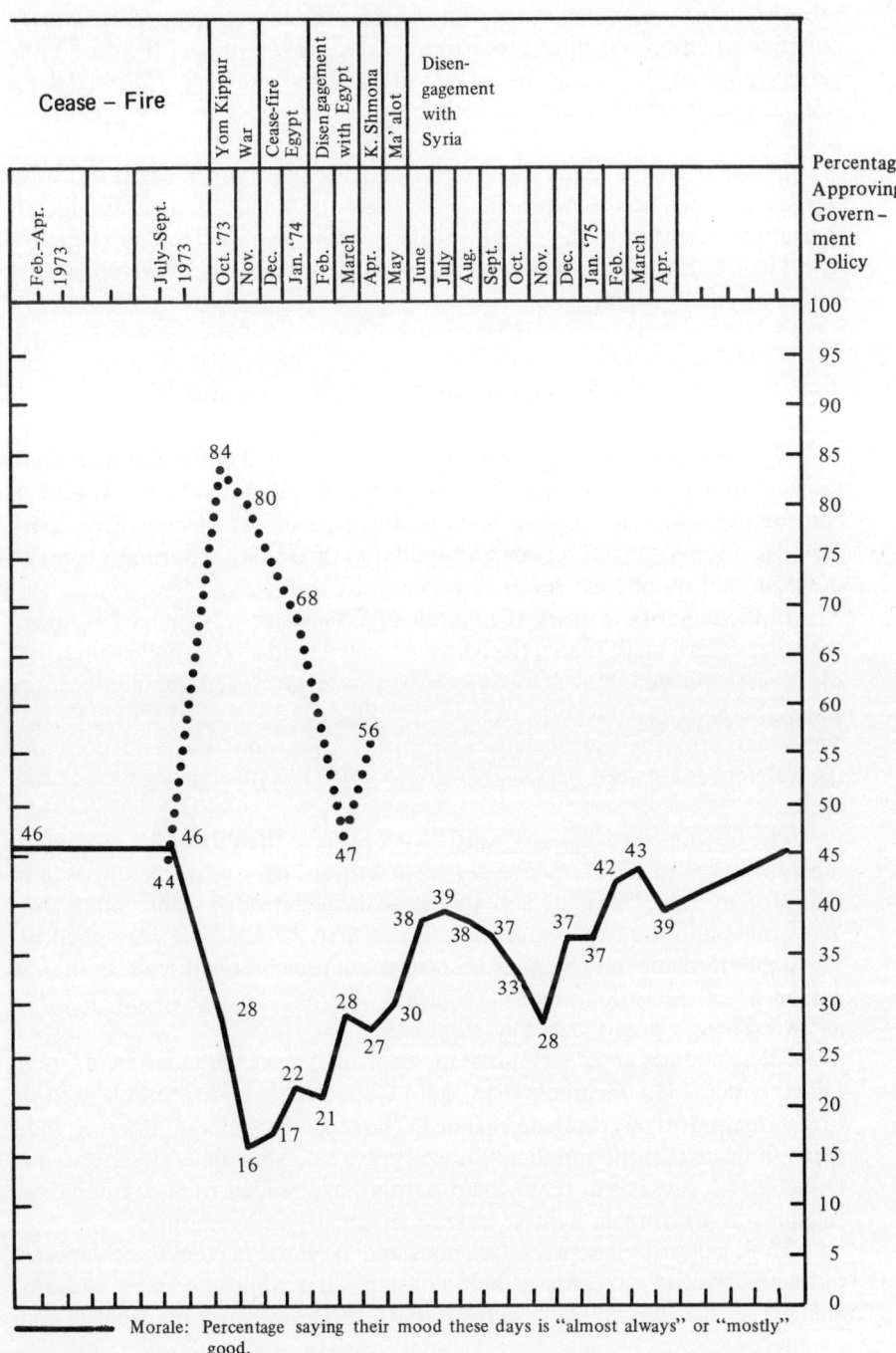

———— Morale: Percentage saying their mood these days is "almost always" or "mostly" good.
• • • • • Solidarity: Percentage saying that the relations between the ethnicities are "very good" or "fairly good"

when both morale and solidarity were on their way down (or were simultaneously low) were rather short. But contrary to expectation, when Israel's objective situation was most precarious (excluding the peak of the crisis), the perseverance of the public reached its greatest vulnerability. Fortunately, a state such as this has been the exception; we can only hope that it will continue to be so.

In conclusion, it seems that, in exploring the effect of conflict, it is fruitful to make a distinction between the major crisis itself and the stage at which it is abating. Apparently the social unit may be more vulnerable at the latter stage; hence this stage deserves special attention both in sociological analysis and in practical concern.

The Relevance of Social Background

Have any groups or categories of people contributed more than their share to maintaining Israel's tenacity? The survey data published by the IIASR in conjunction with the Communications Institute of the Hebrew University includes comparisons of morale and solidarity of Israelis of various countries of origin and of different levels of education.

In the majority of cases, the morale of Westerners was somewhat higher than that of Orientals; that of the better-educated tended to be higher than that of the less-educated. Since Orientals have a lower average level of education, could the level of education explain the differences between Orientals and Westerners? In the few instances in which education was held constant, the differences between persons of various countries of origin tended to disappear.

The findings for solidarity were less consistent than those for morale. In most instances in which differences existed at all, they were the opposite of those for morale. Orientals and the less-educated tended (more often than Westerners and the better-educated) to feel that the relations were good between the ethnicities and between observant and nonobservant Jews. In the one case in which education was held constant, the differences between Orientals and Westerners were practically eliminated.

These findings about solidarity are surprising, since the situation of Orientals in Israel is less favorable than that of Westerners and Orientals are said to feel themselves discriminated against. The reported findings, however, indirectly indicate that the situation is not as grave as is sometimes described; had Orientals felt aggrieved, they would hardly have tended to view interethnic relations in a favorable light at least as frequently as Westerners.

Thus, differences between Orientals and Westerners seem to be canceled out when level of education is held constant; and while the better-educated contribute somewhat more towards morale, the lesser-educated seem to contribute somewhat more towards solidarity. Neither category, therefore, contributes disproportionately towards Israel's standing power, and neither can be held disproportionately responsible for periods of vulnerability.

MORALE, SOLIDARITY, AND THE ISRAELI ESTABLISHMENT

It was our contention that both morale and solidarity have positive implications for support of the political regime, and therefore for the government as its representative. With regard to solidarity, this contention was borne out: in the IIASR survey for March-April 1971 a positive correlation (monotonous coefficient: .40) was reported between sense of interethnic solidarity and support for government policy.* Data from this survey also enabled us to examine both parts of the contention simultaneously. A multiple regression analysis was employed in which support for government policy (consent) served as the dependent variable, while morale (as measured by mood and worries), sense of intergroup solidarity (as measured by perception of interethnic relations), and four background factors (age, education, income, and country of origin) served as independent variables. The social background variables were included to see whether they, rather than attitudes, would account for consent.† Table 9.1 gives the net effects (standardized regression coefficients) calculated for that equation.

The table shows that morale has little effect on support of government policy, while sense of intergroup solidarity, as measured,‡ does have a significantly greater net effect on such support.** The net effect of solidarity, is clearly greater than that of background variables, and is maintained even when the latter are held constant.

Similar conclusions emerge when developments of all three items are plotted jointly over time. This can be illustrated by using the same indicators for morale and solidarity as in Figure 9.3, and adding developments in support for government policy as established by the various surveys (see Chapter 5). These data are presented in Figure 9.4.

Except for the Six-Day War period when all three items reached their peak and then declined simultaneously, consent for government policy and

---

*See Levy and Guttman (June 1971). No correlation coefficients between morale and support for government policy are reported.

†It will be recalled that education and country of origin were found to hold some relationship to consent (see Chapter 7).

‡Only one question on intergroup solidarity was included in this survey.

**Since we are dealing with ordinal (rather than with interval) scales, we emphasize the relative (rather than the absolute) weight of the various items in affecting support for the government.

TABLE 9.1

Net Effect (Standardized Regression Coefficients) of Morale, Solidarity, and Social Background Variables on Support for Government Policy, in **1971**

	Beta
Morale	
Mood	.09*
Worries	.04
Intergroup Solidarity	
Perception of interethnic relations	.20*
Social Background	
Age	.15*
Education	-.14*
Income	-.05
Country of Origin	.01

*Significant $p < 0.001$ N = 1,620

Explanatory Remarks: 1. The questions for morale and solidarity were identical to those reported in Figures 9.1 and 9.2.
2. Country of origin refers to Europe-America vs. Asia-Africa.

Source: Supplied by the IIASR on the basis of data from the survey of March–April, 1971, (Levy and Guttman June 1971A).

morale did not tend to ascend and decline at the same time; on the contrary, there were several periods in which they moved in opposite directions. On the other hand, sense of solidarity and consent for government policy showed a conspicuous tendency to parallel development, especially after the Six-Day War, in the 1970–73 cease-fire period, and during and after the Yom Kippur War.*

The fact that morale and consent are not related and do not show parallel developments over time is rather surprising, because a relationship is reported in various surveys between the respondents' assessment of Israel's situation

---

*Similar conclusions can be reached when developments in the other two indicators of morale and solidarity are compared to that of consent for government policy.

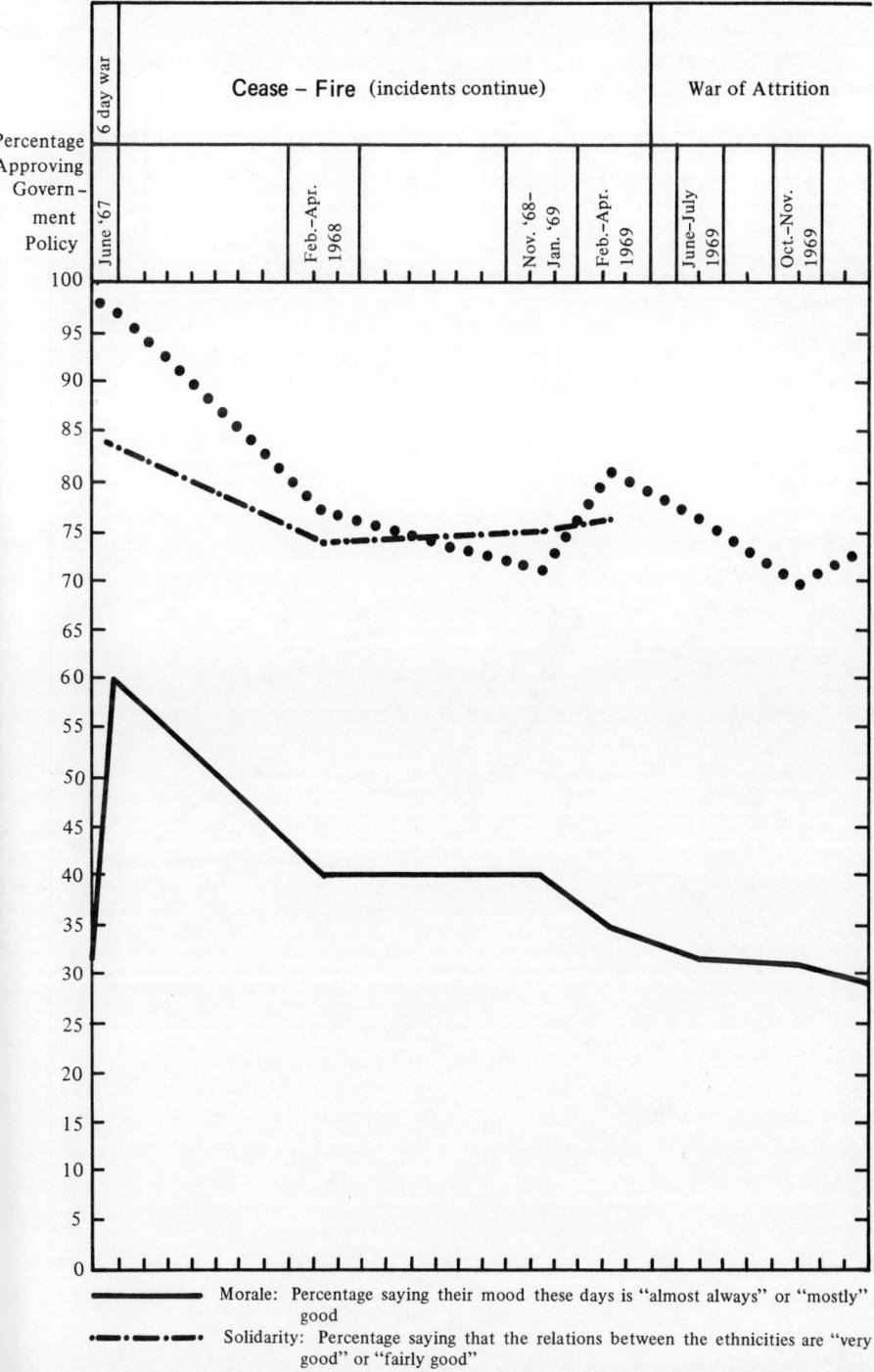

Figure 9.4

Morale, Solidarity, and Consent for Government Policy, 1967–75 (in percentages)

Morale: Percentage saying their mood these days is "almost always" or "mostly" good

Solidarity: Percentage saying that the relations between the ethnicities are "very good" or "fairly good"

(continued)

Figure 9.4 (continued)

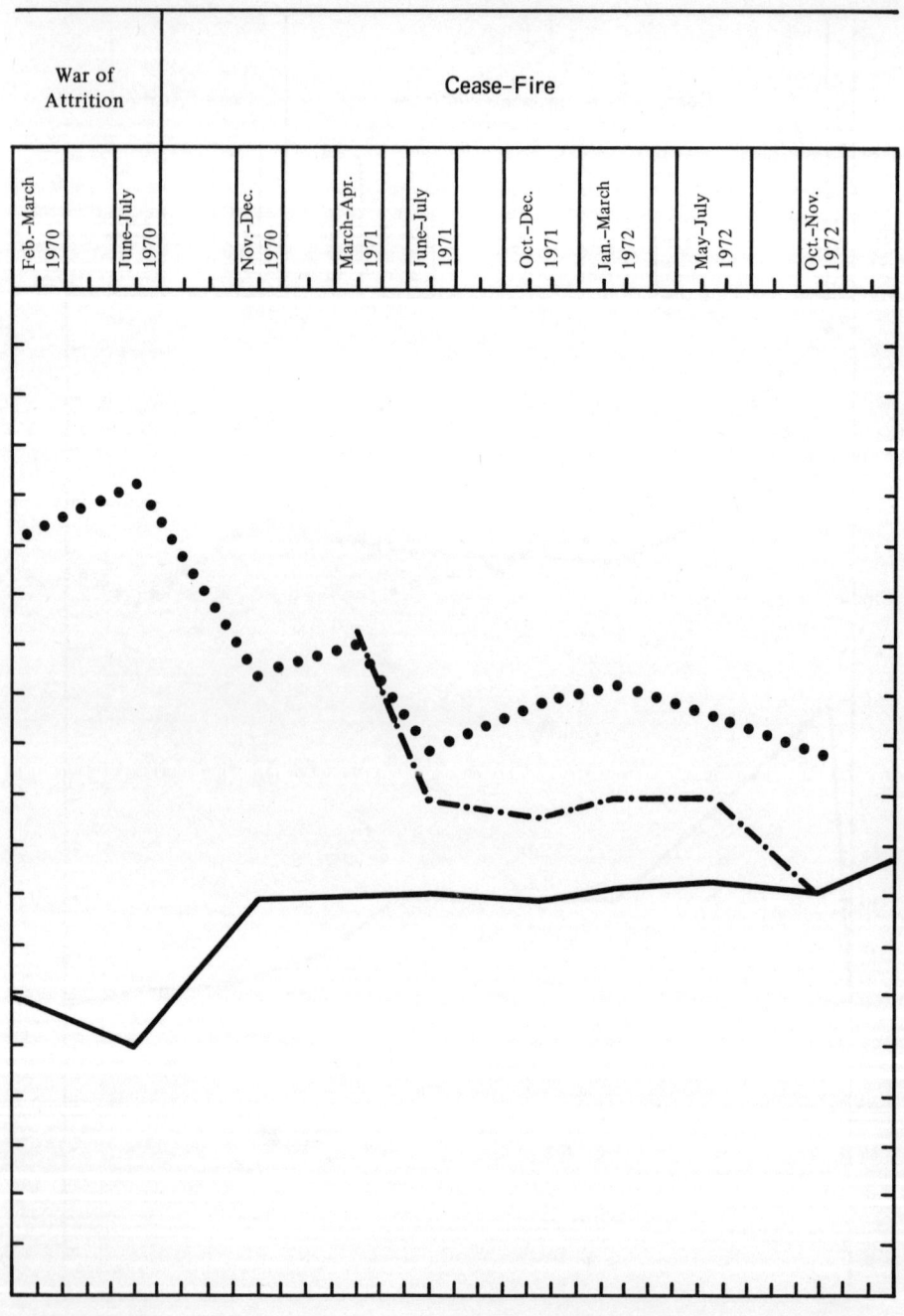

• • • • • • • • • Consent to government policy: Percentage saying the government is dealing "very well" or "well" with the problems of the present situation (see Chapter 5)

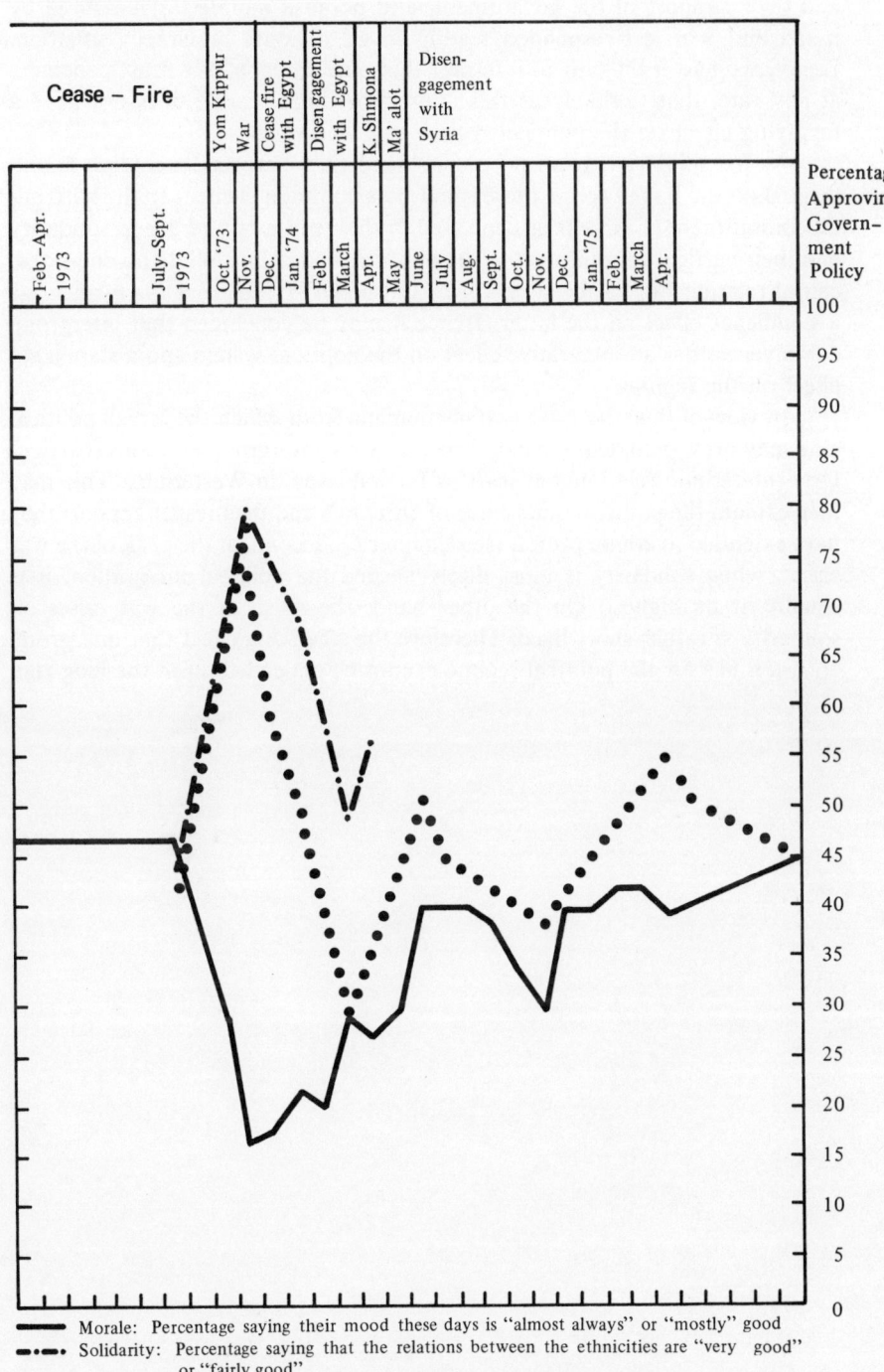

and their support of the government, and because morale (as measured by mood and worries) responded readily to all changes in Israel's situation. Hence, we find it difficult to interpret this phenomenon. We must conclude, at any rate, that (unlikely as this may seem) high morale does not have a fortifying effect on the political regime and vice versa.

As for solidarity, it must be concluded that Verba's conception is vindicated on the Israeli scene: there is indeed a common element to the horizontal commitment of Israelis as expressed in their sense of intergroup solidarity and their vertical commitment to the political leadership. While no one-sided, causal relationship has been established, it could be seen that the former has a significant effect on the latter. Hence it may be concluded that intergroup cohesiveness has an integrative effect on the political system and a stabilizing effect on the regime.

In view of this, there are two phenomena from which the Israeli political elite may draw confidence. First, Orientals view intergroup relations (particularly interethnic relations) at least as favorably as do Westerners. This may help explain the political quiescence of Orientals and the meager support they have extended to ethnic protest (see Chapter 6). Second, at the peak of the war crises, when solidarity is most direly needed for political integration, it is usually at its highest. On the other hand, the effect of the war crises on solidarity is rather short-lived. Therefore the steadying effect that intergroup cohesion has for the political regime cannot be depended on in the long run.

CHAPTER

10

CONCLUSION

Many ingredients go into the making of a political system, and a variety of forces may be pulling in different directions. At the risk of oversimplification, some of these may be characterized as tension-provoking forces and others as integrative mechanisms. Both kinds of forces have clearly been active on the Israeli political scene. It is our contention that some strains resulting from discrepancies between the political elite and the Israeli public have been attenuated by integrative mechanisms that as such, have been extraneous to this relationship. The Israeli political scene may thus be seen as an intricate balance in which distintegrative and integrative mechanisms constantly counteract each other.

POLITICAL CLEAVAGES

Cleavages between the political establishment and the public have been evident in several spheres. There is the great and growing power gap between the political center and the public resulting from the elite's near monopolization of resources, from administrative centralization, from the marked politization of social institutions, and especially from pervasive government control over the economy. The counterpart of this power amassed at the elite level is the excessive dependence of various segments of the population on the center for their subsistence and for a wide array of benefits (Chapter 1).

A certain degree of governmental control over the economy is probably inevitable in contemporary society, and especially in Israel, where a large proportion of the economic resources flows from abroad and is necessarily channeled through the government and its affiliated agencies. Also, some governmental guidance of the economy is considered to be desirable by many

Western liberals. But it can hardly be doubted that the tight control that the Israeli government and its affiliated agencies exercise over the economy is above and beyond what is commonly prevalent in Western societies, and probably exceeds what many Western liberals would consider to be optimal.

At any rate, the issue considered here is not whether such control is desirable, but what its ramifications are for the Israeli political scene. It appears that, on one hand, the dependence of the public has aided the establishment in stabilizing its position. In fact it has enabled the establishment to employ, with relative success, a variety of nonsymbolic devices for marshalling electoral consent (Chapter 5); thus this dependence may be regarded as a major reason why the establishment has maintained itself in power. But, at the same time, it must also be regarded as a tension-provoking mechanism, for it is doubtful that this pattern fits in with the changing political orientations of the Israeli public.

The centralized control of the economy concurs with a left-of-center, socialist ideology; it has frequently been disparaged by the right in the name of "free enterprise." The moderate shift toward the right in the orientations of the Israeli public (Chapter 3) might well signify decreasing approval of this system.

Hence, closely related to the excessive power discrepancy between the Israeli political elite and the public at large is an apparently increasing ideological gap between the two. While the public has shifted towards the right, the Labor Party-Alignment (the major force in the political establishment) still formally adheres to a left-of-center socialist ideology, and in actual fact still retains considerable affinity with it. Although this leftist adherence has been attenuated in recent years, it has never been abandoned. It has not prevented growing inequality in Israel's (government controlled) salary scale but, as noted, tight state control of the economy still clearly attests to this allegiance. At the same time, only about a quarter of the public has recently identified itself with the left (Chapter 3).

Traditionally, the Israeli Labor Party has been considered to embody the major ideological doctrine of Israeli society (Arian 1975). In view of the foregoing, it seems that this has been decreasingly so in recent years. It is true that the Labor Party-Alignment has always been a pragmatic rather than a dogmatic political body; therefore, assuming that this shift away from the left will continue, the Alignment may well be able to adjust to this change to a greater extent than it has done so far. But at present, at any rate, it seems to be somewhat out of step. Moreover, experience has shown (Chapter 6) that the Israeli establishment finds it easier to be flexible where its own power positions are not directly concerned. Consequently, to the extent that a shift away from the left involves a certain loosening of the reins over the economy (and thus the partial relinquishing of power positions), it is not clear whether the elite will be able or willing to evince such a flexibility.

What has been said so far does not imply a "recommendation" for the adoption of a right-wing ideology by the Israeli establishment. The proportion of rightist adherents among the Israeli public does not exceed the proportion of those who are aligned with the left. At the same time, it is clear that the traditional socialist ideology is no longer capable of gripping large proportions of the Israeli public; if the present trend in the public's political orientations continues, a further shift away from such an ideology by the dominant party would probably aid the party in maintaining itself in power. Possibly what is called for, to use Duverger's terms, is a new doctrine for a new epoch, perhaps one that no longer fits neatly into the traditional left-right continuum. Perhaps the fact that the present Israeli leadership has not come up with a political doctrine that could grip the public is in itself a source of cleavage.

Another cleavage between the establishment and the public results from the "mechdal" of the Yom Kippur War. We know that the majority of the public held the government responsible for Israel's performance during the war (Chapters 3 and 6), a fact that evidently did nothing to boost the confidence of the public in its leadership. While most of the personalities directly responsible for the waging of the war are not in the present government, basically the same political elite is still in charge—and it may well take some time before it succeeds in restoring public confidence to its prewar level.

Further, a certain discrepancy could be discerned between professed widespread political involvement among the public and a widespread sense of political impotence. Political involvement implies the wish to exercise influence in the political arena. This tendency of the majority of the Israeli public was found to be at odds with perceived blocking of upward channels of political communication. Such a discrepancy between involvement and efficacy is of special significance, since it turned out to be associated with a lack of confidence in the political establishment (Chapter 4).

This brings us to the final point: the growing divergencies discussed above, in conjunction with a variety of other factors, have recently found expression in a decline in consent for the dominant party as evidenced in the last two elections and a decline in orally expressed consent for the government as well. It is impossible to tell whether this decline is innocuous and temporary, or if it is likely to continue and become more pronounced. At any rate, it certainly attests to the cleavages between the "center" and the "periphery," despite the proficiency of the former in employing various devices for eliciting consent (Chapter 5). In fact, it is quite possible that these devices themselves are being resented. Although on the whole they probably restrained the decline in consent, they may well have had an alienating effect on some segments of the population and may thus have served as yet another source of political cleavage.

In sum, then, several points of stress have recently been evident, expressed in decreasing rapport between the public and the political establishment. Yet we know that these discrepancies have found no clear, overt expression in Israel's political life, which has been basically quiescent. No radical tendencies on the part of Israeli youth have been evident; protest has been sparse, mild, and moderate, and has had but marginal effects on the political establishment (Chapter 6). Practically no totally alienated groups have appeared on the scene; the fundamental political framework of Israeli society has never been jeopardized, and basically the same political elite has maintained its position for more than four decades. Despite the recent decrease in electoral support for that elite, the public has not indicated any clear intention of demoting it.

Israel, apparently, is not the only country in which a decrease in rapport between the public and the political establishment is evident. Some observers have claimed that in the United States, too, growing disaffection with the political system has been evident in the last decade, and has found expression in growing political discontent.* Concomitantly, however, the American political scene has been much more turbulent than has the Israeli scene. *What seems to be peculiar to Israel, then, is not the growing political disaffection as such, but rather growing discontent coupled with basic political stability and quiescence.* How can this apparent inconsistency be explained?

The sparsity of dissent can probably be attributed partly to the establishment's skillful absorption of protest (Chapter 6), and the mildness of the decline in electoral consent is probably due, inter alia, to the fact that no more attractive alternatives are in sight. Beyond this, however, it seems the strain between the public and the political elite has been mitigated by factors originating from outside this relationship. These are mainly of two kinds: collective national identifications and individual mobility channels.

INTEGRATIVE MECHANISMS

Collective National Identifications: The pronounced collectivism that characterized the prestate era and the beginning of statehood later became greatly attenuated and individualism came to be more pronounced. At the same time, the Israeli public's identification with certain basic collective values and ideologies remains extensive. These include the ideology of Zionism; attachment to the Land of Israel; Israeli identification; and, to a somewhat lesser extent, Jewish identification.

Israel's national movement, Zionism, which has exacted staunch collective commitments, is still in the process of routinization, in contrast to the West, where national entities have had a chance to become more fully routi-

---

*See Converse (1972); Miller (1974A); House and Mason (1975). For a different view, see Citrin (1974). Citrin's view is rejected by Miller (1974B).

nized. Moreover, the core values of many Western societies (especially the United States) were more individualist to begin with. Hence (and in view of the cohesive effect of Israel's ongoing external conflict) it may be presumed that collective commitments and cohesiveness in Israel are still particularly strong compared to parallel commitments in the West.

The collective commitments of Israelis were found to have positive implications for support of the political establishment and for tolerance of the regime's deficiencies. A sense of intergroup loyalty was found to have similar implications. Hence, we conclude that in Israel these collective loyalties have been especially significant in contributing to political integration.

Avenues of Individual Mobility: Observers have pointed out that blocked aspirations (especially for achievement and advancement) may be conducive to widespread resentment of the regime—and, hence, to protest and rebellion—while a balance between aspirations and actual opportunities for advancement is conducive to political quiescence. It has further been pointed out that Western countries have been approaching a situation in which extensive mobility has had an integrative impact on the political systems (Germani 1966, p. 379).

It may be added, however, that excessive affluence does not seem to be conducive to political quiescence either. Thus it has been claimed that the student protest in the United States had its source, inter alia, in the country's abundance (Adler 1972). This contention is further supported by the fact that student protest in the United States subsided precisely at a time when the economic situation suffered a setback and the job market tightened up.*

It seems, then, that blocked mobility is not conducive to political quiescence, and neither is excessive affluence. The necessity of investing major efforts in order to advance seems optimal from this point of view. In this respect, at any rate, Israel seems to have struck a lucky middle road. Compared to the United States, it can hardly be regarded as an affluent society; still, the standard of living has been rising and the numbers engaged in higher-ranking occupations (such as those in various bureaucracies) have been increasing beyond those in other countries with similar (or even higher) levels of economic development. Thus, hard-working, ambitious persons have found various avenues of social mobility open to them (Chapter 7), including avenues into some sectors of the political establishment itself. Since the blocking of political mobility has been considered to be as detrimental to political quiescence as the blocking of social mobility, this relative openness is especially significant.

---

*This is not to underrate the importance of the termination of the Vietnam War in bringing an end to the protest movement; however, other factors seem to have been of relevance as well.

Moreover, channels of individual mobility have been opened not only for Ashkenazim but for Orientals as well, and to a greater extent than have parallel channels of advancement for blacks in the United States. While the overall socioeconomic gap between Westerners and Orientals has not narrowed, talented and ambitious Orientals have had various channels of mobility open to them; those who took advantage of such channels have been absorbed into the mainstream of Israeli society and are unlikely to supply the leadership for ethnic protest. In view of the explosiveness of racial protest in the United States in the late 1960s, this feature of the Israeli social scene seems to have contributed considerably to political quiescence.

The Israeli system has been open not only objectively, but subjectively as well, as shown by the fact that most Israelis were found to be satisfied with their occupational situation. Such satisfaction with one's situation, as well as perceived improvements in one's situation and expectations for further improvement, were all found to have positive implications for support of the political regime (Chapter 7). Hence, we can tentatively conclude that individual mobility too, has been conducive to political integration.

Furthermore, there is one channel of mobility that is quite frequently utilized by Israelis when they find other channels closed to them—the channel of horizontal or geographical mobility (which, for many, may turn into a channel of vertical mobility as well)—namely, emigration from Israel. Since the establishment of the State, more than 250,000 Israelis have left the country to seek their fortunes elsewhere. Given the small size of the population, this seems to be a larger percentage of emigrants than may be found in many Western countries. According to various studies, those who favored emigration (as well as those who actually emigrated) were frequently the ones who did not evince strong identification with Israel's collective values, or who perceived their mobility as blocked in this country. Thus, it may be said that the emigrants were the ones for whom the other integrative mechanisms did not work very well. Therefore, although emigration has been a constant drain on Israel's minute population and has therefore weakened Israel considerably, it has also served as a mechanism for removing disgruntled elements and less than fully committed citizens—and, thus, for releasing potential tensions. It is in this manner, we suggest, that the balance between strain and tension on one hand, and integration and support on the other, has been maintained.

However, some of the integrative mechanisms on the Israeli scene are rather precarious. Intergroup solidarity has had its ups and downs; Zionist commitment and attachment to the Land of Israel are less pronounced among the younger generation than among the older generation; and, given intergenerational decline in religious adherence, there are some indications that Jewish identification may decline in the future. Since Jewish identification was found to be closely related to Israeli identification and to attachment to Israel, the possibility must be faced that all these collective-national identifications may diminish to some extent in the future.

As for avenues of social mobility, these depend largely on various factors that cannot be fully controlled by the political elite (not even by one that holds tight control over the economy): such as the amount of foreign aid Israel may be able to obtain, and Israel's resulting financial situation. In fact, lately there have been some indications that the trend of a rising standard of living has been halted or even reversed, that the occupational system is closing up to some extent, and that some cuts in higher-ranking occupations are imminent.

We would expect that if (as seems likely) the integrative mechanisms were to become less effective, the strains in the political arena would become increasingly prominent. In that case, the Israeli political establishment would have to find ways of increasing its rapport with the public if it is to keep itself in power and if it is to maintain the present stability and quiescence of the political system. Will the establishment be able to effect this rapprochement and replenish its depleted resources of political support, or will political strains become paramount so that the political elite will eventually be replaced? Is a major restructuring of Israeli politics imminent, or will the dominant party succeed in keeping itself in power by adapting itself to shifts in the public's orientations; for instance in forming a coalition or even a national unity government with the right-wing Likud? These are questions that can be answered only by future developments.

Recently some voices in the Israeli public have been calling for a "strong leadership" capable of navigating the country with a surer hand. Various signs of political distress suggest that the scene is ripe for a more charismatic type of leadership (Weber 1969, p. 245). But whether such leadership will be forthcoming, and, if so, whether it will remain within the confines of the established democratic procedures, are again questions that only the future can decide.

THE WAR IMPACT

Leaving the future to supply its own answers, we turn once more to the recent past and regard the same developments from a different perspective: that of the impact of the War. While it is reasonable to presume that the overall Israeli-Arab conflict, the state of siege, and the continuous threat to Israel's existence have had a cohesive effect on Israeli society, this presumption cannot be examined on the basis of empirical data. On the other hand, some evidence exists with regard to the specific implications of active warfare on the Israeli public.*

---

*The causative effect of the warfare has not been empirically established but tentative conclusion can be reached on the basis of time sequences.

It is popularly believed that both the 1967 and 1973 wars made a major impact on Israeli society. Is this in fact the case? One important change that definitely occurred in the wake of the Six-Day War was the unprecedented blooming of empirical social research. The reader will have noticed that most of the research on which the present analysis is based was done during and after this war—the reason being that little had been done before. For this same reason, there are few areas in which the situation before and after this war could be compared. More extensive data exist with regard to the Yom Kippur War, but here there is a different problem. That war is still a relatively recent occurrence and the last word is not yet in on the changes it brought about. Therefore, whatever conclusions we have reached must necessarily be tentative.

Keeping this qualification in mind, we may attempt some preliminary observations; of necessity, they must be focused chiefly on the Yom Kippur War. We saw that the political orientations of the Israeli public as expressed on the left-right continuum were only slightly affected by this war. The trend toward the right was not reversed, but a certain polarization occurred; somewhat more people opted for either the left or the right, and fewer aligned themselves with the center. In a way, this indicates a growing tendency to prefer the extremist view, but this tendency was so slight that no far-reaching significance may be attributed to it. Besides, the latest survey on this topic was conducted very shortly after the war. Only later research could have indicated whether this trend was subsequently perpetuated.

We further saw that electoral consent for Israel's ruling Alignment declined after the war, as did orally expressed consent for the government's policy. Since the evidence indicates that after the war, the majority of the public held the government responsible for the aggravation of Israel's situation, it is reasonable to presume that the war had something to do with this decline in consent. Yet we also noted that this decline had begun well before the war. Furthermore, public opinion research has indicated that the results of the election (which closely followed the war) could have been predicted rather accurately before the war (Peres et al. 1975). At most, then, the war gave further impetus to a trend that had begun before and that was due mainly to other factors.

After the war more persons than before expressed the wish to influence government policy, while the widespread sense of inability to do so remained more or less as it had been before. Hence we conclude that the existing gap between rather widespread professed involvement and a much less widespread sense of efficacy that we noted in recent years became somewhat more pronounced after the war.

This is further attested by the fact that shortly after the war a protest movement sprung up that was focused precisely on this issue. While it started out protesting the "mechdal" and demanding the resignation of those directly

CONCLUSION

responsible for it, the movement soon came to voice complaints focused on more pervasive and fundamental issues, especially the imperviousness of the political elite, and the weakness of democratic procedures designed to furnish channels of upward political communication. But this protest movement subsided as suddenly as it had appeared. What is more, it achieved only marginal changes; the substantial transformations in Israel's political system for which it had clamored did not come about.

One area in which both the Six-Day War and the Yom Kippur War have clearly made an impact is that of national identifications. The national commitments of Israelis that had been strong and pervasive even before the wars were clearly strengthened in the wake of the Six-Day War. In the Yom Kippur War, a certain intensification of some national commitments was similarly evident. But some time after this war these had reverted to their prewar level (which in any case had been very high to begin with). Consequently, it looks as if the Yom Kippur War did have some intensifying effect on Israelis' collective national commitments, but that this was not a lasting effect.

A similar conclusion emerges with regard to morale and solidarity. The Six-Day War brought in its wake a rising of morale and solidarity, while the Yom Kippur War produced a lowering of morale and a heightening of solidarity. But in both cases the effects were transitory; some time after the wars were over, solidarity and, especially, morale reverted to typical interwar (or rather semiwar) levels.

In conclusion, it seems that in practically all areas examined the wars (and mainly the Yom Kippur War) have had some effects. But these were either a further intensification of trends that had been evident beforehand, or else were rather short-lived. Contrary to what is popularly believed, we must conclude, then, that in none of the areas studied did the wars result in any basic and lasting transformations.

It is possible, of course, that the long-range effects of the Yom Kippur War will become evident only at a later time. It is also possible, though we hope that this will not be the case, that yet another war will further intensify tendencies that have barely become visible after the Yom Kippur War. But other contingencies are equally feasible. The Jewish tradition maintains that since the destruction of the Temple in Jerusalem, prophecy has been confined to minors and fools. As the authors stand no chance of being subsumed under the first category, they do not wish to incur the risk of being included in the second one; hence it seems preferable to abstain from prophesying for the future. As Israelis are used to saying: "We shall live and we shall see."

APPENDIX A
LIST OF QUESTIONS

The following is a list of the questions* employed in the various studies and surveys referred to in this book.†

Questions appearing in one or more IIASR surveys

1) How is your mood these days? (Good almost always or always; mostly good; sometimes good and sometimes not good; mostly not good; almost always not good)
2) Are you worried these days? (Always; almost always; frequently; sometimes; almost never or never)
3) What is your opinion on the manner in which the government is handling the problems of the present situation? (Very well; well; not too well; not at all well)
4) What is your opinion on the manner in which the government is handling the problems of children's education? (Very well; well; not too well; not well; not at all well)
5) What is your opinion on the manner in which the government is handling terrorism? (As above)
6) What is your opinion on the manner in which the government is handling the country's security problems? (As above)
7) What is your opinion on the manner in which the government is handling the country's economic problems? (As above)
8) Would you say that the government is doing enough to aid the disadvantaged? (Much too much; too much; the right extent; too little; much too little)
9) Do you think the government should spend a lot of money to aid the disadvantaged? (Definitely yes; yes; perhaps; no; definitely not)
10) Would you support an aggressive policy of Israel toward the Arab countries? (Definitely; to a large extent; no; definitely not)
11) Do you think that Israel's policy toward the Arab countries should be more adamant or more moderate than it is at present? (Much more adamant; somewhat more adamant; as it is; somewhat more moderate; much more moderate)

---

*With slight abbreviations.
†Precoded response categories are listed in parentheses. Standard social background questions are not listed. Only questions analyzed in this essay are listed.

APPENDIX A

12) With regard to the held territories—what is the greatest concession that should be made in order to attain a peace agreement with the Arab countries? (Give up all or almost all territories; most territories; small part of territories; no territories whatsoever)
13) Do you think that now the relations between the observant and the nonobservant are good? (Very good; fairly good; not so good; not good at all)
14) Do you think that now the relations between the ethnicities are good? (As above)
15) With what political trend do you identify? (Left; moderate left; center; right)
16) Do you plan to vote in the forthcoming Knesset elections? For what party do you intend to vote? (List of parties; not decided; will not vote)
17) Is it personally important to you to vote in the Knesset elections? (Very important; important; not too important; not at all important)
18) Do you support a party, are you a party member and/or do you hold a party post? (Member and holds paid post; member but holds no post; party supporter; not party supporter)
19) Did you listen to parties' election campaigns on the radio? (Every day; frequently; rarely; never)
20) Did you see parties' election campaigns on television? (As above)
21) Are you active in the present election campaign? (Very active; active; not too active; not active at all)
22) How important is it for you to criticize the government's actions when they are unjustified? (Very important; important; not too important; not at all important)
23) Do you personally wish to influence government policy? (Definitely; yes; no; definitely not)
24) Do you think that you and people like you (or you and your friends) can exert an influence on the government's policy decisions? (Greatly; to some extent; to a small extent; not at all) (Sometimes with 5 response categories—see Chapter 4)
25) Do you discuss politics with your friends? (Frequently; sometimes; rarely; not at all)
26) Has your family's economic situation improved or deteriorated recently? (Great improvement; some improvement; no change; some deterioration; great deterioration)
27) Do you expect your family's economic situation to improve or to deteriorate in the coming year? (As above)
28) To what extent are you satisfied with your situation? (Greatly; somewhat; no; not at all)
29) Do you observe the religious tradition? (Yes, absolutely; to a great extent; a little; not at all)

30) Do you feel yourself to be part of the Jewish people of the world? (Definitely; yes; no; definitely not)
31) Do you regard yourself as a Zionist? (As above)
32) Do you think the Jews in Israel and the Jews abroad have a common fate? (As above)
33) If you had a chance, would you like to live outside of Israel? (As above)
34) The Jews abroad have an obligation to support Israel. (Definitely agree; agree; don't agree; definitely don't agree)
35) Are you sure that you will remain in Israel? (Sure; pretty sure; possibly but not sure; probably won't remain; almost certainly won't remain)
36) Do you want your children to live permanently in Israel? (Very much; yes; pretty much; not too anxious; no; very much don't want)
37) To what extent are the following topics influential in making you think that perhaps it would be a good thing to leave Israel?
    - The political regime (Very influential; influential; not too influential; not at all influential)
    - The tax policy (As above)
    - The authorities' handling of citizens (As above)
38) The youth in Israel should be educated toward Zionism (Definitely agree; agree; don't agree; definitely don't agree)

The Arian Study (Arian 1973) Questions: 10; 15; 16; 18; 20; 24; 29.

39) Among the following factors, does any one stand out as the most important one in determining your vote for the Knesset? Which is the most important in your opinion? (Identification with the party; the party's candidate; the party's stand on various issues)
40) In the event that the party would change its position on the subject which you mentioned in a previous question (i.e., the topic most important in determining his party support), would you change your vote? (Yes; no; would not vote at all; did not cite a topic in previous question)
41) Do you usually go to lectures on political subjects? (Often; rarely; never)
42) In the period before the elections, do you participate in meetings organized by the parties? (As above)
43) What do you usually prefer on the radio: entertainment and amusement; culture and education; or news and information? (Entertainment, culture, information; information, entertainment, culture, etc. ....)
44) To what extent are you interested in the Knesset voting results? (Very interested; interested; not interested; not at all interested)
45) To what extent do you take an interest in the foreign affairs of Israel? (As above)
46) To what extent do you take an interest in the economic problems of Israel? (As above)
47) To what extent do you take an interest in the social problems of Israel? (As above)

48) Do you occasionally discuss subjects concerned with the State of Israel with acquaintances, friends, colleagues at work, or family? About how frequently?
 - Topics of foreign policy and security? (Very often; sometimes; rarely; not at all)
 - Economic topics? (As above)
 - Social topics? (As above)
49) Concerning the structure of the country's economic life—do you support the socialist approach or the capitalist approach? (Absolutely capitalist; more capitalist than socialist; more socialist than capitalist; absolutely socialist)

The General and Panel Study (1973)   Questions: 5; 7; 8; 9; 12; 15; 16; 17; 18; 24; 25; 29; 41; 42; 45.

50) Are you generally interested in politics? (Greatly; fairly; not too much; not at all)
51) Lately it has been claimed that there is a socioeconomic gap (between different groups) in this country. Are you generally interested in these problems? (As above)
52) To what extent will this topic influence your voting in the next elections? (As above)
53) Would you say that the socioeconomic gaps in this country are too great? (Definitely; yes; no; definitely not)
54) When you think of employees on a lower vocational level—would you say that the differences between their incomes and yours are: (Too great; as they should be; too small)
55) And what about employees on a higher level than you are—would you say that the differences between their incomes and yours are: (As above)
56) Do you agree that the Histadrut should be both the owner of enterprises and the representative of employees? (Definitely; yes; no; definitely not)
57) Some people say that through elections politicians utilize citizens for their own ends. Do you agree with this opinion? (As above)
58) Some people claim that a few strong leaders would benefit the country more than do laws and discussions. Do you agree or disagree? (As above)
59) Do you think that elections impair the nation's unity? (To a great extent; to some extent; to a small extent; not at all)
60) Do you think that the government will solve (Israel's two most important problems) in the near future? (Both; the first only; the second only; neither)
61) Think of an ideal party you would like to see in office. How would you classify such a party:

Leftist	1	2	3	4	5	6	Rightist
Working class		1	2	3	4	5	6	Middle class

Panel Survey (1973)   Questions: 15; 17; 18; 19; 20; 21; 23; 24; 25; 50.
62) Do you read parties' advertisements in newspapers? (Yes; no)
63) How important is it for you to gain a better understanding of politics in this country? (Very; to some extent; to a small extent; not at all)
64) How important is it for you to gain a better understanding of how democracy works? (As above)
65) How important is it for you to have a say on which party will be in office? (As above)

The Accompanying Survey (1973)   Questions: 15; 61.
Shapira and Etzioni-Halevy Students Project (Shapira and Etzioni-Halevy 1973).

Question: 49.

66) Please give your opinion on the following statements: Every Jew, wherever he may be, ought to feel some obligation toward Israel. (Definitely agree; agree; don't agree; definitely don't agree)
67) Every Israeli ought to feel some obligation toward Jews in the Diaspora. (As above)
68) Our government may make mistakes occasionally, but basically it is going in the right direction. (As above)
69) Every person in Israel has a chance of getting ahead if only he invests the necessary efforts. (As above)
70) A person's success in Israel depends mainly on his talent and education. (As above)
71) To succeed in Israel, it is not enough to be talented and educated; one also needs connections with the "right people." (As above)
72) Concerning an Israeli university graduate who has some difficulties in finding work, would you say that:
    - If he cannot find work in Israel, he should live wherever he can work in his field. (As above)
    - The place of every Israeli is in Israel and he should stay here under any circumstances. (As above)
    - If he can get ahead better in another country, he should live there. (As above)
    - If in another country he can contribute more to the development of science, he should live there. (As above)
73) How would you define your feelings concerning the situation in Israel today:

1	2	3	4	5	6

Satisfied   Unsatisfied

74) How would you define your political orientation:

| 1 | 2 | 3 | 4 | 5 | 6 | 7 |

Leftist   Rightist

75) Do you feel that being Jewish is important in your life?

| 1 | 2 | 3 | 4 | 5 | 6 |

Unimportant   Important

76) Do you feel that being Israeli is important in your life?

| 1 | 2 | 3 | 4 | 5 | 6 |

Unimportant   Important

77) Please place yourself on the following continua:

| 1 | 2 | 3 | 4 | 5 | 6 |

Weak Jewish feeling   Strong Jewish feeling

78)

| 1 | 2 | 3 | 4 | 5 | 6 |

Weak Israeli feeling   Strong Israeli feeling

79) In your opinion, what are the chances that you will be able to realize your occupational aspirations in Israel?

| 1 | 2 | 3 | 4 | 5 | 6 |

Very good   Not good at all

Shapira et al.'s Project on High School Students and Graduates (Shapira et al. 1975). Questions: 49; 66; 67; 69; 70; 71; 72; 74; 77; 78.

80) Are you satisfied with the manner in which the government is handling the problems of the present situation?

| 1 | 2 | 3 | 4 | 5 | 6 |

Unsatisfied   Satisfied

The Katz-Gurevitz Study (Katz-Gurevitz 1973)

81) Are you a member of any organizations? If so, which? (Political, vocational; voluntary; others—which?; not member)
82) Do you read newspapers? (Morning paper only; evening paper only; both; none)
83) How often? (Daily; a few times a week; Saturdays only; less frequently)
84) How important is it for you:

- To understand what is going on in Israel and in the world? (Very important; somewhat important; not important; no opinion)
- To keep track of how the government fulfills its task? (As above)
85) State your opinion on the following: The State of Israel cannot survive without strong ties with Jews in the Diaspora. (Definitely agree; agree; don't agree; definitely don't agree; no opinion)
86) The Jewish people cannot survive without Israel. (As above)

The Herman Study (Herman 1970)
87) Does the fact that you are Jewish play an important part in your life? (A very important part; an important part; is of little importance; plays no part)
88) Does the fact that you are Israeli play an important part in your life? (As above)
- Are you: (Religious; traditionalist; nonreligious)?
89) Are your parents: (As above)?
90) Are you: (More religious than your parents; as religious as your parents; less religious than your parents)?

The Fein Project (Fein 1962) Questions: 25; 42; 50.
91) In the last elections, did you work in any way for the election of any party? (Yes; no)
92) People like you have no influence over the government. (Strongly agree; agree; disagree; strongly disagree; undecided)
93) How often do you read a daily newspaper? (Every day; several times a week; once a week; less than once a week; never)

Voter Questionnaire; Youth Survey; New Immigrant Survey (1973) Questions: 15; 25.

Antonovsky Project (Antonovsky 1963A and B) Questions: 15; 29; 49. Question on support of Zionist idea (not specified)

Cohen High School Project (Cohen 1975) Questions: 29, 30.
To what extent does the following influence your desire to be part of the Israeli society?:
- The Zionist ideology (Greatly; somewhat; no; not at all)
To what extent is it important for you to understand Zionism? (As above)

Zloczower Project (Zloczower 1972) Questions not specified.

APPENDIX B
MILESTONES IN THE ISRAELI-ARAB CONFLICT

This book is not directly concerned with foreign policy or Israeli-Arab relations. However, to make developments in Israel's political culture meaningful to the non-Israeli reader, it is necessary to call to his attention the major milestones in the Israeli-Arab conflict in recent years:

June 1967: The Six-Day War, which ended in a spectacular victory for Israel; the Golan Heights, the West Bank, and the Sinai Peninsula were conquered.

July 1967–April 1969: Ceasefire period (although incidents continued).

May 1969–July 1970: War of Attrition between Israel and Egypt, with a less successful outcome for Israel.

August 1970–September 1973: Ceasefire period.

October–November 1973: The Yom Kippur War, in which Israel was taken unaware and whose outcome was even less successful from the Israeli point of view.

December 1973: Ceasefire with Egypt.

January 1974: Disengagement agreement with Egypt.

April 1974: Terrorist onslaught on Kiryat Shmona, in which civilians (including children) were massacred.

May 1974: Terrorist onslaught on Ma'alot, in which school children were massacred.

June 1974: Disengagement agreement with Syria.

September 1975: Interim agreement with Egypt, in which Israel agreed to withdraw from the strategic Sinai passes and the Sinai oil fields.

APPENDIX C
GLOSSARY OF MAJOR PARTIES IN THE YISHUV AND IN ISRAEL

Hebrew Name   *Translation*

IN THE YISHUV

The Radical Left

Hebrew Name	Translation
Komunistim	Communists
Poalei Zion Smol	Zion's Workers - Left

The Left

Hebrew Name	Translation
Hashomer Hatzair	The Young Guard
Poalei Zion	Zion's Workers
Hapoel Hatzair	The Young Worker
Achdut Ha'avoda	The Unity of Labor
Mifleget Poalei Eretz Israel (MAPAI)	The Land of Israel Workers' Party

The Center-Right

Hebrew Name	Translation
Aliya Hadasha later: Progressivim	New Immigration later: Progressives
Various "Citizens' Groups" (e.g., The Farmers' Association; The Craftsmen's Association)	
Zionim Klalliyim	General Zionists
Harevisionistim	The Revisionists

The Religious Bloc

Hebrew Name	Translation
Hamizrachi	Religious Party (literally: The Oriental)
Hapoel Hamizrachi	Religious Workers' Party (literally: The Oriental Worker)
Agudat Israel	Orthodox Religious Party (literally: The Collectivity of Israel)
Poalei Agudat Israel	Orthodox Workers' Party (literally: The Collectivity of Israel's Workers)

IN ISRAEL

The Radical Left

Miflaga Komunistit Israelit (MAKI)	Israel Communist Party
Moked	Focus
Reshima Komunistit Chadasha (RAKACH)	New Communist List

The Left

Mifleget Hapoalim Hameuchedet (MAPAM)	United Workers' Party
Achdut Ha'avoda	The Unity of Labor
Mifleget Poalei Eretz Israel (MAPAI)	Land of Israel Workers' Party
Reshimat Poalei Israel (RAFI)	Israel Workers' List
Mifleget Ha'avoda Haisraelit	Israel Labor Party (ILP)
Maarach	Alignment

The Center-Right

Progressivim - later: Liberalim Azmaim (LAMED-AIN)	Progressives - later: Independent Liberals
Zionim Klaliyim later: Liberalim	General Zionists later: Liberals
Herut	Freedom Party
Gush-Herut Liberalim (GACHAL)	Herut-Liberals Bloc
Hamerkaz Hachofshi	Free Center
Hareshima Hamamlachtit	State List
Likud	Center Right Alignment (literally: Cohesion)

The Religious Bloc

Hamizrachi	Religious Party (literally: The Oriental)
Hapoel Hamizrachi	Religious Workers' Party (literally: The Oriental Worker)
Miflaga Datit-Leumit (Mafdal)	National Religious Party
Agudat Israel	Orthodox Religious Party (literally: Collectivity of Israel)

Poalei Agudat Israel Orthodox Workers' Party
(literally: Collectivity of
Israel's Workers)

APPENDIX D
ELECTORAL BASIS OF ISRAEL'S GOVERNMENTS AND OF THE MAJOR OPPOSITION PARTIES

(IN PERCENTAGES)

			Electoral Support for Coalition Parties	Total Electoral Support for Government	Electoral Support for Major Opposition Party*
First Knesset	First Government (1949-50) Premier: D. Ben-Gurion	Mapai	35.7		
		Religious Party	12.2	57.2	Mapam 14.7
		Independent Liberals (Progressives)	4.1		
		Others	5.2		
First Knesset	Second Government (1950-51) Premier: D. Ben-Gurion	Same as First Government		57.2	Same as before
Second Knesset	Third Government (1951-52) Premier: D. Ben-Gurion	Mapai	37.3		
		Religious Party	11.9	55.6	General Zionists 16.2 (Liberals)
		Others	6.4		
Second Knesset	Fourth Government (1952-54) Premier: D. Ben-Gurion	Mapai	37.3		
		General Zionists (Liberals)	16.2		
		Religious Parties	8.3	72.6	Mapam 12.5
		Independent Liberals (Progressives)	3.2		
		Others	7.6		
Second Knesset	Fifth Government (1954-55) Premier: M. Sharet	Same as Fourth Government		72.6	Same as before

(continued)

(Appendix D continued)

			Electoral Support for Coalition Parties	Total Electoral Support for Government	Electoral Support for Major Opposition Party*
Second Knesset	Sixth Government	Mapai	37.3		
		Religious Parties	8.3		
	(1955-56)			53.5	General Zionists (Liberals) 16.2
		Independent Liberals			
	Premier:	(Progressives)	3.2		
	M. Sharet	Others	4.7		
Third Knesset	Seventh Government	Mapai	32.2		
	(1955-58)	Religious Party	9.1		
		Achdut Ha' avoda	8.2		
	Premier:				
	D. Ben-Gurion	Mapam	7.3	65.6	Herut 12.6
		Independent Liberals (Progressives)	4.4		
		Others	4.4		
Third Knesset	Eighth Government				
	(1958-59)	Same as Seventh Government		65.6	Same as before
	Premier:				
	D. Ben-Gurion				
Fourth Knesset	Ninth Government	Mapai	38.2		
	(1959-61)	Religious Party	9.9		
		Mapam	7.2		
	Premier:			69.4	Herut 13.5
		Achdut Ha' avoda	6.0		
	D. Ben-Gurion	Independent Liberals (Progressives)	4.6		
		Others	3.5		
Fifth Knesset	Tenth Government	Mapai	34.7		
	(1961-63)	Religious Parties	11.7		
		Achdut Ha' avoda	6.6	56.5	Herut 13.8
	Premier:				
	D. Ben-Gurion	Others	3.5		
Fifth Knesset	Eleventh Government				
	(1963-64)	Same as Tenth Government		56.5	Same as before
	Premier:				
	L. Eshkol				

Knesset	Government	Parties	%	Total %	Opposition
Fifth Knesset	Twelfth Government (1964-66) Premier: L. Eshkol	Same as Tenth Government		56.5	Same as before
Sixth Knesset	Thirteenth Government (1966-67) Premier: L. Eshkol	Mapai/Achdut Ha' avoda Religious Parties Mapam Independent Liberals (Progressives) Others	36.7 10.7 6.6 3.8 3.8	61.6	Gachal† 21.3
Sixth Knesset	Fourteenth Government (1967-69) Premier: L. Eshkol	Gachal (21.3) and Rafi (7.9) joined the Thirteenth Government coalition to form a National Unity Government		90.8	
Sixth Knesset	Fifteenth Government (1969) Premier: G. Meir	Same as Fourteenth Government		90.8	
Seventh Knesset	Sixteenth Government 1970 Premier: G. Meir	Alignment of Israel Labor Party (Mapai, Rafi, Achdut Ha' avoda) + Mapam Gachal Religious Parties Independent Liberals (Progressives) Others	46.2 21.7 9.7 3.2 3.5	84.3	
Seventh Knesset	Seventeenth Government (1970-73) Premier: G. Meir	Gachal 21.7 resigned from the Sixteenth Government coalition		62.6	Gachal 21.7
Eighth Knesset	Eighteenth Government (March 1974 April 1974) Premier: G. Meir	Alignment Religious Party Independent Liberals Others	39.6 8.3 3.6 3.3	54.8	Likud‡ 30.2

(continued)

(Appendix D continued)

			Electoral Support for Coalition Parties	Total Electoral Support for Government	Electoral Support for Major Opposition Party*
Eighth Knesset	Nineteenth Government (June 1974 - Oct.1974) Premier: Y. Rabin	Alignment Independent Liberals Others	39.6 3.6 5.5	48.7	Same as before
Eighth Knesset	Twentieth Government (Oct. 1974 -) Premier: Y. Rabin	Alignment Independent Liberals Religious Party Others	39.6 3.6 8.3 3.3	54.8	Same as before

Explanatory Remarks: 1) For the sake of brevity, the table does not report *which* religious party or parties are part of any particular government coalition, and does not enumerate which parties are included in the category of "others."

2) The Nineteenth Government had an electoral support of less than 50 percent; nevertheless it had the support of 61 members of Parliament. This was so because the Israeli system of proportional representation always leaves a handful of seats undistributed and it leaves each party with varying numbers of votes that are not enough to credit it with another "whole" Knesset seat. In the past, a party's claim for one of the undistributed seats depended on how many leftover votes it had. Recently, however, an amendment to the Knesset Election bill was passed by which surplus votes are redistributed to the advantage of the largest parties.

*For details on the various parties see, Chapters 1 and 3.
†Composed of Herut plus General Zionists (Liberals).
‡Composed of Gachal, Hareshima Hamamhachlit plus Hamerkaz Hachofschi.
Source: Israel Government (1950-76).

BIBLIOGRAPHY

GENERAL

Adar, Lea, and Haim Adler. 1965. *Education For Values in Schools For Immigrant Children in Israel.* Jerusalem: School of Education of the Hebrew University and the Ministry of Education.

Adler, H. 1972. "The Student Revolt: A Special Case of Youth Culture." *Megamot* 18: 313–23. (Hebrew).

Almond, Gabriel A., and Sidney Verba. 1965. *The Civic Culture.* Boston: Little Brown.

Antonovsky, Aaron. 1963A. "Israeli Political-Social Attitudes." *Amot* 6: 11–22. (Hebrew).

———. 1963B. "Political Ideologies of Israelis." *Amot* 7: 21–28. (Hebrew).

Apter, David E. 1955. *The Gold Coast in Transition.* Princeton: Princeton University Press.

Arian, Alan. 1975. "Were the 1973 Elections in Israel Critical?" In *The Elections in Israel—1973,* ed. Alan Arian, pp. 287–308. Jerusalem: Academic Press.

———. 1973. *The Choosing People: Voting Behavior in Israel.* Cleveland: Press of Case Western Reserve University.

———. 1972. *The Elections in Israel—1969.* Jerusalem: Jerusalem Academic Press.

———. 1971. "Stability and Change in Israel Public Opinion and Politics." *Public Opinion Quarterly* 35: 19–35.

———. 1968. *Ideological Change in Israel.* Cleveland: Press of Case Western Reserve University.

Aronoff, Myron J. 1975. "The Power of Nominations in the Israeli Labor Party." in *The Elections in Israel—1973,* ed. Alan Arian, pp. 21–38. Jerusalem: Academic Press.

———. 1972. "Party Center and Local Branch Relationship: The Israel Labor Party." In *The Elections in Israel—1969,* ed. Alan Arian, pp. 152–83. Jerusalem: Academic Press.

Barkai, Haim. 1964. *The Public Sector, the Histadrut Sector and the Private Sector in the Israeli Economy. Sixth Report.* Jerusalem: Falk Project. (Hebrew).

Ben Raphael, Eliezer. 1973. *The Student Revolution—A Comparative Research: The U.S.A., Germany, France.* Jerusalem: Hebrew University of Jerusalem. (Hebrew).

Blau-Luksemburg, Joana. 1976. "Status Inconsistency, Voting and Support of Government Policy" M.A. Thesis, Tel Aviv University. (Hebrew).

Bluhm, William T. 1974. *Ideologies and Attitudes.* Englewood Cliffs, N.J.: Prentice-Hall.

Blumer, Herbert. 1967. "Society as Symbolic Interaction." In *Symbolic Interaction,* eds. Jerome G. Manis and Bernard M. Meltzer, pp. 145-63. Boston: Allyn & Bacon.

Boim, Leon. 1971-72. *Financing of the Parties and of the Elections in Israel.* Tel Aviv: Mifal Ha-Shichpul. (Hebrew).

Brichta, Abraham. 1972. "The Social and Political Characteristics of Members of the Seventh Knesset." In *The Elections in Israel—1969,* ed. Alan Arian, pp. 109-31. Jerusalem: Academic Press.

Brinton, Crane. 1959. *The Anatomy of Revolution.* New York: Vintage Books.

Campbell, Angus, Philip E. Converse, and Donald E. Stokes. 1960. *The American Voter.* New York: Wiley.

Carter, April. 1973. *Direct Action and Liberal Democracy.* London: Routledge & K. Paul.

Citrin, Jack. 1974. "Comment: The Political Relevance of Trust in Government." *American Political Science Review* 68: 973-88.

Chanoch, Giora. 1961. *Income Differentials in Israel.* Jerusalem: Falk Project, Fifth Report, 1959-1960. (Hebrew).

Cohen, Erik. 1972. "The Black Panthers in Israeli Society." *Jewish Journal of Sociology* 14: 93-110.

_____. 1968. "Emigration in the Eyes of Emigrants." In *Immigrants in Israel,* ed. Moshe Lissak, Beverly Mizrachi, and Ofra Ben-David, pp. 787-808. Jerusalem: Akademon. (Hebrew).

Cohen, Erik, Lea Shamgar, and Yael Levi. 1962. *Research on Absorption of Immigrants in Development Towns. A Summary Report.* Jerusalem: Department of Sociology, Hebrew University. (Hebrew).

Cohen, Oved. 1975. "The Conflict Between Religious and Non-Religious Jews in Israel: Solidarity and Social Distance Among High School Students." Ph.D. Dissertation, Hebrew University.

Converse, Philip E. 1972. "Change in the American Electorate." In *The Human Meaning of Social Change,* eds. Angus Campbell and Philip E. Converse, pp. 263-338. New York: Russell Sage Foundation.

_____. 1964. "The Nature of Belief Systems in Mass Publics." In *Ideology and Discontent,* ed. David Apter, pp. 206-61. London: Free Press of Glencoe.

Coser, Lewis A. 1956. *The Functions of Social Conflict.* New York: The Free Press.

Dahl, Robert A. 1961. *Who Governs? Democracy and Power in an American City.* New Haven: Yale University Press.

Dahrendorf, Ralf. 1959. *Class and Class Conflict in Industrial Society.* Stanford, Calif.: Stanford University Press.

Darin-Drabkin, Haim. n.d. "Financing Residence Construction." In *Israel Economy—Theory and Practice,* ed. Joseph Ronen, pp. 464–73. Tel Aviv: Dvir. (Hebrew).

———. 1957. *Housing in Israel: Economic and Sociological Aspects.* Tel Aviv: Gadish.

Davies, James. 1962. "Toward a Theory of Revolution." *American Sociological Review* 27: 5–15.

De Tocqueville, Alexis. 1955. *The Old Regime and the French Revolution.* Garden City, N.Y.: Doubleday & Company, Anchor Books Edition.

Derber, Milton. 1970. "Israel Wage Differential: A Persisting Problem." In *Integration and Development in Israel,* eds. Shmuel N. Eisenstadt, Rivkah Bar-Yosef, and Chaim Adler, pp. 185–201. Jerusalem: Israel Universities Press.

Deshen, Shlomo A. 1975. "Israeli Judaism: Introduction to the Major Pattern." Unpublished.

———. 1972. "The Business of Ethnicity is Finished? The Ethnic Factor in a Local Election Campaign." In *The Elections in Israel—1969,* ed. Alan Arian, pp. 278–302. Jerusalem: Academic Press.

———. 1970. *Immigrant Voters in Israel; Parties and Congregations in a Local Election Campaign.* Manchester: Manchester University Press, 1970.

Devine, Donald J. 1972. *The Political Culture of the United States.* Boston: Little Brown.

DiPalma, Giuseppe. 1970. *Apathy and Participation.* New York: Free Press.

Downes, Bryan T. 1969. "Social and Political Characteristics of Riot Cities: A Comparative Study." In *Blacks in the United States,* eds. Norval D. Glenn and Charles M. Bonjean, pp. 427–43. San Francisco: Chandler.

Duncan, Otis D. 1966. "Methodological Issues in the Analysis of Social Mobility." In *Social Structure and Mobility in Economic Development,* eds. Seymour M. Lipset and Neil J. Smelser, pp. 51–97. Chicago: Aldine.

Duverger, Maurice. 1964. *Political Parties: Their Organisation and Activity in the Modern State.* London: Methuen.

Easton, David. 1965. *A Systems Analysis of Political Life,* New York: Wiley.

Eckstein, Harry. 1966. *Division and Cohesion in Democracy; A Study of Norway.* Princeton, N.J.: Princeton University Press.

Edelman, Murray J. 1971. *Politics as Symbolic Action.* New York: Academic Press.

———. 1964. *The Symbolic Uses of Politics.* Urbana: University of Illinois Press.

Eisenstadt, Shmuel N. 1970. "Israel: Traditional and Modern Social Values and Economic Development." In *Integration and Development in Israel,* ed. Shmuel N. Eisenstadt, pp. 107–22. Jerusalem: Israel University Press.

———. 1968. "Ideology and Social Change." In *American Sociology,* ed. Talcott Parsons, pp. 304–18. New York: Basic Books.

———. 1967. *Israeli Society.* London: Weidenfeld and Nicolson.

———. 1966. *Modernization: Protest and Change.* Englewood Cliffs, N.J.: Prentice-Hall.

Eisenstadt, Shmuel N., ed. 1956. *Political Sociology.* Tel Aviv: Am-Oved. (Hebrew).

Eshkol, Levi. n. d. "The Israeli Development Policy." In *Israel Economy—Theory and Practice,* ed. Joseph Ronen, pp. 4–27. Tel Aviv: Dvir. (Hebrew).

Etzioni, Amitai, 1966A. "Change in the System: Alternative Ways to Democracy—The Case of Israel." In his *Studies in Social Change,* pp. 157–79. New York: Holt, Rinehart and Winston.

———. 1966B. "Change in the System: The Decline of Neo-Feudalism in Israel." In his *Studies in Social Change,* pp. 180–97. New York: Holt, Rinehart and Winston.

Etzioni, Eva, 1969. "Jewish Identification of Tel Aviv University Students." M.A. Thesis, Tel Aviv University.

Etzioni-Halevy, Eva. 1975A, Fall. "Protest Politics in the Israeli Democracy." *Political Science Quarterly* 90: 497–520.

———. 1975B, June. "Patterns of Conflict Generation and Conflict 'Absorption'. The Cases of Israeli Labor and Ethnic Conflicts." *Journal of Conflict Resolution* 19: 286–309.

———. 1975C, February. "Some Patterns of Semi-Deviance on the Israeli Social Scene." *Social Problems* 22: 356–67.

———. 1973. "The Other Gap." *Maariv,* September 12. (Hebrew).

———. 1971. "Attitudes of Israeli Students Towards Emigration: Confrontation of Individual Aspirations with Collective Value Orientations." Ph.D. Thesis, Tel Aviv University.

Etzioni-Halevy, Eva, and Zvi Halevy. "The Jewish Ethic and the Spirit of Achievement." Forthcoming in *The Jewish Journal of Sociology.*

Etzioni-Halevy, Eva, and Moshe Livne. 1976. "The Response of the Israeli Establishment to the Yom Kippur War Protest." Unpublished.

Etzioni-Halevy, Eva, and Rina Shapira. 1975. "Jewish Identification of Israeli Students: What Lies Ahead." *Jewish Social Studies,* 37: 251–66.

Farago, Uri. 1968. "Time Perspectives in Jewish Identity of High School Students." Report to the Blumenson Foundation, Unpublished.

Fein, Leonard J. 1967. *Politics in Israel.* Boston: Little Brown.

———. 1962. *The Political Worlds of Jerusalem's People.* Michigan State University, Ph.D.

Free, Lloyd A., and Hadley Cantril. 1967. *The Political Beliefs of Americans.* New Brunswick, N.J.: Rutgers University Press.

Gamson, William A. 1968. *Power and Discontent.* Homewood, Ill.: Dorsey Press.

Germani, Gino. 1966. "Social and Political Consequences of Mobility." In *Social Structure and Mobility in Economic Development,* eds. Neil J. Smelser and Seymor M. Lipset, pp. 364–94. Chicago: Aldine Publishing Co.

Goldberger, Arthur S. 1964. *Econometric Theory.* New York: Wiley.

Gosnell, Harold F. 1969. *Boss Platt and His New York Machine.* New York: Russell & Russell.

———. 1968. *Machine Politics—Chicago Model.* Chicago: University of Chicago Press.

Green, Robert W., ed. 1959. *Protestantism and Capitalism: The Weber Thesis and its Critics.* Boston: D. C. Heath.

Guttman Louis E., and Dov Elizur. 1972. "Factors Influencing the Remigration of Israelis Living Abroad." In *The Israel Yearbook—1972,* pp. 141–44. Tel Aviv: Israel Yearbook.

Halevi, Nadav, and Ruth Klinov-Malul. 1968. *The Economic Development of Israel.* New York: Praeger.

Hartman, Moshe. 1975. "Grading of Occupations by Sociologists." Paper read at the Israeli Sociological Convention, May, at Ben-Gurion University. Mimeographed.

Hauser, Robert L., and David L. Featherman. 1974. "White-Nonwhite Differentials in Occupational Mobility Among Men in the United States, 1962–1972." *Demography* 11: 247–65.

———. 1973. "Trends in Occupational Mobility of U.S. Men, 1962–1970." *American Sociological Review* 38: 302–10.

Heidenheimer, Arnold J., ed. 1970. *Political Corruption—Readings in Comparative Analysis.* New York: Holt, Rinehart and Winston.

Heilbroner, Robert L. 1972. *The Making of Economic Society.* Englewood Cliffs, N.J.: Prentice-Hall.

Hendelman, Don, and Shlomo A. Deshen. 1975. *The Social Anthropology of Israel.* Tel Aviv University Institute for Social Research, Department of Sociology and Anthropology. (Hebrew).

Hendles, Yeoshua. 1975. "Ego Involvement and the Reaction to a State of Cognitive Imbalance." M.A. Thesis, Tel Aviv University.

Herberg, Will. 1960. *Protestant—Catholic—Jew.* Garden City, N.Y.: Doubleday.

Herman, Simon N. 1970. *Israelis and Jews.* New York: Random House.

Hofman, John E. 1970. "The Ethnic Identity of Jewish Youth in Israel." *Megamot,* Vol. 17, No. 1: 5–14. (Hebrew).

Horowitz, Dan, and Moshe Lissak. 1971. "Authority Without Sovereignty." In *Political Institutions and Processes in Israel,* eds. Moshe Lissak and Emanuel Gutmann. Jerusalem: Akademon.

House, James S., and William M. Mason. 1975. "Political Alienation in America, 1952–1968." *American Sociological Review* 40: 123–47.

Huntington, Samuel P. 1968. *Political Order in Changing Societies.* New Haven: Yale University Press.

Kamen, Charles S. 1975. "The Effect of Crisis on Social Integration: Israel and the Six-Day War." Unpublished.

Katz, Elihu, and Michael Gurevitz. 1973. *The Culture of Leisure in Israel.* Tel Aviv: Am-Oved. (Hebrew).

Kavanagh, Dennis. 1972. *Political Culture.* London: Macmillan Press Ltd.

Key, Valdimer O. 1970. "Techniques of Political Graft." In *Political Corruption—Readings in Comparative Analysis,* ed. Arnold J. Heidenheimer, pp. 46–53. New York: Holt, Rinehart and Winston.

———. 1961. *Public Opinion and American Democracy.* New York: Alfred A. Knopf.

Keydar, Adam. 1972. "The Effect of Political Socialization Within the Family and The Age Groups on Intergenerational Continuity and Change in Patterns of Political Behavior." M.A. Thesis, Tel Aviv University.

Kies, Naomi. 1969. "Consistency Support and the Israeli Party System: An Analysis of Elections in Jerusalem 1959–1965." Ph.D. Dissertation, Massachusetts Institute of Technology.

Kluckhohn, Florence R. 1953. "Dominant and Variant Value Orientations." In *Personality in Nature, Society and Culture,* eds. Clyde Kluckhohn and Henry A. Murray, pp. 342–60. New York: Alfred A. Knopf.

Kornhauser, William A. 1959. *The Politics of Mass Society.* Glencoe, Ill.: The Free Press.

Kriesberg, Louis. 1973. *The Sociology of Social Conflicts.* Englewood Cliffs, N.J.: Prentice-Hall.

Krivine, David. 1965. *Housing in Israel.* Jerusalem: Israel Digest.

Laidler, Harry W. 1947. *Social Economic Movements.* New York: Thomas Y. Crowell.

Lane, Robert E. 1962. *Political Ideology: Why the American Common Man Believes What He Does.* New York: Free Press.

———. 1959. *Political Life: Why People Get Involved in Politics.* Glencoe, Ill.: Free Press.

Leeds, Ruth. 1964. "The Absorption of Protest: A Working Paper." In *New Perspectives in Organization Research,* eds. William W. Cooper, Harold J. Leavitt, and Maynard W. Shelly, pp. 115–35. New York: Wiley.

Lippmann, Walter. 1961. *Public Opinion.* New York: Macmillan.

Lipset, Seymour M. 1972. *Rebellion in the University.* London: Routledge & Kegan Paul.

———. 1963. *Political Man: The Social Bases of Politics.* Garden City, N.Y.: Anchor Books, Doubleday & Company.

Lipset, Seymour M., and Philip G. Altbach. 1966. "Student Politics and Higher Education in the United States." *Comparative Education Review* 10: 320–49.

Lipset, Seymour M., and Hans L. Zetterberg. 1964. "A Theory of Social Mobility." In *Sociological Theory,* eds. Lewis A. Coser and Bernard Rosenberg, pp. 427–53. New York: Macmillan Company.

———. 1959. "Social Mobility in Industrial Societies." In *Social Mobility in Industrial Society,* eds. Seymour M. Lipset and Reinhard Bendix, pp. 11–75. Berkeley, Calif: University of California Press.

Lissak, Moshe. 1970. "Patterns of Change in Ideology and Class Structure in Israel." In *Integration and Development in Israel,* eds. Shmuel N. Eisenstadt, Rivka Bar-Yosef, and Chaim Adler, pp. 141–61. Jerusalem: Israel University Press.

———. 1961. "Expectations for Social Mobility and Choice of an Occupation Among Urban Youth in Israel." Ph.D. Dissertation, Hebrew University.

Lopreato, Joseph. 1967. "Upward Social Mobility and Political Orientation." *American Sociological Review* 32: 586–92.

Lukes, Steven. n. d. "Power—A Radical View." Unpublished.

McClelland, David C. 1961. *The Achieving Society.* Princeton, N.J.: D. Van Nostrand.

McClosky, Herbert. 1964. "Consensus and Ideology in American Politics." *American Political Science Review* 58: 361–82.

MacIntyre, Alasdair C. 1971. "Is A Science of Comparative Politics Possible." In his *Against the Self Images of the Age: Essays on Ideology and Philosophy*, pp. 260–79. London: Duckworth.

Marcuse, Herbert. 1964. *One Dimensional Man.* London: Sphere Books.

Marx, Emanuel. 1971. "The Power Relations between the Authorities and the Citizens." *Davar*, October 1, p. 16. (Hebrew).

Matras, Judah. 1965. *Social Change in Israel.* Chicago: Aldine.

Medding, Peter Y. 1972. *Mapai in Israel.* Cambridge: Cambridge University Press.

Milbrath, Lester W. 1965. *Political Participation: How and Why Do People Get Involved in Politics?* Chicago: Rand McNally.

Miller, Arthur H. 1974A. "Political Issues and Trust in Government: 1964–1970." *American Political Science Review* 68: 951–72.

———. 1974B. "Rejoinder to Comment by Jack Citrin: Political Discontent or Ritualism?" *American Political Science Review* 68: 989–1001.

Mills, C. Wright. 1956. *The Power Elite.* New York: Oxford University Press.

———. 1953. *The Sociological Imagination.* New York: Grove Press.

Moore, Wilbert E., "Changes in Occupational Structures." In *Social Structure and Mobility in Economic Development*, eds. Neil J. Smelser and Seymour M. Lipset, pp. 194–212. Chicago: Aldine Publishing Co.

Mueller, Claus. 1973. *The Politics of Communication.* New York: Oxford University Press.

Nachmias, David. 1973. "Status Inconsistency and Political Opposition: A Case Study of an Israeli Minority Group." *The Middle East Journal*, (Autumn): 456–70.

Neumann, Franz L., ed. 1957. *The Democratic and the Authoritarian State: Essays in Political and Legal Theory.* Glencoe, Ill.: Free Press.

Ofer, Gur. 1967. *The Service Industries in a Developing Economy. Israel as a Case Study.* New York: Praeger.

Pareto, Vilfredo. 1935. *The Mind and Society: A Treatise on General Sociology.* Trans. A. Bongiorno and A. Livingston. New York: Dover.

Parsons, Talcott. 1973. "A Functional Theory of Change." In *Social Change*, eds. Amitai Etzioni and Eva Etzioni-Halevy, pp. 72–86. New York: Basic Books.

Partridge, Percy H. 1971. *Consent and Consensus.* London: Macmillan.

Pateman, Carole. 1970. *Participation and Democratic Theory.* Cambridge: Cambridge University Press.

Patterson, C. L. 1968. "The Political Cultures of the American States." In *Public Opinion and Public Policy,* ed. Norman R. Luttbeg, pp. 275–92. Homewood, Ill.: Dorsey Press.

Peres, Yochanan. 1976. *Ethnic Relations in Israel.* Tel Aviv: Sifriat Poalim. (Hebrew).

_____. 1971. "Ethnic Relations in Israel." *American Journal of Sociology* 76: 1021–47.

Peres, Yochanan, Ephraim Yuchtman (Yaar), and Rivka Shafat. 1975. "Predicting and Explaining Voters' Behavior in Israel." In *The Elections in Israel—1973,* ed. Alan Arian, pp. 189–202. Jerusalem: Academic Press.

Pitkun, Hanna. 1966. "Obligation and Consent—II." *American Political Science Review* 60: 39–52.

_____. 1965. "Obligation and Consent—I." *American Political Science Review* 59: 990–98.

Plamenatz, John P. 1970. *Ideology.* London: Macmillan and Co.

_____. 1968. *Consent, Freedom and Political Obligation.* 2nd. ed. London: Oxford University Press.

Pye, Lucian W. 1965. "Introduction: Political Culture and Political Development." In *Political Culture and Political Development,* eds. Lucian W. Pye and Sidney Verba, pp. 3–26. Princeton, N.J.: Princeton University Press.

Riesman, David. 1973. "From 'Inter-Directed' to 'Other-Directed'." In *Social Change,* eds. Amitai Etzioni and Eva Etzioni-Halevy, pp. 410–20. New York: Basic Books.

Robinson, John P., Jerrold G. Rusk, and Kendra B. Head. 1968. *Measures of Political Attitudes.* Survey Research Center, Institute for Social Research. Ann Arbor, Mich.: University of Michigan Press.

Rose, Richard. 1974. *Electoral Behavior: A Comparative Handbook.* New York: Free Press.

Rosenbaum, Walter E. 1975. *Political Culture.* London: Nelson.

Schrift, Ruth. 1975. "Interethnic and Interracial Marriage." M.A. Thesis, Tel Aviv University. (Hebrew).

Scott, James C. 1970. "Corruption, Machine Politics and Political Change." In *Political Corruption—Readings in Comparative Analysis,* ed. Arnold J. Heidenheimer, pp. 549–63. New York: Holt, Rinehart and Winston.

Seligman, Lester G. 1966. "Political Mobility and Development." In *Mobility in Economic Development,* eds. Seymour M. Lipset and Neil J. Smelser, pp. 340–63. Chicago: Aldine.

Shapira, Rina, Chaim Adler, Miri Lerner, Rachel Peleg, and Zarchovitch Nechemia. 1975. "The Social World of Youth-Movement Graduates in Israel." Research Report, unpublished. (Hebrew).

Shapira, Rina, and Eva Etzioni-Halevy. 1973. *Who is the Israeli Student?* Tel Aviv: Am-Oved. (Hebrew).

Shapiro, Yonathan. 1975. *The Organization of Power.* Tel Aviv: Am-Oved. (Hebrew).

Shils, Edward A. 1975. "Center and Periphery." In his *Center and Periphery: Essays in Macrosociology,* pp. 3–16. Chicago: University of Chicago Press.

———. 1965. "Charisma, Order and Status." *American Sociological Review* 30: 199–213.

Shils, Edward A., and Morris Janowitz. 1948. "Cohesion and Disintegration in the Wehrmacht in World War II." *Public Opinion Quarterly* 12: 280–315.

Smith, Hanoch. 1971. "Analysis of the Election Results of The Sixth Knesset." In *Political Institutions and Processes in Israel,* eds. Moshe Lissak and Emanuel Gutmann, pp. 238–56. Jerusalem: Akademon.

Smith, Herbert. 1972. "Analysis of Voting." In *The Elections in Israel—1969,* ed. Alan Arian, pp. 63–80. Jerusalem: Academic Press.

Smith, Gordon. 1972. *Politics in Western Europe: A Comparative Analysis.* London: Heinemann Educational Books.

Smith, Robert B. 1971. "Some Effects of Limited War." Unpublished.

Smocha, Sammy, and Yochanan Peres. 1974. "The Dynamics of Ethnic Inequalities: The Case of Israel." Unpublished.

Sombart, Werner. 1951. *The Jews and Modern Capitalism.* Trans. M. Epstein. Glencoe, Ill.: Free Press.

Special Committee on Campus Tensions. 1970. *Campus Tensions: Analysis and Recommendations.* Washington, D.C.: American Council on Education.

Stein, Herman D., and Richard A. Cloward. 1958. *Social Perspectives on Behavior.* Glencoe, Ill.: Free Press.

Tal, Avraham. 1975. "Not Master in its House." *Ha'aretz,* July 25. (Hebrew).

Tanter, Raymond. 1966. "Dimensions of Conflict Behavior Within and Between Nations, 1958–1960." *Journal of Conflict Resolution* 10: 55–64.

Teodori, Massimo, ed. 1970. *The New Left.* London: Jonathan Cape.

BIBLIOGRAPHY

Thomas, William I. 1927. *The Unadjusted Girl.* Boston: Little, Brown.

Tumin, Melvin M. 1953. "Some Principles of Stratification: A Critical Analysis." *The American Journal of Sociology* 18: 387–93.

Urwin, Derek W., ed. n.d. "Elections in Western Nations 1945–1968." *Occasional Papers* Nos. 4/5. Glasgow, Scotland: Survey Research Center, University of Strathclyde.

Verba, Sidney. 1965. "Comparative Political Culture." In *Political Culture and Political Development,* eds. Lucian W. Pye and Sidney Verba, pp. 512–60. Princeton, N.J.: Princeton University Press.

Verba, Sidney; and Norman H. Nie. 1972. *Participation in America.* New York: Harper & Row.

Weber, Max. 1969. "The Sociology of Charismatic Authority." In *From Max Weber: Essays in Sociology,* eds. Hans H. Gerth and C. Wright Mills, pp. 245–52. New York: Oxford University Press.

_____. 1958. *The Protestant Ethic and The Spirit of Capitalism.* New York: Charles Scribners's Sons.

Weiss, Shevach. 1975. "Knesset in Decline." *Yediot Achronot,* September 9, p. 14. (Hebrew).

_____. 1971. "The Composition of the Labor Party's 'Lishka': Presumed Political and Social Significance." *Medina Umimshal* 1: 124–28. (Hebrew).

Wilensky, Harold L. 1966. "Measures and Effects of Mobility." In *Social Structure and Mobility in Economic Development,* eds. Neil J. Smelser and Seymour M. Lipset, pp. 98–140. Chicago: Aldine.

Werlin, Herbert H. 1973. "The Consequences of Corruption: The Ghanaian Experience." *Political Science Quarterly* 88: 71–85.

Yatsiv, Gadi. 1974. "The Class Basis of Party Affiliation." Ph.D. Thesis, Hebrew University. Jerusalem.

Yuchtman, Ephraim, and Gidon Fishelson. 1970. "Inequality in Distribution of Income." *The Economic Quarterly* 17: 75–88. (Hebrew).

Zamir, Rina. 1964. *Beer-sheba: 1958/59, Social Processes in a Development Town.* Sociological Research, Notebook 5. Jerusalem: Department of Sociology, Hebrew University. (Hebrew).

Zloczower, Avraham. 1972. "Occupation, Mobility and Social Class." *Social Science Information* 11: 329–57.

_____. 1968. "Mobility Patterns and Status Conceptions in an Urban Israeli Setting." Ph.D. Thesis, Hebrew University.

SURVEYS

(Within each category, surveys [and statistical data] are listed by date of publication).

Surveys by the Israel Institute of Applied Social Research (IIASR) in conjunction with the Communications Institute of the Hebrew University, Jerusalem*

Institute Staff. 1967A. *Before and During the War.* Jerusalem.

_____. 1967B. *Public Attitudes After the War: Social Solidarity.* Jerusalem.

_____. 1967C. *Selected Findings of the Three War Surveys.* Jerusalem.

Peled, Tziona. 1968. *Changes in Public Opinion and Attitudes Since the Six-Day War and up to April 1968.* Jerusalem.

Peled, Tziona, and Shmuel Shye. 1969. *The Continuing Survey of Public Opinion and Public Problems.* Jerusalem: January.

Peled, Tziona. 1969. *Changes in Public Opinion and Public Problems Since the Six-Day War.* Jerusalem: May.

Schwartz, G., and T. Biran. 1970. *Summary of Findings on Change in Public Opinion and Public Problems Since the Six Day War and Up to November 1969.* Jerusalem: January.

Adi, Pessach, and Daniela Froelich. 1970A. *Attitudes Concerning Political Security and Topics of Public Morale in February–March 1970.* Jerusalem: May.

_____. 1970B. *Attitudes with Regard to Political and Social Topics in June–July 1970.* Jerusalem: September.

Levy, Shlomit, and Louis E. Guttman. 1970. *Structure and Dynamics of Worries: A Multivariate Analysis of Worries Relating to the Public and the Individual Since the Six Day War up to July 1970.* Jerusalem: December.

_____. 1971A. *The Public's Reactions to Current Problems: Worries, Evaluations and Readiness to Concessions.* Jerusalem: June. (Hebrew).

_____. 1971B. *Zionism and the Jewish People as Viewed by Israelis.* Jerusalem: August.

---

*Unless otherwise stated, all Survey Reports are in Hebrew.

BIBLIOGRAPHY

Peled, Tziona. 1971. *The Public Views the Current Situation—June-July 1971.* Jerusalem: October.

Peled, Tziona, and Haviva Schimmerling. 1972A. *The Public Views the Current Situation—October-December 1971.* Jerusalem: March.

———. 1972B. *The Public Views the Current Situation.* Jerusalem: July.

Ben Sira, Zeev. 1972. *The Public Views the Current Situation—May-July 1972.* Jerusalem: December.

Levy, Shlomit, and Louis E. Guttman. 1973A. *Feelings of Well-Being and Distress Among the Israeli Public—Analysis of Social Indicators—February-April 1973.* Jerusalem: August.

Institute Staff. 1973A. *Yom Kippur War Surveys.* Jerusalem: October–November.

Levy, Shlomit, and Louis E. Guttman. 1973B. *Jewish Identification of Israelis During the Yom Kippur War.* Jerusalem: November.

Institute Staff. 1973B. *Toward the Election for the Eighth Knesset.* Jerusalem: December.

Ben Sira, Zeev, and Rivka Winter. November 1973A; December 1973B; January 1974. *Survey of Political Attitudes.* Jerusalem.

Levy, Shlomit, and Louis E. Guttman. 1974A. *Social Indicators for Israel: The Reactions of the Public to Current Problems—January 22-March 12, 1974—The Continuing Survey.* Jerusalem: March.

Levy, Shlomit, Yael Nathan, and Louis E. Guttman. 1974B. *Social Indicators for Israel March 18-April 30, 1974—The Continuing Survey.* Jerusalem: May.

Levy, Shlomit, and Louis E. Guttman. 1974C. *The Wish to Remain in Israel.* Jerusalem: June.

Nathan, Yael, and Israel Adler. 1974. *Social Indicators for Israel: The Reactions of the Public to Current Problems—May 6-June 11, 1974—The Continuing Survey.* Jerusalem: July.

Levy, Shlomit, and Louis E. Guttman. 1974D. *Values and Attitudes of Israel High School Youth.* Jerusalem. (Hebrew, with English Translation of Introduction and Summary.)

Elizur, Dov, and Miki Elizur. 1974. *The Long Way Back: Attitudes of Israelis Residing in the United States and in France—Toward Returning to Israel.* Jerusalem.

Institute Staff. 1975A. *Social Problems Indicators for the Month of March 1975.* Jerusalem: April.

———. 1975B. *Social Problems Indicators for the Month of January-February 1975.* Jerusalem.

———. 1975C. *Social Problems for the Month of April 1975.* Jerusalem.

Other Surveys

The Israel Elections Research Group (headed by A. Arian and E. Torgovnik). 1973. "General and Panel Study." Tel Aviv: Spring. (Unpublished).*

———. 1973. "Accompanying Survey." Tel Aviv: Spring. (Unpublished).

The Society for Sociological Services. 1973. "Youth Questionnaire." Ramat-Gan: Spring. (Unpublished).

The Israel Elections Research Group (headed by A. Arian and E. Torgovnik). 1973. "Panel Survey." Tel Aviv: September. (Unpublished).

The Society for Sociological Services. 1973. "Voter Questionnaire." Ramat-Gan: November. (Unpublished).

The Society for Sociological Services. 1973. "New Immigrant Survey." Ramat-Gan. (Unpublished)

STATISTICAL DATA

Israel

Central Bureau of Statistics. 1957. *Labor Force Survey, June 1954.* Special Series No. 56, Jerusalem.

———. 1969. *Statistical Abstract of Israel,* Vol. 20.

The Ministry of Housing. *The Minister of Housing's Speech on the Ministry of Housing's Activities 1971/1972.* Jerusalem: June 28, 1971, and May 8, 1972.

Central Bureau of Statistics. 1972. *Young Couples Survey, 1971.* Jerusalem.

———. 1973. *Statistical Abstract of Israel,* Vol. 24.

The Ministry of Housing. 1973. *Survey of the Ministry of Housing's Activities.* Jerusalem.

Central Bureau of Statistics. 1974A. *Monthly Price Statistics.* Vol. 25, No. 3. Jerusalem: March.

———. 1974B. *Israel Statistical Monthly Supplement,* Vol. 25, No. 4, April.

---

*For details, see Chapter 2.

———. 1974C. *Israel Statistical Monthly Supplement,* Vol. 25, No. 7, July.

———. 1974D. *Statistical Abstract of Israel,* Vol. 25.

———. 1974E. *Results of Elections to the Eighth Knesset and to Local Authorities—December 31, 1973.* Special Series, No. 461, Jerusalem.

———. 1975A. *Monthly Bulletin of Statistics,* Vol. 26, No. 5, May.

———. 1975B. *Statistical Abstract of Israel,* Vol. 26.

Israel Government Information Center. *Government Yearbooks.* Jerusalem: 1950–1976. (Hebrew).

The United States

Bureau of Labor Statistics, U.S. Department of Labor. 1962. "A Century of Change: Negroes in the U.S. Economy, 1860–1960," *Monthly Labor Review* (December): 1363–64.

Bureau of the Census. 1972. *Statistical Abstract of the United States: 1972.* (93d. edition). Washington, D.C.

NAME INDEX

Adar, L., 23
Adi, P., 61, 77, 166
Adler, H., 23, 209
Almond, G., 35, 67, 76, 82, 83
Antonovsky, A., 57, 59, 65, 138, 139, 167, 173
Apter, D. E., 150
Arian, A., 10, 13, 25, 28, 29, 30, 33, 34, 38, 44, 48, 51, 52, 56, 59, 65, 69, 70, 73, 75, 77, 78, 79, 90, 113, 173, 206
Aronoff, M. J., 17, 94, 113

Barkai, H., 18, 19
Ben Raphael, E., 121
Ben Sira, Z., 45, 51, 56, 62, 70, 73, 75, 80, 81, 141
Blau-Luksemburg, J., 142
Blumer, H., 27
Boim, L., 92, 96
Brichta, A., 113
Brinton, C., 150

Campbell, A., 42, 68, 77
Cantril, H., 43, 140
Carter, A., 112
Chanoch, G., 62–63
Citrin, J., 208
Cloward, R. A., 26
Cohen, E., 94, 118, 130
Cohen, O., 173, 189
Converse, P. E., 42, 82, 128, 208
Coser, L. A., 180, 181

Dahrendorf, R., 26
Darin-Drabkin, H., 115
Derber, M., 63
Deshen, S. A., 28, 92, 94, 108, 114, 174
DiPalma, G., 68
Downes, B. T., 121
Duncan, O. D., 148
Durkheim, E., 27
Duverger, M., 10, 25, 44, 90, 207

Easton, D., 92
Eckstein, H., 179
Edelman, M. J., 89

Eisenstadt, S. N., 3, 5, 9, 15, 17, 18, 20, 21, 23, 24, 26, 28, 64, 66, 67, 83, 91, 115, 134
Erikson, E., 157
Eshkol, L., 18
Etzioni, A., 15, 17, 44, 113
Etzioni-Halevy, E., 19, 52, 54, 76, 128, 131, 142, 144, 160, 162, 164, 165, 167, 168, 169, 171, 173, 175

Farago, U., 170
Fein, L. J., 17, 68, 69, 70, 73, 75, 77, 79, 113
Fishelson, G., 63
Free, L. J., 43, 140
Froelich, D., 61, 77, 166

Gamson, W. A., 92
Germani, G., 150, 209
Goldberger, A. S., 49
Gosnell, H. F., 109
Gurevitz, M., 54, 69, 73, 75, 164, 169
Guttman, L. E., 49, 50, 105, 141, 160, 162, 163, 165, 166, 167, 172, 173, 175, 176, 199, 200

Halevi, N., 151
Hartman, M., 146, 150
Heidenheimer, A. J., 109
Heilbroner, R. L., 20
Hendelman, D., 108
Hendles, Y., 48
Herberg, W., 173
Herman, S. N., 159, 164, 167, 169, 170, 172, 173, 174, 175
Hofman, J. E., 170
Horowitz, D., 3, 11
House, J. S., 49, 82, 208

Janowitz, M., 182

Kamen, C. S., 181, 193
Katz, E., 54, 69, 73, 75, 164, 169
Key, V. O., 109
Keydar, A., 48
Kies, N., 55, 56, 95
Kishon, E., 77, 180
Klinov-Malul, R., 151

244

Kluckhohn, F. R., 26
Kornhauser, W. A., 112
Kriesberg, L., 181
Krivine, D., 115

Laidler, H. W., 28
Lane, R. E., 72
Leeds, R., 134
Levy, S., 49, 50, 105, 106, 160, 162, 163, 165, 166, 167, 172, 173, 175, 176, 199, 200
Lippmann, W., 89
Lipset, S. M., 28, 55, 121, 128, 139, 140, 142, 150
Lissak, M., 3, 11, 62, 63, 64, 140, 146, 150
Livne, M., 113, 127
Lopreato, J., 142
Lukes, S., 107

MacIntyre, A. C., 82
Marcuse, H., 68
Marx, E., 18
Mason, W. M., 49, 82, 208
Matras, J., 145, 174
Medding, P. Y., 24, 95
Merton, R. K., 27, 109
Milbrath, L. W., 68, 76
Miller, A. H., 31, 82, 92, 111, 208
Mills, C. W., 26, 67, 84
Moore, W. E., 150, 151
Mueller, C., 89, 91

Nie, N. H., 68
Neumann, F. L., 84

Ofer, G., 151

Pareto, V., 150
Parsons, T., 26
Partridge, P. H., 88, 89
Pateman, C., 35, 86, 113
Peled, Z., 70, 141, 145, 166
Peres, Y., 21, 50, 51, 55, 56, 60, 61, 62, 130, 132, 151, 154, 189, 212
Pitkin, H., 88
Plamenatz, J. P., 28, 90

Robinson, J. P., 43
Rose, R., 54, 139
Rosenbaum, W. E., 82

Schrift, R., 131, 152, 153, 154
Scott, J. C., 109
Seligman, L. G., 150
Shafat, R., 50
Shapira, R., 52, 54, 76, 131, 142, 144, 146, 160, 162, 164, 165, 167, 168, 169, 171, 173, 175
Shapiro, Y., 3, 10
Shils, E. A., 86, 89, 142, 182
Shimmerling, H., 141
Simmel, G., 180
Smith, G., 139
Smith, H., 45, 47
Smith, R. B., 181
Smocha, S., 21, 151, 154
Stein, H. D., 26

Tal, A., 18
Tanter, R., 129, 181
Teodori, M., 121
Thomas, W. I., 27
Torgovnik, E., 29
Tumin, M. M., 137

Urwin, D. W., 72

Verba, S., 35, 67, 82, 83, 157, 158, 179, 182, 204

Weber, M., 91, 211
Weiss, S., 16, 17
Wilensky, H. L., 142
Winter, R., 48, 51, 62, 70, 73, 75, 81

Yatsiv, G., 48, 56
Yuchtman, E., 50, 63

Zamir, R., 95
Zetterberg, H. L., 142, 150
Zloczower, A., 30, 32, 139, 140, 142, 143

SUBJECT INDEX

Achdut Ha'avoda, 6, 7, 41, 46, 47, 65, 222, 223, 226–27
affinity with Jews abroad, 159–60, 161, 165, 167–168, 169, 172–73, 175–76
age (groups), 51–55, 56–57, 60
agricultural: colonies (moshavot), 4, 8; settlements, 6 (*see also*, collective settlements)
Agudat Israel, 6, 13, 46, 47, 222, 223
alienation (*see*, political alienation)
alignment, 41, 45–47, 49–52, 56, 60, 65, 94, 96–97, 110, 126, 206, 212, 223, 227
aliya (aliyot), 3–5, 20, 56, 57–58, 60, 71, 93, 115
Arab(s), 8, 19, 41, 47, 62, 105, 158–59; countries, 19, 33, 34, 42, 61–62, 188; labor, 4; parties, 47; terrorism, 49, 50
attachment to Israel, 159–62, 166–67, 169–70, 173, 177

Black Panthers, 114, 115, 116–18, 119–20, 122–23
British mandate, 3, 10–12, 15, 21
bureaucracies, 108, 118, 150, 155

capitalism, 33, 34, 40, 138, 144, 146
centralization, 15–17, 205
"citizens" groups, 7, 8, 12, 222
citizens, types of, 84–86
cleavages: ideological, 11, 40, 61, 101; intergroup, 52, 71, 179, 189; political, 25, 33, 36–38, 39, 41–43, 91, 109, 138, 159, 205–08 (*see also*, gaps)
coalition, 10–11, 14, 16, 93–94, 97, 101, 110, 211
cohesion, cohesiveness, 177, 179–81, 204, 208, 211
collective: commitments, 20, 23–24, 130, 159, 163–68, 177, 208–09, 210; identifications, 130, 176, 208–09, 213; values, 130–31, 179, 208–09, 210 (*see*, ideology, national identifications)
collective settlements (Moshavim, Kibbutzim), 5, 7, 9, 18, 23, 24, 167
collectivism, 23–24, 62–64, 177, 209
communist parties, 46, 47, 222–23

conflict, 133, 180–82, 198; ethnic, 114; external, 129, 177, 180–98, 209; Israeli-Arab, 41, 101–06, 155, 183, 211
consensus, 10, 41, 176
consent (support, confidence, approval) for political establishment, 20, 48, 81–83, 84–87, 140–41, 144–45, 179, 182, 199–200, 207–08, 209, 210–11, 212; by social background, 140–41; decline of, 97–110, 129, 155; definition of, 90; impact of, 110–11; measures of, 90–91; mechanisms for fostering, 92–96, 108–09
cooptation, 95, 122, 128

democracy, 35, 79, 90, 91, 111, 119, 133, 134; criteria of, 112–13; protest in, 112, 133–34; theory of, 86, 87; Western type, 54, 72, 76, 89, 109
democratic procedures, 33, 35–37, 40, 112, 117, 133, 211, 213
demonstrations, 110, 114, 120, 121, 122
doctrine, 206; dominant, 25, 29, 44
dominant party, dominant party system, 10, 14, 44, 65, 66, 79, 92, 94, 95, 109, 207, 211 (*see also*, ruling party)

economic: activity, 66; benefits, 19; dependence, 19–20, 108–09; development, 209; facilities, 15; resources, 11, 18, 20, 205; policy, 70, 101–06; rewards, 24
economy: public and private sectors of, 13, 17–19, 40, 66; state (government, political) control of, 17–19, 20, 28, 44, 49, 50, 66, 205–06, 211
education, 38, 39, 198, 199
educational system, 9, 10, 15, 23, 55
egalitarianism, 28, 32, 36, 40–41, 62–64 (*see also*, ideology)
elections, 15, 16–17, 46, 48, 50, 60, 70, 72, 79, 80–81, 90–92, 93–96, 107, 119, 127, 146; campaigns, 72, 76, 80, 93, 94, 96; results, 45, 51, 55, 70, 72, 78, 79, 90, 91, 95, 212; turnout, 71–72, 79, 80 (*see also*, voting)
electoral: support, 48, 50, 51, 60, 94, 96–97, 107, 110, 207; system, 14, 118

246

emigration, 8, 10, 11, 14, 167, 210; approval or disapproval of, 160, 161, 162, 163, 173
ethnic: groups, 56, 61, 94, 189; relations, 21–22, 40, 188–89, 194, 198, 200, 204; solidarity, 189, 199 (*see also,* protest, solidarity)

Gachal, 46, 47, 55, 223, 226–27
gaps, ethnic and socioeconomic, 19–22, 30, 31, 36, 39–40, 114, 117, 123, 159, 210 (*see also,* cleavages)
General Zionists, 6, 12, 45, 46, 47, 222, 223
grievances, 114–17, 129, 130, 132, 134

Haganah, 8, 15, 23
Hamerkaz Hachofshi, 46, 47, 223, 227
Hamizrachi, 6, 12, 222, 223
Hapoel Hamizrachi, 6, 12, 222, 223
Hapoel Hatzair, 6, 7, 222
Hareshima Hamamlachtit, 46, 47, 223, 227
Hashomer Hatzair, 6, 222
Herut, 12, 45, 46, 47, 140, 223, 226
Histadrut, 5, 7, 9, 11, 12, 13–15, 18, 19, 40, 93
housing: projects, 11, 15, 189; problems, 115–16, 124–25, 132; "solutions," 124

ideological: affinity, 36, 44, 45, 206; development, 3–24; incongruence, 25, 29, 43, 44, 206
ideology, 25, 28, 48, 62, 66, 114, 132, 137, 140, 142, 146, 155; collectivist, 62, 66; egalitarian, 62–63, 140; leftist, 44, 206; nationalist, 4, 13, 23, 41, 42; of democracy, 88; of national unity, 130; of status quo, 142; of Zionism, 64, 130, 131, 145, 146, 167, 168, 169, 170, 176; rightist, 207; socialist, 5, 28, 40, 44, 60, 64, 66, 81, 206 (*see also,* collective commitments, collectivism, egalitarianism national identifications, socialism, Zionism)
immigrants, immigration (*see,* Aliya)
Independent Liberals, 14, 46, 47, 97, 223, 225–27
individualism, 9, 23, 177, 208
integrative mechanisms, 129–33, 134, 138, 142–45, 148–51, 154, 155–58, 162–63, 178–79, 199–200, 208–11
interest groups, 17, 93, 95
intermarriage, 152–53
Irgun Zvai-Leumi, 8

Israel Defense Forces, 15, 118, 188
Israeli identification, 158, 159–62, 163–65, 167–68, 170, 177–78, 208, 210 (*see also,* national identification)
Israel Labor Party (ILP), 5, 12, 14, 15, 17, 44, 46, 47, 65, 81, 93, 96, 97, 126, 127, 139, 206, 223

Jewish Agency Executive, 15
Jewish identification, 158, 159–62, 163–65, 167–69, 170–73, 174–75, 177–78, 208, 210 (*see also,* national identification, sense of belonging to Jewish people)

Knesset, 14, 16, 22, 118, 126, 127; committees, 16, 17
Knesset Israel, 10

labor: movement, 5–13, 20, 23, 28, 36, 44, 55; organizations, 7, 8, 11; party, 139; sector, 13 (*see,* Israel Labor Party)
Labor Movement for a Greater Israel, 41
Lechi, 8
legitimation, 26, 91–92
Liberals, 12, 37, 46, 47, 223, 225–27
Likud, 41, 45, 48, 50, 51, 55, 81, 97, 110, 140, 211, 223, 227

Mafdal, 13, 14, 46, 223
Maki (*see,* communist parties)
Mapai, 6, 7, 10, 12, 14, 44, 46, 47, 65, 95–97, 139, 222, 223, 225–27
Mapam, 12, 46, 47, 65, 223, 225–27
middle class, 36, 38
mobility (*see,* social mobility)
Moked (*see* communist parties)
morale, 179–88, 189, 193–200, 212–13
multiparty system, 79, 109

national commitments (*see,* national identification, collective commitments)
national council, 10, 15
national identification: and support for the regime, 157–59, 161–63, 168, 177; by age, 169–70, 177–78; by religiousness, 169, 170–77; depletion of, 169–78; relationship among various identifications, 159–61, 175–76; strength of, 163–68, 175–76; vulnerability of, 169, 178; war impact on, 168, 212–13
national institutions, 8, 10–12, 15

oligarchy, 17, 113
opposition, 50, 91, 96
Our Israel, 114, 118, 119

Palmach, 15, 23
party, 16–17, 30, 32, 48, 51, 52, 55–56, 60, 65, 80, 81, 92, 93–96, 101 (*see also,* dominant party; ruling party)
party political key, 11, 14, 15
pioneering, 4, 5, 9, 20, 23–24
Poalei Agudat Israel, 6, 13, 46, 47, 222, 224
Poalei Zion, 6, 222
Poalei Zion Smol, 6, 222
political alienation, 84–86
political apathy, 67–68
political center, 7, 10–11, 20, 114, 140, 205; and periphery, 207; charisma of, 141–42; imperviousness of, 129
political cleavages (*see,* cleavages)
political culture, 35, 51, 69, 82, 188
political efficacy, 67–68, 70, 76–79, 80, 81–84, 85–86, 106, 117, 129, 207, 212
political integration (*see,* integrative mechanisms)
political involvement, 27, 28, 30, 36–37, 42, 48, 67–72, 76–77, 78–80, 81–84, 85–86, 106, 129, 155, 212
political mobility, 148, 150, 209
political participation, 67–68, 69, 71–76, 80, 86, 113
political quiescence, 137, 148, 150, 156, 209, 211
political socialization, 7–8, 55
power, 10, 15, 16, 19, 26, 44, 183, 188, 199, 205–07, 211; economic, 3, 7, 9, 17–20, 134 (*see also,* economic); gap, 3, 205, 206; political, 10, 14, 16, 19, 20, 40, 134, 179; positions, 22, 206; structures, 26, 128
prestate era (*see* yishuv)
Progressives, 6, 46, 222, 223, 225–27
protest, 39, 47, 56, 112–34, 189, 208–09, 212–13; absorption of, 117–18, 128, 133–34; democratic role of, 112, 133; ethnic, 114–15, 117–20, 122–23, 129–30, 151, 154; housing, 114–16, 117–19, 122, 123–24, 129, 132; in France, 120–21; in Germany, 120–21; in the United States, 120–21; 128, 133; limitation of, 119–20, 129–32; mildness of, 120, 131, 133; moderation of, 117–21, 129–32, 154; radical, 121, 129, 130, 132–33, 134; response to, 121–28; student, 114, 121, 131, 144; Yom Kippur War, 114, 116–20, 126, 129, 131, 132 (*see also,* grievances)

Rafi, 46, 47, 223, 227
Rakach (*see* communist parties)
religious parties, 45, 46, 49, 97, 110, 222, 223, 225–27; sector, 5, 6, 12, 13, 14, 36
religiousness: and national identifications, 169, 170–73, 174–77; diminution of, 173, 175, 176, 177, 210
Revisionist Party, 6, 7, 11, 23, 222
ruling party, 49, 95, 107, 108, 110, 113, 127, 141, 154 (*see also,* dominant party)

secularization, 174
sense of belonging to the Jewish People, 160, 161–63, 165, 166, 168–69, 172, 175–76 (*see also,* national identification; Jewish identification)
social mobility, 131–32, 134, 137, 142–56, 208–11; blocking of, 137, 142, 144, 150; intergenerational, 143, 145 (*see also,* political mobility)
socialism, 4, 9, 30, 32, 33, 34, 37, 40, 44–45, 54–55, 60–61, 63, 66, 138–39, 142–43, 144, 146 (*see also,* ideology, labor movement)
socialist: movement, 28, 40, 47; Zionism, 4, 5, 9, 13, 17, 20, 176
solidarity, 130, 131, 179–83, 188–204, 213; with Jews abroad (*see,* affinity with Jews abroad)
standard of living, 125, 154, 156
state control of economy (*see,* economy)
status: discrepancy, 142; satisfaction, 144

tension: external, 180, 188, 189; internal, 12, 22, 25, 89, 90, 109, 111, 158, 162, 189, 210; provoking mechanisms, 205
territories, administered, 35, 36, 41–42, 49, 147

Vadi Salib, 114
values, 22–28, 42, 86–89, 157, 178 (*see also,* collective commitments, ideology, national identifications)
voting, 72, 79–81, 90, 94, 95–96, 101, 108; decisions, 30, 39, 48, 49; patterns, 48, 54, 109; studies, 52

war (impact), 116–17, 129, 168, 181, 209, 211–13; of Attrition, 182, 187, 188,

189; Six-Day, 41, 49–50, 62, 80, 106, 130, 155, 168, 182, 183, 187, 189–94, 200, 213; veterans, 117, 127, 154, 156, 168; Yom Kippur, 49–50, 60, 62, 80–82, 97, 106, 110, 116–17, 182–88, 189–94, 200, 207, 212–13

withdrawal (from territories), 35, 36, 42, 49

working class, 36

yishuv, yishuv era, 3–12, 19, 20, 44, 145, 177, 208

young couples, 114–20, 122–25, 132

youth movements, 9, 55

Zionism, 22, 23, 47, 54, 119, 176–77

Zionist: commitment, 158, 159, 160, 161, 163, 165–69, 172–73, 175–78, 210; movement, 8; organizations, 10, 11, 12 (*see also,* ideology)

ABOUT THE AUTHORS

EVA ETZIONI-HALEVY is a graduate of the Hebrew University, Jerusalem. She received her Ph.D from Tel Aviv University. Presently she is senior lecturer at the department of Sociology and Anthropology, Tel Aviv University. Her previous publications are in the area of political sociology, national identifications, and higher education in Israel.

RINA SHAPIRA is a graduate of the Hebrew University, Jerusalem. She received her Ph.D from Columbia University, New York. Presently she is associate professor at the department of Sociology and Anthropology, Tel Aviv University, and Dean of Students at that university. Her previous publications are in the area of sociology of education, higher education, and national identifications in Israel.

The authors have collaborated on several articles and are coauthors of *Who is the Israeli Student* (in Hebrew).

RELATED TITLES
Published by
Praeger Special Studies

ISRAEL: An Economic Survey
    Shlomo Sitton

POLITICAL PARTIES IN ISRAEL: The Evolution of Israeli Democracy
    David M. Zohar

CRISIS DECISION MAKING: Israel's Experience in 1967 and 1973
    Abraham R. Wagner

POVERTY IN ISRAEL
    Harold Greenberg and Samuel Nadler

WAR AND FOREIGN POLICY: Issues and Policy Making in Four Middle Eastern States
    R. D. McLaurin, Mohammed Mughisuddin, and Abraham R. Wagner

RURAL COMMUNITIES: Inter-Cooperation and Development
    edited by Yehuda H. Landau, Maurice Konopnicki, Henri Desroche, and Placide Rambaud

LIBRARY OF DAVIDSON COLLEGE

Books on regular loan may be checked out for **two weeks**. Books must be presented at the Circulation Desk in order to be renewed.

A fine is charged after date due.

Special books are subject to special regulations at the discretion of library staff.

NOV -7 1982			
MAY 10 1985			
APR 0 3 1992			